MASTERING RESEARCH

-DEVELOPING COUNTRIES' CHALLENGES

BEN ODIGBO

DEDICATION

Dedicated to the Almighty God,

for His immeasurable

Mercies and Kindness.

ACKNOWLEDGEMENTS

My heart of gratitude goes to my numerous students who spurred me to write this book. Not to be forgotten are my academic colleagues for their cooperation and support. Then, all the individuals and organizations that have consulted me for research assistants, which helped in enriching and sharpening my research skills. Finally, what could I have done without my 'sweet-heart,' Barrister Ada Odigbo, and my little boy, Chidubem Odigbo. May the Almighty God reward you all.

TABLE OF CONTENTS

CHAPTER ONE

RESEARCH FUNDAMENTALS

1.1 Introduction

The chapter one of this book is intended to furnish us with the fundamentals or foundational knowledge about research: what research is all about, with specific emphasis on marketing research and the social sciences. It will showcase the two broad research classifications and the reasons why individuals, organizations, institutions, and governments devote their time and resources to researchers. The fundamental concepts in research and marketing research are highlighted. Finally, the chapter will look into the underlying marketing research process.

The objectives of this chapter include to acquaint you with an in-depth understanding of the meanings of research and marketing research, the importance and benefits of marketing research and the roles it plays in management decision makings. You will also arm yourself with knowledge of what basic and applied research are, the fundamental concepts in marketing research and the critical conventional marketing research process. With this foundational knowledge, you will be on a better footing to take-off soundly in this course.

1.2 The Meaning of Research and Marketing Research

Research is a scientific exercise, which entails a systematic, planned, organized, objectives, formal process of problem identification, gathering data, processing the data, analyzing the data, interpreting the data and generating information for solving the problem identified. Other authorities captured some aspects of this in their definitions. For instance, The Zambia Education and Training Unit (2016), defined research as a systematic inquiry to describe, explain, predict and control an observed phenomenon. On the other hand, the College of San Mateo (2017), says research is the organized and systematic method of finding answers to questions.

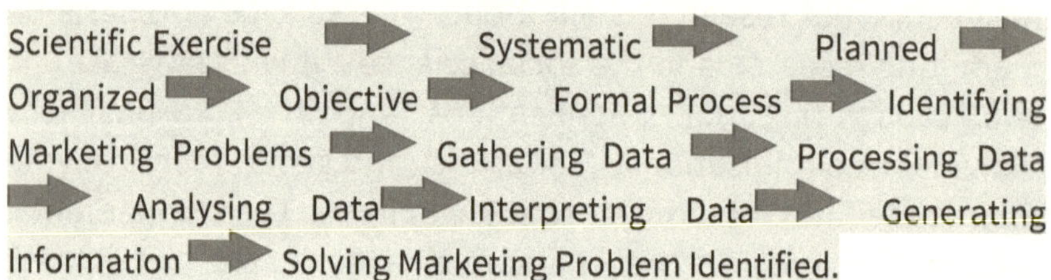

Fig. 1.1: The meaning of marketing research and the marketing research cycle.

Based on figure 1.1, marketing research is, therefore, a scientific exercise, which involves a systematic, planned, organized, objective and a formal process of identifying marketing problems, gathering data on it, processing the data, analyzing the data, interpreting the data and generating information for solving the marketing problem identified. The question could be price-related, product-related, promotional issues, distribution challenges, or based on general market demographics or consumer characterized.

Meanwhile, mark the key words underlined in this definition, because they capture all the essence of what marketing research entails. So, let us now look at them one after another.

1.2.1 Explaining the Key Elements in Marketing Research Definition

A Scientific Exercise: This means that research and indeed marketing research is purely scientific and adheres strictly to all the rules of scientific inquiry. Any slightest deviation from this invalidates or renders the outcome a nullity. The scientific method is a process of searching for answers to issues or investigating a phenomenon, acquiring and analyzing data on it and gaining new knowledge, for correcting, improving and adding to what is known previously. It is also a set of principles for systematic observation of phenomena and arriving at conclusions, for our improved understanding of the world around. For it to be a scientific exercise, however, the results must be verifiable and reproducible, as a fundamental basis for universal acceptance for knowledge.

The significant steps in the scientific method are as shown in figure 1.2 as follows:
1. Posing a question;

2.   Setting out objectives;
3.   Constructing a hypothesis;
4.   Test the hypothesis by analyzing the data;
5.   Concluding; and
6.   Reporting the results.

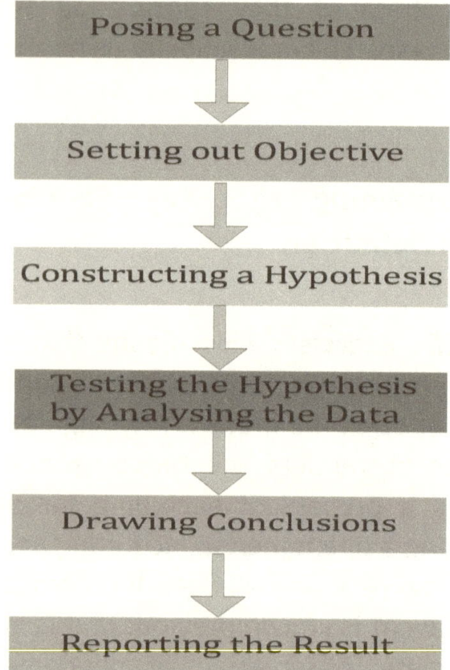

Fig. 1.2: The scientific method.

See also figure 1.3 from New York University (2017) on this.

Systematic Method: Systematic in that definition entails that research follows a led down step by step process in achieving its set objectives. The College of San Mateo (2017), adds that the investigation is systematic because it is a process broken up into clear steps that lead to conclusions.

Planned: This means that research is not an off-chance or half-hazard affair. It must be carefully designed for and assiduously executed.

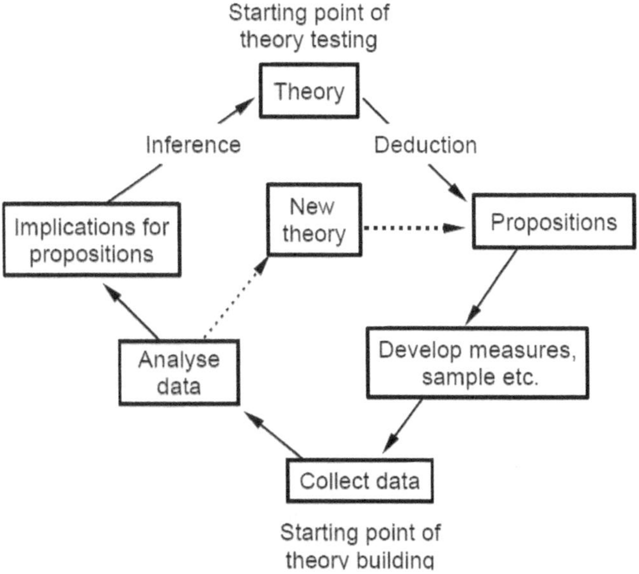

Fig. 1.3: Theory and basic research designs. Source: New York University (2017), What is research design?
https://www.nyu.edu/classes/bkg/methods/005847ch1.pdf

Organized: Research is designed to involve an astute sourcing and methodical management of human and material resources in achieving results. On the other hand, College of San Mateo (2017), observes that research is organized because there is a planned structure or method used to reach a conclusion.

Objective: The objectivity element of research entails that the researcher(s) must on no account input personal sentiments or biases into the study or its results. Any adopted research format, formulas, and designs must be strictly followed. There should be no bending of rules half-way to favor any interest. The data, the instruments, the statistical tools and the result(s) must be undoctored. Any attempt to the contrary renders the outcome of the study null and void.

Formal Process: The formality element in research entails that it is not a personal exercise, so, you must go by the rules, not your hunch, no matter the temptation.

Identifying Marketing Problem: Every marketing research comes under the realm of applied research, not basic research. That means marketing research are motivated by recognized management or marketing problems, and the need to find answers to the problem(s).

Gathering Data: Every research involves the gathering of some data which must be either primary or secondary. Some research, however, involves the use of both primary and secondary data.

Processing Data: This involves the preparation, sorting, collation, editing, coding and sometimes reduction of data before final analysis. For the expected research result to be got, raw data sourced from the field must be processed and analyzed.

Analyzing Data: To generate the needed information from research, the data procured from the fields must be analyzed, qualitatively or quantitatively. Data analysis often involves the testing of hypothesis.

Testing Hypothesis: Hypotheses are postulations, suppositions, propositions, educated predictions or declarations, informed guesses, testable statements or likely answers to a study, which must, however, be subjected to tests in order to ascertain the veracity or otherwise. In most studies, there are usually two types of hypotheses: the null and the alternative hypotheses. They provide the guidance for further investigation.

Interpreting Data: After analysis of most data, the results come out in abstract statistical figures or symbols, which the layman cannot understand. However, for it to serve the desired management decision purposes, these must be explained in the layman's language.

Generating Information: The essence of every marketing research is to generate information for management decisions and action. The information generated must be geared towards solving the marketing problem identified, initially.

However, not all research is motivated by a problem. Hence, research is categorized into two broad classes: basic and applied research. Again, research uses inductive and deductive methods.

1.3 Classification of Research

1.3.1 Basic Research

Basic research is research that is not occasioned by any identified problem but merely intended to increase the boundaries of knowledge. According to the US National

Academy of Sciences, the object of basic research is to "extend human knowledge of the physical, biological, or social world beyond what is already known." Basic research is based on a test of the veracity or otherwise of a theory. See figure 1.4 on this.

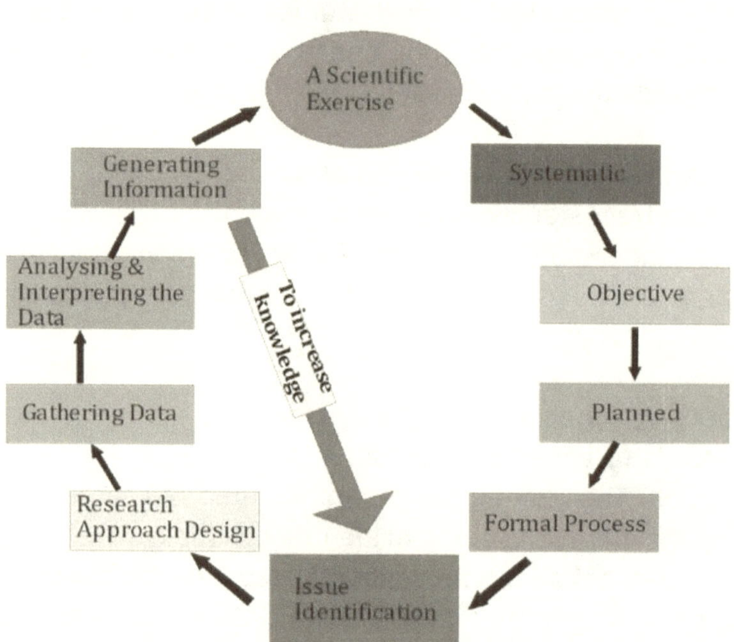

Fig. 1.4 Research Cycle for a basic research

1.3.2 Applied Research

Applied research is research that is informed by an identified problem, seeking vital information to address. Here belong marketing research and others useful for enhanced management decisions and actions. See figure 1.5 for a pictorial view of an applied research cycle.

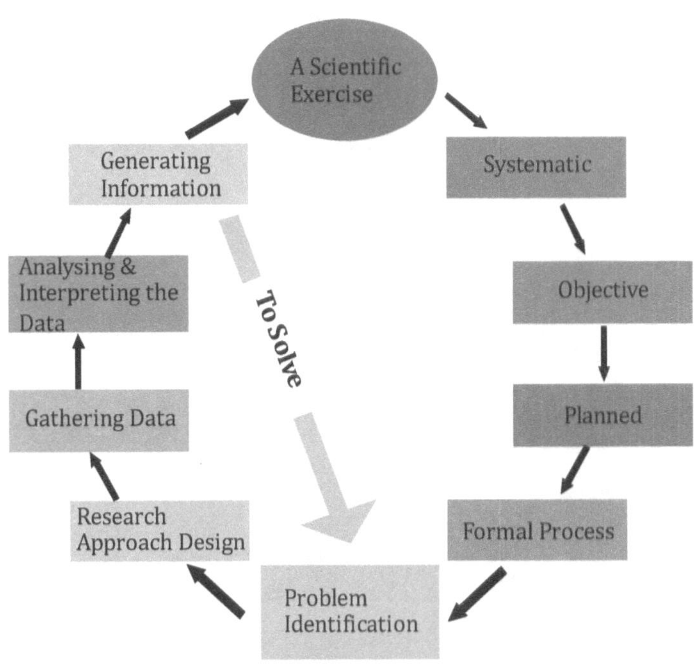

Figure 1.5 Applied research cycle

1.3.3 Inductive Research

Inductive research is a research method in which the premises of the study are meant to supply substantial evidence for the truth of the conclusion. It is a research approach concerned with the generation of new theory emerging from the data. See a graphic picture of this depicted by Professor Paresh (2017), in figure 1.6.

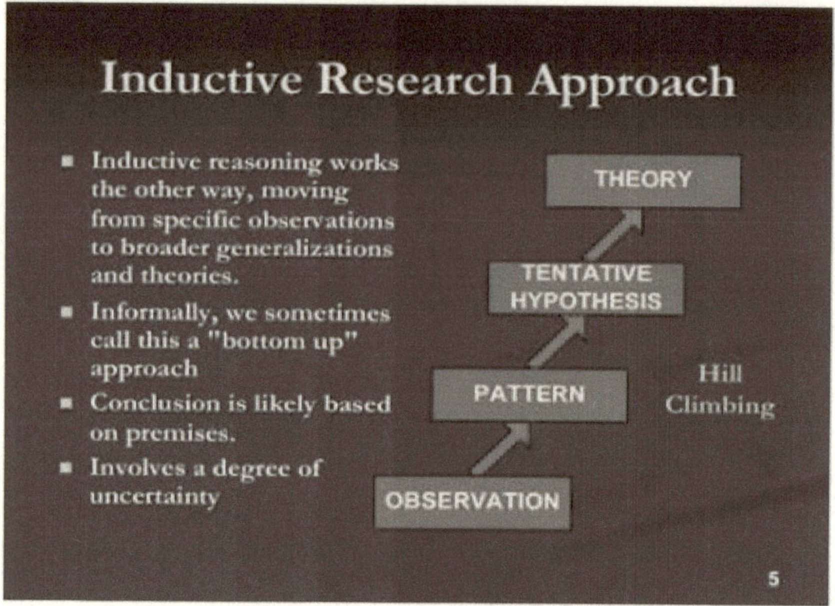

Fig. 1.6: Inductive Research. Source: Shah, Paresh (2017), Inductive vs. Deductive Research Approach. https://profparesh.in/inductive-vs-deductive-research-approach/

1.3.4   Deductive Research

Deductive research is research aimed at testing a theory or theories. Deductive analyses seek answers to problems that are more in agreement with known theories or hypotheses rather than attempt to refute them. That is in deductive research hypotheses are derived from existing theories, while data are sourced and analyzed to test the hypotheses.

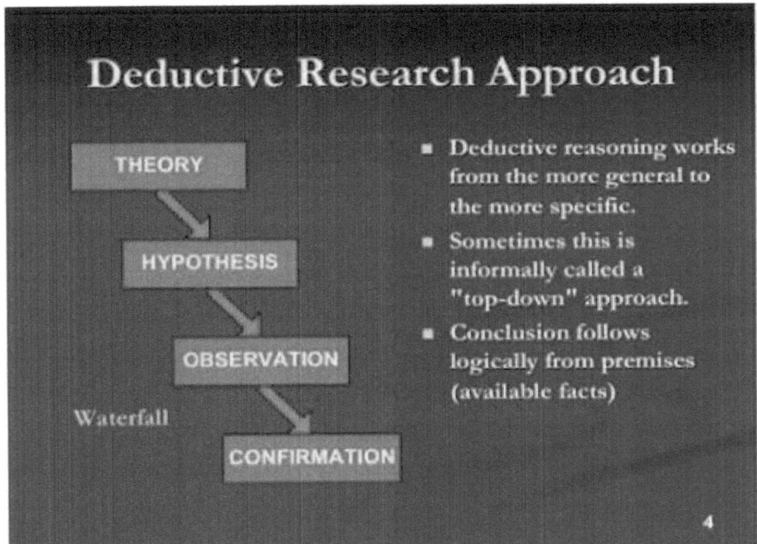

Fig. 1.7: Deductive Research. Source: Shah, Paresh (2017), Inductive vs. Deductive Research Approach. https://profparesh.in/inductive-vs-deductive-research-approach/

1.4. The Role/Rationale/Importance of Research in Business and Marketing

In business and marketing, research holds a very critical role which is quite inevitable for business survival. The rationale and importance of study in business and marketing include the following:

i. Research helps to reduce the level of business uncertainties, by arming you with valuable information for decisions and actions.

ii. Study helps to minimize business risks since the accruable decisions are based on research-ascertained facts.

ii. Research leads to the taking of quality business decisions and actions that improve business and marketing performance.

iv.   Research helps in the optimal allocation of business resources, based on research-ascertained facts.

v.   Research arms businesses and marketers with valuable information for performance evaluations.

vi.   Research provides businesses and marketers useful information for the planning and controls of their operations.

vii.   When organizational resources are allocated based on research-ascertained facts, it helps to reduce or avoid corporate conflicts/crises amongst workers.

viii.   Research provides businesses and marketers with knowledge of consumers, consumer characteristics, demographics, perceptions, behavior, etc., necessary for successful business planning, strategies, and executions.

ix.   Research also helps organizations in effective media evaluation, media selection, media buying and media placement.

1.5 Marketing Research Process

As shown in figure 1.8 below, the seven critical steps or processes in research are: Problem Identification & Definition, Specification of Information Needed, Development of an Approach, Development of the Research Design, Field Work, Data Analysis and Report Writing/Presentation.

Step 1	⟹	Problem Identification & Definition
Step 2	⟹	Specification of Information Needed
Step 3	⟹	Development of the Research Approach
Step 4	⟹	Development of the Research Design
Step 5	⟹	Field Work (E.g. Questionnaire Administration, Interview, Observation, Etc.)
Step 6	⟹	Data Analysis
Step 7	⟹	Research Report Writing/Presentation

Fig. 1.8: The key research process.

Problem Identification & Definition: The problem motivating the research must be appropriately identified, adequately defined and stated.

Specification of Information Needed: Information needed in research are organization-centric. That is, every organization needs research information peculiar to their operations. Hence, there must be a precise specification of the information required by an organization or its department(s) before the research kicks off.

Development of an Approach: The approach to be adopted in the research must be chosen, agreed upon and developed. That is to say, is it going to be inductive or deductive research, qualitative or quantitative, empirical or desk research, and many more?

Development of the Research Design: Having agreed on a research approach, the next step is to undertake the research design. The design is the roadmap or master plan to be used in conducting the research.

Field Work: This includes the administration of your questionnaire, conducting your interview, undertaking study group(s) observation, conducting a focus group exercise, conducting an experiment, or simulation exercise, depending on the type of research approach adopted.

Data Analysis: This entails the collation, processing and analysis of data procured from the field, and interpretation of the result(s).

Report Writing/Presentation: Study reports are written in unambiguous languages that must be understood by those who commissioned it, those who need the information and those who would wish to reference it tomorrow. They are also reported in such a way as to contribute to the body of knowledge.

A summarized and not detailed marketing research process from Slideshare (2017), is also presented herein figure 1.9 for your attention.

Compare figures 1.7, 1.8 and 1.9, also with figure 1.10, another detailed marketing research process from Philip Kotler as reported by Civil Service India (2018).

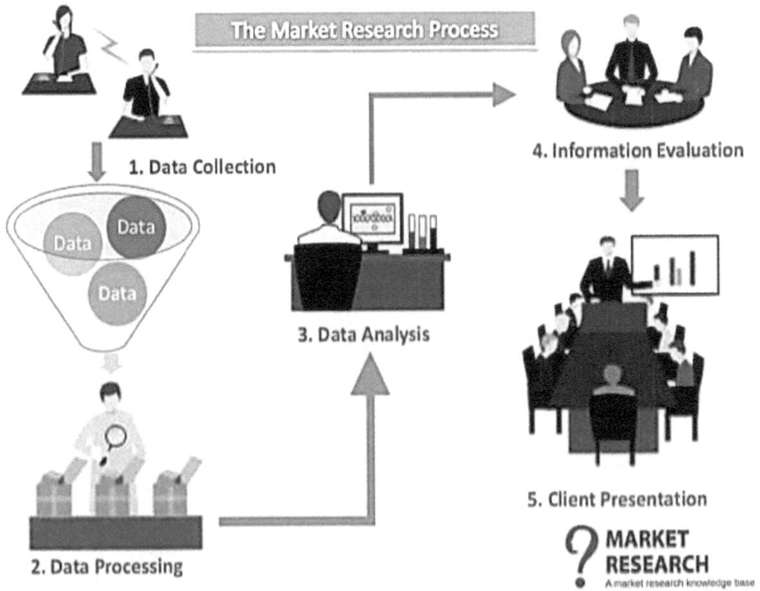

Fig. 1.9: A summarized marketing research process. Source: Slideshare (2017), Syndicated sources of secondary data.

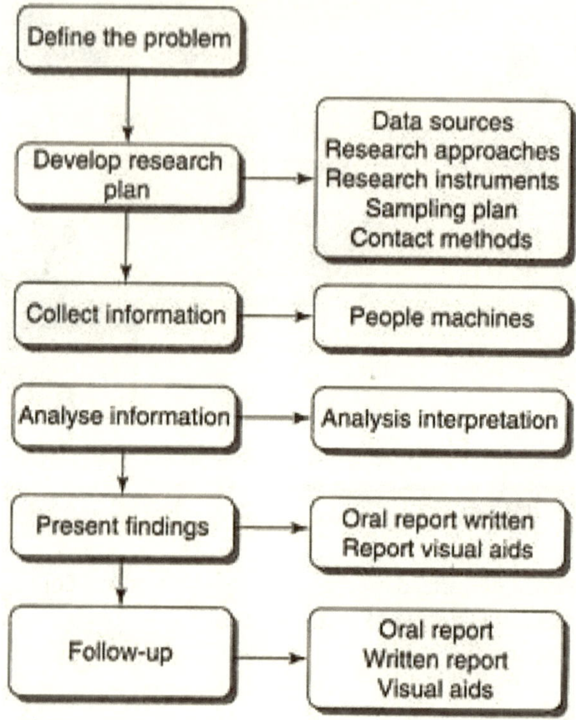

Fig. 1.10: Marketing research process. Source: Civil Service India (2018). https://www.civilserviceindia.com/subject/Management/notes/market-research.html

1.7 Summary and Conclusion

In this chapter, we have learned the meaning of research and marketing research, the critical elements in its definition and the necessary classification of scientific studies. We also acquired the differences and or similarities between basic research and applied research on the one hand, inductive and deductive research on the other hand. The role, rationale and importance of research in business and marketing were treated in this chapter, with details of the marketing research process.

The essence of this chapter is to lay a fundamental foundation for our understanding of marketing research. That makes it easier for us to follow the building blocks on the following topics that are coming up in the book. All these are designed in sequential order to ease our learning and appreciation of research and marketing research.

Exercises

1. Explain in detail the meaning and implications of the underlined words in the definition of marketing research: "Marketing Research is, therefore, a scientific exercise, which involves a systematic, planned, organized, objective, formal process of identifying marketing problems, gathering data on it, processing the data, analysing the data, interpreting the data and generating information for solving the marketing problem identified."

2. Give and justify two practical examples each of inductive research and deductive research.

3. Defend or debunk with adequate reasons the claim that individuals, organizations, institutions or government should not invest their hard-earned resources in research.

4. Outline and explain the step by step marketing process.

References

Civil Service India (2018).
https://www.civilserviceindia.com/subject/Management/notes/market-research.html

College of San Mateo (2016), What is Research?
https://collegeofsanmateo.edu/csmlibrary/tutorials/what.html

Explorable.com (2017), What is Research? Definition and steps of the scientific method. https://explorable.com/what-is-research

New York University (2017), What is research design?
https://www.nyu.edu/classes/bkg/methods/005847ch1.pdf

Shah, Paresh (2017), Inductive vs. Deductive Research Approach.
https://profparesh.in/inductive-vs-deductive-research-approach/

Slideshare (2017), Syndicated sources of secondary data.
https://www.slideshare.net/velibahceci/syndicated-sources-of-secondary-data

CHAPTER TWO

TYPES OF RESEARCHES

2.1   Introduction

Having laid the foundation for our understanding of the underlying fundamentals about research in the first chapter, this chapter tries to consolidate upon that, by taking us on a journey of the most general types of research that are usually conducted.

This is to enable us to learn the basic types of general research and how they apply in the scientific method. The justification for the adoption of each of them will also be studied here.

2.2   Types of Research General

These are research that is common and applies to all fields of learning. They include the following:

2.2.1 Opinion Survey

This is a form of research in which a target population's public opinion is sampled to determine some facts, as shown in figure 2.1. Here, the beliefs, viewpoints or feelings of a selected sample frame is chosen from the given population. The sample frame and sample size selected must, however, reflect a true representative of the demographic, sociographic, economic, political and other characteristics of members of the population. Another name for opinion survey is opinion poll. The target population's opinion could be sampled through the filling of a questionnaire as shown in figure 2.2, or through interviews as shown in figure 2.3.

Figure 2.1 shows a pool of opinions of different people a researcher is sampling.

Figure 2.2 is an example of a respondent filling a questionnaire given to him by a researcher. People should not be afraid to help researchers in filling surveys, as it is the case in some developing countries.

Fig.2.1: Asia Research Partners LLP (2017), Opinion survey. https://www.asianresearchpartners.com/opinion.php

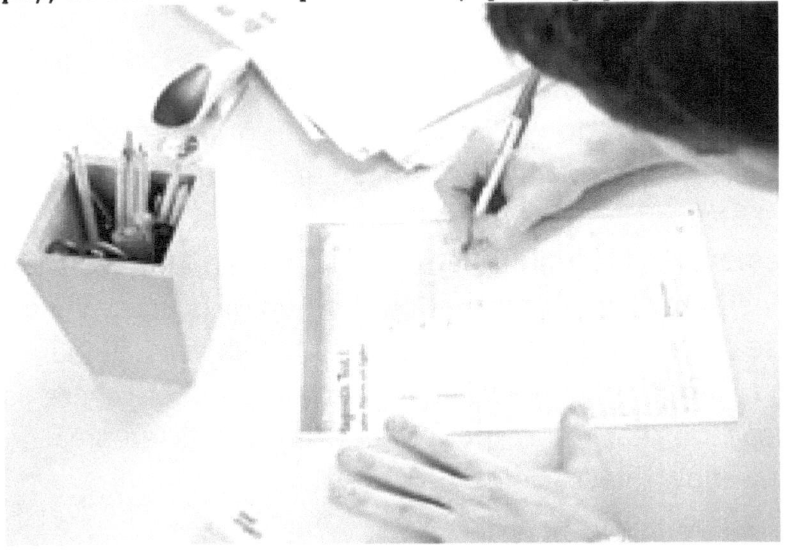

Fig. 2.2: Opinion survey through the filling of a questionnaire. Source: Australia Department of Education (2014), School Opinion survey. http://www.education.qld.gov.au/schoolopinionsurvey

Figure 2.3 shows a researcher conducting opinion survey via telephone interviews. In developing countries, this could be a challenging task, due to inadequate telecommunications facilities and high costs.

2.2.2 Observation Research

Observation research is a form of non-experimental social and psychological research technique during which a researcher(s) observes the behavior of a chosen sample elements in a given population, for informed generalizations about that population. It is used when the researcher doesn't need to control the sample elements as in a laboratory experiment, and also when there is a suspicion that the respondents will give biased answers if they know they're being watched.

Hence, the researcher observes them performing in their natural setting unaware they're being watched, and not their opinion which could sometimes be diluted to suit personal interests or fears.

Figure 2.4 shows a researcher, observing and recording the behavior of a child. While figure 2.5 shows two medical personnel, watching and recording the health status and response of a patient.

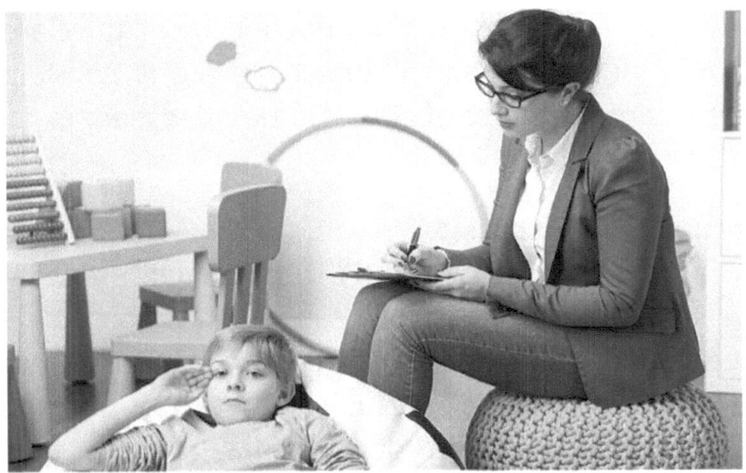

Fig. 2.4: Observation research. Source: Holah (2016), Observation research. http//holah.co.uk/investigations/observation

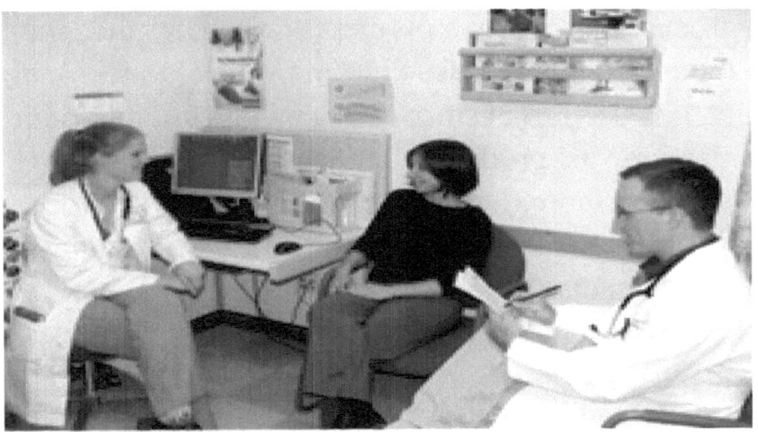

Fig. 2.5: Observation research. Source: Holah (2016), Observation research. http//holah.co.uk/investigations/observation.

This is why the US Center for Disease Control (CDC, 2016), adds that observations can be overt (everyone knows they are being observed) or covert (no one knows they are being observed and the observer is concealed). The benefit of covert observation is that people are more likely to behave naturally if they do not know they are under watch. However, you will typically need to conduct covert inspections because of ethical issues in research.

2.2.3 Focus Group Discussion

A focus group discussion (FGD) is a small group of people, selected in a study in such a manner to represent a given target population indeed, demographically, used in a guided open discussion on a subject matter or specific topic of interest. It is a form of qualitative research that tracks the participants' opinions, perceptions, beliefs, feelings, and attitude towards a subject matter, like product's taste, price, packaging, advertising, distribution, etc. The discussion follows a prepared interview guideline, led by a moderator, who is usually a member of the FGD. In marketing, it is used to elicit consumers' perception about an organization, its products, services, prices, customer cares, and many more. See a pictorial example of a focus group discussion on figure 2.6 from Bloustein Center for Survey Research (2017).

Fig. 2.6: Focus Group discussion. Source: Bloustein Center for Survey Research (2017). http://bcsr.rutgers.edu/focus-group-discussions/

2.2.4 Descriptive Research

Descriptive Research is a form of research used to elicit information that will describe the characteristics of a target population or variable of interest studied. It is used to uncover new facts and meanings concerning the current status of a subject matter and describe what obtains. Descriptive studies are also conducted to demonstrate the degree of associations, correlations or relatedness between two variables or phenomena. When it involves a one-time interaction with groups of people, it is called a cross-sectional study, but when it follows individuals over time, it is called a longitudinal study. It is also used in researches targeted at offering answers to the questions – who, what, where, when, how and why, as seen in figure 2.7.

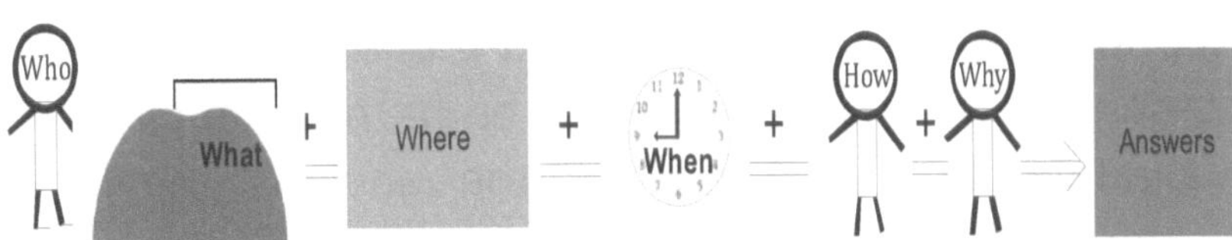

Fig. 2.7: Focus and end of descriptive research

Exploratory Research is research usually done on a subject matter, issue or problem that has not been studied more clearly. It is, therefore, a form of initial investigation to test a hypothetical or theoretical idea, to understand more about it. It is used to lay the groundwork for an in-depth future study, or to determine if what is being studied is supported by an existing theory. Most often, exploratory research lays the initial groundwork for future research, by helping develop and improve the research design (College of San Mateo, 2016).

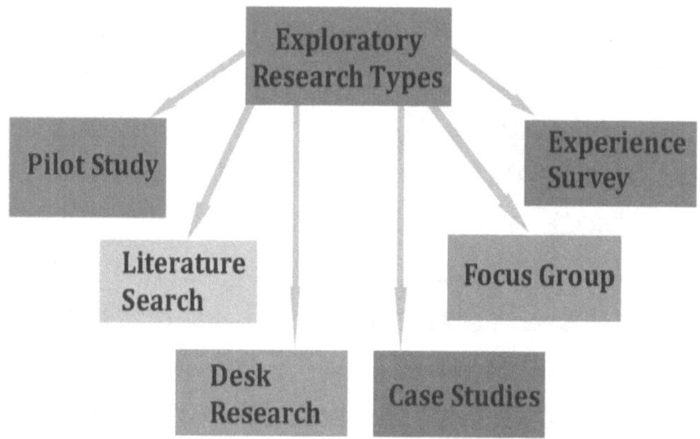

Fig. 2.8: Exploratory research types.

2.2.6 Explanatory Research

Explanatory Research is a form of causal research used to establish degree and nature of a cause-and-effect relationship. In such study, both quantitative and qualitative data are used in the analysis. Here, the researcher collects and analyses some quantitative data, followed by a collection and analysis of some qualitative data. The aim is to use the qualitative data to interpret and explain the quantitative data. The essence is to tell why, how and the extent a phenomenon or event occurs.

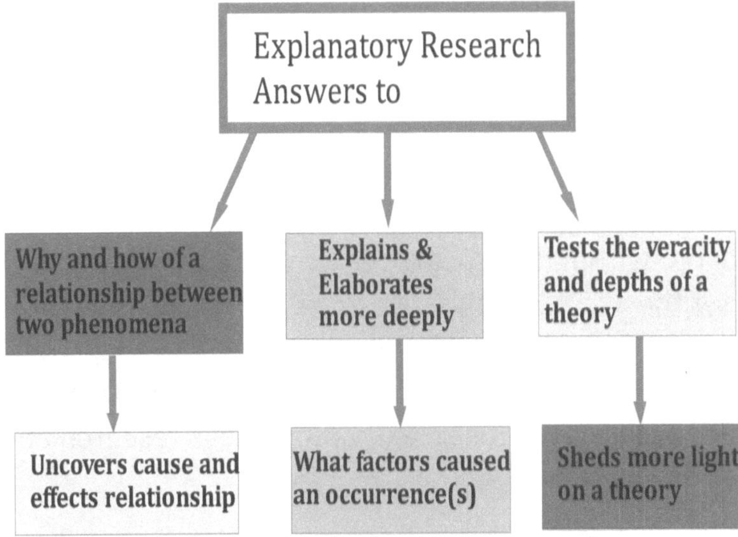

Fig. 2.9: The focus and ends of explanatory research.

2.2.7 Predictive Research

Predictive research involves extracting data from existing datasets to ascertain the likely trends and patterns. The directions or models are subsequently used to make informed predictions about the future occurrence, hence the name predictive research. See an example in figure 2.10 from Iot Analytics (2017).

Figure 2.10 gives the current and future trends of events within a market segment, by examining current and expected expenditures across 13 vertical-industry segments and seven technology areas, from 2016 and projected to 2022. Trend analysis research, issues analysis research and situation analysis studies, geared towards predicting the future implications, are good examples of predictive research.

2.2.8 Desk Research

Desk Research is a form of research in which fieldwork is not usually done, but which involves the use of secondary data or literature search or internet materials gathered within the researcher's confines. It may also entail the synthesis and analysis of some other existing studies or data, as opposed to primary research in which data are sourced from the field(s). See figure 2.11 from University of Portsmouth (2012), for an example of desk research and the potential sources of its data.

2.2.9 Critical Analysis Research

Eleje (2009) defines critical analysis as subjective writing because it expresses the writer's opinion or evaluation of a text. Writing a critical paper requires two steps: critical reading and critical writing. According to Palm Grave (2006), to do this effectively, the rules to follow include identifying the focus of the assignment, identifying your own point of view, considering how you'll persuade other people of your point of view, finding the proof, engaging in the debate, and structuring the argument. The

University of Washington Tacoma Learning Centre (2014), says for a critical analysis to be valid it must offer a solution to the problem(s) it raised, it must be plausible and it must have contemporary relevance.

2.2.10 Doctrinaire Research

Doctrinaire research usually done by people in law is a form of research devoted mainly to the application of some doctrines or theories in a study, as opposed to empirical studies. It is a form of persuasive essay targeted at defending an opinion or belief.

2.2.11 Expo Facto Research

Expo Facto Research is a quasi-experimental study also known as after-the facts research that examines how an independent variable affects a dependent variable. Here the participants are not randomly selected but are grouped based on particular characteristics or traits. It is called after the facts research because the investigation begins after the events have occurred without interference from the researcher. It is used when it is not possible or acceptable to manipulate the characteristics of the human participants. It follows a causal-comparative format.

2.3 Summary and Conclusion

In this chapter, we have learned the major types of scientific studies like opinion survey, observation research, focus group discussion, descriptive research, exploratory research, explanatory research, predictive research, desk research, critical analysis research, expo-facto research, and doctrinaire. The chapter has also given us an overview of the major types of research, especially in the social sciences. The justifications for researchers' choice of each of them at a given time were also highlighted.

Exercises

1.	Design an 'interview schedule' for a focus group discussion on consumers' perception of a product in the food and beverages sub-sector.
2.	The President of Nigeria wants to issue loans to Graduates for a Farming programme, as a way of curbing youths' unemployment in the country. Mention and explain two types of research you will recommend to him, stating your justifications for the choices.

References

Asia Research Partners LLP (2017), Opinion survey.
	https://www.asianresearchpartners.com/opinion.php

Australia Department of Education (2014), School Opinion
	survey.http://www.education.qld.gov.au/schoolopinionsurv
	ey

Bloustein Center for Survey Research (2017).
	http://bcsr.rutgers.edu/focus-group-discussions/

IoT Analytics (2017), Predictive Maintenance Market Report 2017-
	22.https://iotanalytics.com/product/predictive-
	maintenance-market-report-2017-2022/

North County Daily Star (2016), Opinion Survey.
	http://ncdailystar.com/city-conducting-marijuana-public-
	opinion-survey/

Palgrave Macmillan (2006), Critical analysis,
http:www.palgrave.com/studentstudyskills/.../critical%20an
alysis%20.pdf.

U. Eleje (2009), Critical Writing,
http://www2.southeastern.edu/Academics/Faculty/elejeune
/critique.htm.

University of Portsmouth (2012), What is Secondary Data Analysis?
http://compass.port.ac.uk/UoP/file/...

US Center for Disease Control (CDC, 2016), Observation Research
Method. https://www.cdc.gov/healthy
youth/evaluation/pdf/brief16.pdf

UW.edu (2014), How to Write a Critical Analysis.
https://www.tacoma.uw.edu/sites/.../files/.../howtowriteacr
iticalanalysis.pdf

CHAPTER THREE

MARKET AND MARKETING RESEARCH

3.1 Introduction

In the last chapter, we dwelt on general types of research that are common to all fields in the social sciences. In this very chapter, we are going to dwell on the types of marketing research that are peculiar to and mainly conducted in marketing operations. This will be followed by the reasons and justifications for choosing any of the approaches.

The areas to cover include major types of research usually done in the field of marketing like: market research, marketing research, environmental scanning, competitors' research, consumer research (consumer behavior, buyers' perception, studies, etc), trend analysis, audience profile research, market share analysis, market performance analysis, sales force analysis, desk research, *-media effectiveness research, audience profile studies, market share analysis and experimental research.

3.2   Market Research

Market Research is a form of research conducted to gain knowledge about a given market or markets: like the market strength, the type of consumers in the market, their demographic, economic and sociographic characteristics. Apart from all these and how they impact positively or negatively on our organization's marketing operations, market research also tries to track other intervening market variables that might affect the organization's activities. See figure 3.1 on the areas preferably covered by the market research.

Market research is also done when business organizations or entrepreneurs wish to gain knowledge or vital information as to whether to move into a market or not, and the type of marketing strategies to adopt in doing so.

Fig.3.1: Market Research

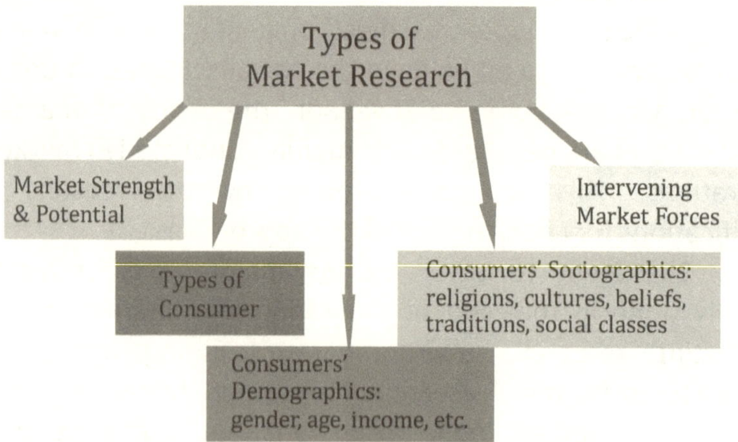

Fig. 3.1: Areas Covered by Market Research.

3.3   Marketing Research

Marketing research is directed toward testing the effectiveness or otherwise of all or any of the marketing-mix elements called the 4Ps (product, price, promotion, and place). Any study done to test consumers' appreciation or acceptance of product taste, product quality, product price, promotion effectiveness, distribution effectiveness, marketing strategy effectiveness, etc., falls within this realm. It is done when organizations want to improve their marketing performance or gain some competitive edge in the market, through the manipulations and management of the traditional 4Ps, the 7Ps of service marketing or the 8Ps of social marketing.

It also involves auditing or wholistic review of the organization's marketing strategy. A company might decide to conduct its marketing research on any of the marketing-mix elements or go into a critical appraisal of all of them, which is their marketing strategy.

3.4 Environmental Scanning

Environmental scanning entails marketing research aimed at analyzing the political, economic, socio-cultural, technological, legal and environmental factors (P.E.S.T.L.E) in a given market, which could impact positively or negatively on our organization's marketing efforts. It is conducted when an organization wants to understand the extraneous variables that affect its operations better or wishes to go into a new market, as it will help her understand the peculiarities existing there, for better decision making.

3.5   Competitors' Research

Competitors' Research is a form of research done to gain a better understanding of our business competitors, what they are doing and how they affect our operations. It entails analyzing what our competitors are doing which could impact positively or negatively on our organizational or marketing efforts. A good example of Competitors' Research may start with first and foremost making a precise identification of who the competitors are, ascertaining their business goals and objectives and how they affect us, identifying the strategies and tactics they use in achieving those goals and objectives, analyzing their strengths and weaknesses vis-à-vis that of your own organization. Then, you can map out your strategies and tactics to counter or checkmate any adverse effect of the activities of the competitors on your operations, and finally evaluating the result.

3.6   Consumer Research

These are researches done to gain a better understanding of our consumers. For instance, consumer behavior research is used to ascertain the buying behavior of the target consumers. While consumers' perception research is used to ascertain what the consumers think, feel or say about our organization, its products, and services. You can categorize your consumers using either consumers' demographic, psychographic, economic, or socio-cultural variables or a combination of these.

3.7 Trend Analysis

Trend Analysis is done to acquaint us with issues, variables or factors that have affected our sales performance positively or negatively in the past over some given number of years. A clear understanding of the pattern of occurrence, helps the organization or marketer to predict the likely repeat in future, hence, plan to take advantage of positive ones, and nip the negative ones in the bud.

3.8 Audience Profile Research

Audience profile research is a form of media research used by marketers to ascertain the type of audience that patronizes a particular media channel (radio, television, newspaper or magazine) and the rate of patronage. The information will enable the marketer and or his organization to select the most appropriate media for advertising their products or services. It is used to ascertain the type of audience that is mainly attracted to a particular media, to know whether they fall within the likely purchasers of an organization's products/services.

For instance, if your product is a youth-based product like sports wears, it may be unwise to place your advert in a news-mainly media like the CNN, BBC, Aljazeera, etc.; it will be better to choose a sports media, patronized and viewed mainly by youths. Audience profile research is also used by marketers to know their consumer audience – who they are and where to reach them.

Slideshare (2017), defines audience research as communication research that is conducted on specific audience segment to gather information about their attitude, knowledge, interest, preferences or behavior.

3.9 Market Share Analysis

Fig. 3.2: Market share analysis. Source: Kovash, Ken (2008), Where will Firefox Reach 50% Market Share?
https://blog.mozilla.org/metrics/2008/07/23/where-will-firefox-reach-50-market-share/

Market Share Analysis is employed to determine our market share in a particular environment vis-à-vis our competitors. See an example of this in figure 3.2 showing Firefox market share in different countries of the world in 2007 and 2008.

Figure 3.2 shows that Firefox market share is highest in Indonesia, Slovenia, Poland, Finland, and Slovakia, with over 45% market share respectively. However, it hit the desired 50% market share only in Indonesia, within the years under review.

3.10   Market Performance Analysis

Market performance analysis is a form of marketing research conducted by organizations to determine whether they are doing well or not in a given target market. For instance, a multinational firm dealing in wears wanted to ascertain how people of all age groups demanded her winter clothes in Asia, Europe and America, and her sweaters in Africa during the winter period and rainy season respectively. Her market performance analysis displayed figure 3.3 shows that older adults of 55 years or above bought more, followed by people in the 46 to 55 years age bracket, while people in the other age ranges purchased almost the same percentage.

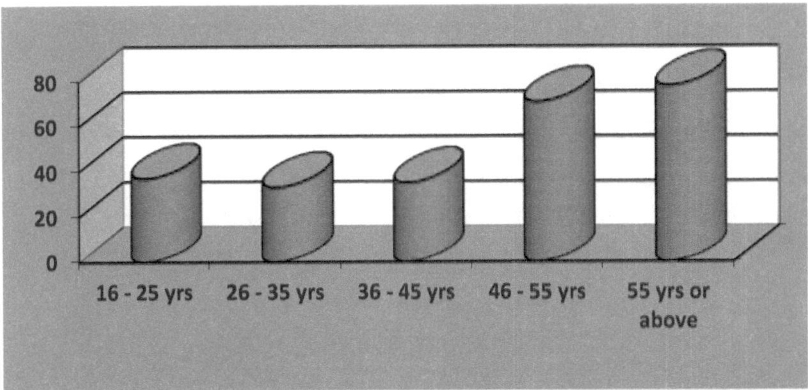

Fig. 3.3: Market performance analysis based on consumers' ages for a firm selling sweater during winter and rainy season.

3.11 Media Effectiveness Research

Media effectiveness research is a form of advertising research used to ascertain the strength/reach/listenership/ viewership of the media we want to place our ads. It is used in determining the strengths of the media regarding the number of listeners for the radio, the number of viewers for the television, the volume of copies sold for the newspapers and magazines, and the number of participants in a social media network.

Armed with this vital information, the marketer or his organization will be in better stead to take decisions in their media selection, media buying, and media placements.

3.12 Consumer Behavior Research

Consumer behavior research is used to ascertain the buying behavior, buying habits and buying preferences of the target consumers in a given market or environment. For instance, in typical African markets, buyers and sellers haggle over prices and negotiate exhaustively before transaction is finally settled as can be seen in figure 3.4.

Fig. 3.4: Sellers and buyers in typical African markets

3.13   Buyers' Perception Studies

Buyers' perception studies are used to determine the opinion or perceptions of the target consumers about an organization, its products and or services, or even the conduct of its sales force.

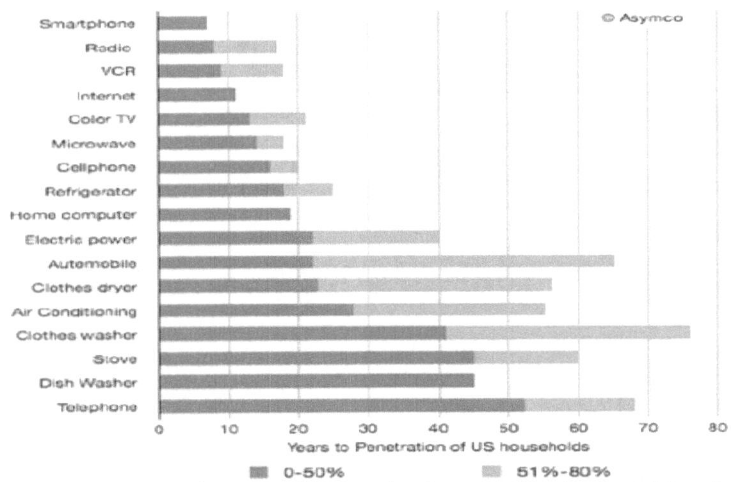

Fig. 3.5: Consumers' perception study. Source: The National Academic Press (2017), Understanding and predicting the adoption of new technologies. https://www.nap.edu/read/21725/chapter/5#38

Figure 3.5 is a study on consumers perception of how long it will take different kinds of electronic gadgets to penetrate the majority of households in the United States of America. This is, however, a different kind of perception research, because it is also a form of predictive analysis.

3.14 Experimental Research

Experimental research is done mainly by consumer goods manufacturers/marketers to ascertain consumers' preferences, mainly with regards to product's taste, product's choice and the remote or immediate reasons behind that. Figure 3.6 from ACC Media (2017), shows us various types of experimental research designs. While figure 3.7 from the Australian Research Council (2015), highlights a typical laboratory experimental setting. However, a consumer panel experimental setting to test product's quality, packaging, taste, etc. acceptability will pose a different outlook.

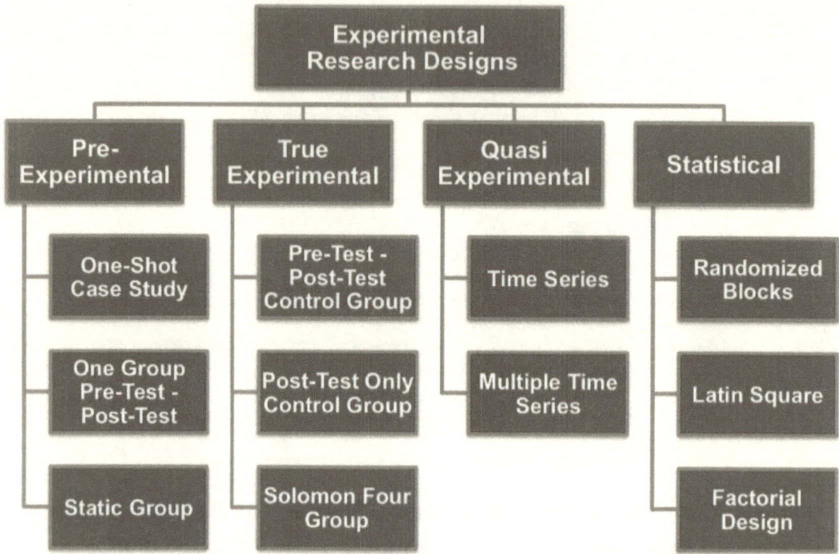

Fig. 3.6: Experimental Research Designs. Source: ACC Media (2017), Types of Experimental Research Designs.
http://media.acc.qcc.cuny.edu/faculty/volchok/causalMR/CausalMR6.html

Fig. 3.7: Example of experimental research. Source: Australian Research Council (2015), Australian facility for taphonomic experimental research. http://www.arc.gov.au/australian-facility-taphonomic-experimental-research.

3.15 Summary and Conclusion

This chapter has treated the various types of research that are conducted mainly in marketing, the reasons, and justifications for adopting any one of them at a given time. These included market research and marketing research, noting their differences. Others include environmental scanning, competitors' research, trend analysis, audience profile research, market share analysis, market performance analysis, media effectiveness research, consumer behavior research, buyers' perception studies and experimental research.

However, we must bear in mind that these types of research are not only peculiar to the field of marketing but also extends to the marketing communication realms like advertising, public relations, publicity, sales promotion, personal selling, social media marketing, internet marketing, etc.

Exercises

1. Outline and explain the differences and similarities between market research and marketing research.
2. Give three practical examples of the following marketing research types using hypothetical organizations and or products of your choice: environmental scanning, competitors' research, trend analysis, audience profile research and market performance analysis.
3. With the aid of a diagram, explain the meaning of experimental research and the types of experimental designs.
4. Outline and explain the differences between consumers' behavior research and consumers' perception research.
5. Explain the differences and similarities between media effectiveness research and audience profile research.

References

ACC Media (2017), Types of Experimental Research Designs. http://media.acc.qcc.cuny.edu/faculty/volchok/causalMR/CausalMR6.html

Australian Research Council (2015), Australian facility for taphonomic experimental research. http://www.arc.gov.au/australian-facility-taphonomic-experimental-research.

Cordura Brand (2010), Consumer Research. http://www.cordura.com/en/marketing-support/market-brand-research.html

IoT Analytics (2017), Predictive Maintenance Market Report 2017-22. https://iot-analytics.com/product/predictive-maintenance-market-report-2017-2022/

Kovash, Ken (2008), Where will Firefox Reach 50% Market Share? https://blog.mozilla.org/metrics/2008/07/23/where-will-firefox-reach-50-market-share/

Launch Engineering (2017), Competitor analysis and competitive intelligence. http://www.launchengineer.com/competionanalysis.htm

National Academic Press (2017), Understanding and predicting the adoption of new technologies. https://www.nap.edu/read/21725/chapter/5#38

Slideshare.net (2017), Audience Profile. https://www.slideshare.net/AnnieRose95/audience-research-22808080.

CHAPTER FOUR

RESEARCH PROPOSALS

4.1 Introduction

In this module, we are going to learn about what research proposal is all about, followed by the major types of research proposals and their applications in marketing research. It is designed to let us properly learn and understand the meaning of research proposal, the major types of research proposals, which include: mini-research proposal, thesis/dissertation research, and business research proposal

4.2 What is a Research Proposal

A research proposal is a brief write-up that proposes and presents the outlook and outlines of a research project and the justifications for it. It is usually a requirement in the academia, sciences and even in the industry. Some research proposals meant for research grants should also contain a request for sponsorship of the research.

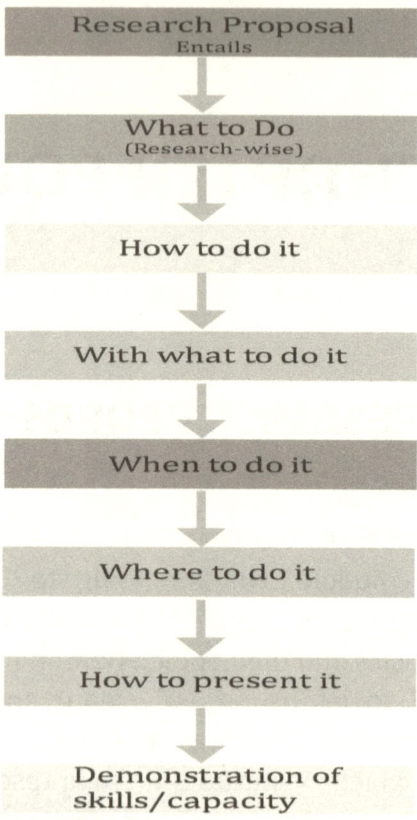

Fig. 4.1: Research proposal's focus.

The chances of your proposal scaling through depend on many factors which include: the quality of the proposal, the relevance of the study, the potential impact of the proposed research, the aptness of the proposed plan for the research, and the potential sponsor's research interest. Some include abstract, but this is wrong. There should be no abstract because an abstract is a tight summary of a completed research project, but there could be an executive summary. Some universities require students applying for postgraduate studies to submit a research proposal, as one of the criteria for admission, grant or assistantship. In summary, every research proposal should specify what to do, how to do it, with what to do it, when to do it, where to do it, how to present it, and demonstration of skills/capacity to do it, as shown in figure 4.1. The question mark there indicates it is a proposal, still begging for approval or rejection.

Businessdictionary (2017) says that the research proposal should outline the research process from beginning to end. While the Academy Study (2017), emphasizes that research proposals are intended to convince people that your ideas and projects are essential. They strive to explain how you can satisfactorily complete the project. A research proposal needs to let people know why the project is a good and necessary idea and that you understand what related studies are already out there. Finally, for academic research, your grammar, the structure, and content of the proposal are equally important and can make a difference in whether or not the proposal is accepted or rejected.

4.3 Pre-Research or Mini-Research Proposal

Means a picture or a brief of what your project will look like, a skeletal presentation or mirror of the work, with their primary elements as will be contained in your research project. When your supervisor asks you to give him a proposal of your project, thesis or dissertation, what he means is a pre-research or mini-research proposal of your work – a skeletal mirror of what the job will look like at completion, with the essential elements. The vital elements of what will be contained in your mini-research proposal are treated in sub-topic 4.5 of this chapter.

4.4 Thesis/ Dissertation Research Proposal

In your thesis or dissertation research proposal, you must follow your university's format. However, conventionally, thesis or dissertation research proposal in the academia embodies your chapters one to three, including the proposed research instrument and other documentary materials for the field work. The essence is to enable a panel of select academics in your department, faculty or college to vet the work so far, assess the outlined research plan and make recommendations for the way forward.

4.5 Business Research Proposal

The business research proposal is a research proposal targeted at solving an identified business problem. It is usually given to an organization by a research consultant wishing to undertake a study for them in one of their areas of need, challenges or problem. For his proposal to succeed, he must exhibit sufficient knowledge about the organization and its issues. However, if it's the organization that approached the consultant for research, he should first request from them a research brief, which will arm him with needed information about the organization, to make a good proposal to them.

4.6 Contents/Structures of a Pre-Research or Mini-Research Proposal

For the benefits of some students who are usually at a loss when asked by their project supervisors to submit a proposal, this unit is designed to aid you in tackling the problem. Remember once more, that when your supervisor demands a proposal before your project proper, what he means is a pre-research or mini-research proposal, which must contain the following:

4.6.1 Brief Introduction or Background

Your introduction or background should not be more than two paragraphs but must capture the issues that motivated the study and show whether you're going to present it historically, in perspectives or otherwise. You must also make a few citations. The aim is to enable your supervisor know whether you're getting it right or not so that he/she will correct and guide you, ab initio.

4.6.2 Brief Problem Statement

You must highlight for your supervisor the problem(s) motivating the study. Some universities demand that you also identify the gaps here and how your research intends to fill it. However, we wish to state that gaps can only be rightly identified after literature review. So, it's better to leave that out at this stage, but avoid running into a collision course with your supervisor. Obey him even when he seems wrong, then find a mild and respectful way of putting across your point.

4.6.3 Broad/Specific Objectives

You must state a summarized version of your tentative broad and specific objectives. We used the word "tentative" here because these might change in the course of your research, especially after your literature review.

4.6.4 The Research Questions

You must highlight your tentative research questions, which must, however, ensue from your research objectives. That is to say, each research question must be in accord with its matching number research objective.

4.6.5 Research Hypotheses

You are also supposed to show your research hypotheses, must be in line with your research objectives and questions.

4.6.6 Scope of the Study

You are expected to state the scope of your proposed research in your mini-proposal. This will include the subject scope, the geographical scope, the time-frame and the sample scope.

4.6.7   Research Methodology

A highlight of your research approach, methodology, and design have to be made here too, for your supervisor's vetting.

4.6.7.1 Area of the Study

You should give your supervisor a picture of the possible area of the study.

4.6.7.2 Population

The ways and means for determining the population of the study have to be given in your mini-proposal. However, the essence is for your supervisor to verify whether you know what demographic of the research is all about and how to go about it.

4.6.7.3 Sample Size

You are not stating the sample size in your proposal because the study proper has not taken off, but the sample size determination formulas to be used in the study and the Justification(s) for the choice.

4.6.7.4 Research Instrument

The likely research instrument to be used and the Justification for that has to be stated.

4.6.7.5 Primary and Secondary Data Sources

The likely sources for gathering your primary and secondary data have to be stated too.

4.6.7.6 Validity/Reliability Method

The methods to be used in validating your instrument and confirming the reliability have to be stated, with the justifications.

4.6.7.7 Data Analysis Techniques

The data analysis techniques or tools to be used in the study must be stated and the justifications for that.

4.8 Literature Review Contents

Some supervisors require that you show them a highlight of the likely sub-topics to be contained in your literature review.

4.9　Citation and Referencing Style

The citation and referencing style to be adopted in your research reporting and the justifications for that have to be given. However, it is advisable that you follow your university's approved citation and referencing style for students.

Note that your supervisor may modify this structure, based on his interest. However, if there is no such guideline from your supervisor, your pre-research or mini-research proposal must be structured as listed in 4.7.1 to 4.10.

4.10　Summary and Conclusion

From this chapter, we have learned the meaning of a research proposal, the various types of research proposals and when they are applied. The differences between pre-research or mini-research proposal, thesis/ dissertation research proposal, and business research proposal were also handled here. Finally, the essential contents and structures of a pre-research or mini-research proposal were also treated for students who usually have challenges with this.

Exercises

1.   Write a business research proposal to any organization of your choice, requesting to undertake a consumer research on one of their products that are not doing well in the market.
2.   Outline and expatiate on the differences between pre-research or mini-research proposal, thesis/ dissertation research proposal, and business research proposal.
3.   Write and submit a mini-research proposal on any hypothetical project topic of your choice.
4.   Write a research proposal to the Vice Chancellor or Chair of your university on the need for a periodic students' perception research in the university. Justify the Proposal.

References

Businessdictionary (2017), What is research proposal? definition and meaning.
http://www.businessdictionary.com/definition/research-proposal.html
Academy Study (2017), What is research proposal? https://study.com/academy/lesson/what-is-a-research-proposal-components-examples.html

CHAPTER FIVE

RESEARCH BRIEF

5.1   Introduction

In this chapter, we will be looking into the meaning of research brief in marketing research, some rationale, and importance of research brief and the contents/structure of a good research brief. This is intending to our understanding correctly what a research brief is all about, the essence of research brief, its importance to both the research seller (researcher or research consultant) and the research buyer (client/organization). The essential contents of a good research brief will also be learned in this module.

5.2   What is a Research Brief

A research brief is provisional information either demanded by or given to a researcher by a client or organization, to guide and help him carry out a research project successfully. It also helps a research consultant in putting up an informed proposal to the client/ organization. The research brief could be given electronically, verbally or documented, depending on which option that is mutually acceptable to the two parties.

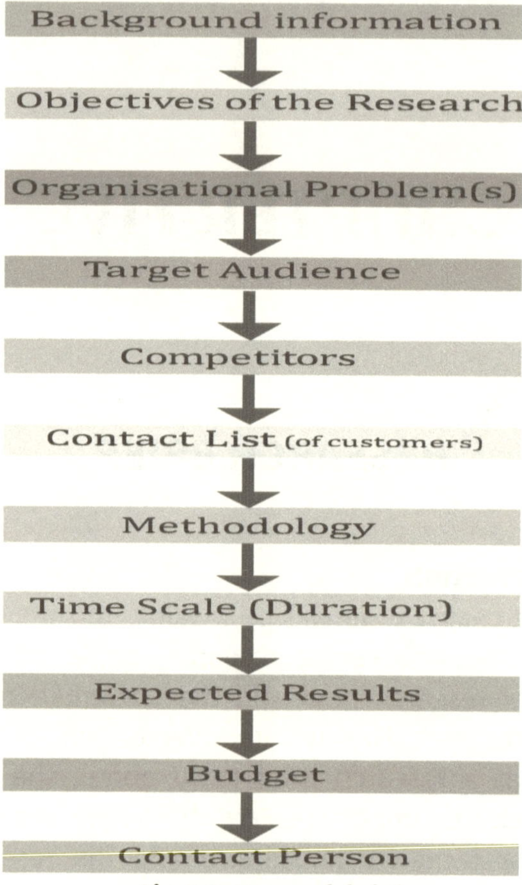

Fig. 5.1: Research brief.

5.3 Rationale/Importance of a Research Brief

The research brief serves many purposes to the researcher or research consultant and the client/ organization. These include:

5.3.1 Importance of a Research Brief to the   Researcher or Research Consultant

The importance of a research brief to the researcher or research consultant include the following:

i. The research brief gives the researcher or research consultant first-hand information about the organization or client, their set goals, and objectives, especially for the study.

ii. The research brief will furnish the researcher or research consultant with vital information regarding the internal and external problem(s) facing the organization or client.

iii. The research brief will let the researcher or research consultant understand the client's or organization's competitors and what they're doing that affects the organization.

iv. The research brief will enable a researcher or research consultant to understand the scope and target audience of a study, which is vital information for putting up an informed proposal, especially in his/her costing of the job.

v. Through the research brief, a researcher or research consultant may demand an organization's or client's contact list of customers or target publics, if that is necessary for the study.

vi. Through the research brief, a researcher or research consultant agrees with an organization or client the research approach and methodology that will be adopted for a study.

vii. The research brief also enables a researcher or research consultant   to know the time scale for a survey, the client's or organization's   expected result,   their budget for the research and the likely contact person(s) to be reached when the researcher or research consultant   needs further clarifications.

5.3.2 Importance of a Research Brief to the Client/Organisation

The importance of a research brief to the client or organization include the following:

i. A research brief arms the research buyer (client or organization) with its first contractual document, in case of any breach or deviation from the research consultant.

ii. The research brief helps the research buyer (client or organization) to work in partnership with the research consultant, towards achieving the set goals/objectives

iii. With a good research brief, an organization or research buyer is now confident that the researcher is adequately armed with vital information for successful research services delivery.

iv. The research brief will aid the client/ organization in getting an informed research proposal from the consultant.

v. The research brief acts as the launch-pad and working tool for discussion between the research buyer (client or organization) and the research consultant.

5.4 Who Needs a Research Brief

The research brief is needed by both research buyer (client or organization) and the researcher or research consultant. These are because of the benefits as mentioned above to the research clients, , and the researcher or research consultant.

5.5 Structures/Contents of a Research Brief

The critical elements of a research brief are as follows:

i. Background information about the organization.

ii.   The Objectives of the research.

iii.   The problem(s) facing the organization.

iv.   Target audience (who are their audience).

v.   Competitors (demand to know who are their competitors).

vi.   Contact List (request for the contact list of their customers).

vii.   Methodology (agree with them on the method to be used in carrying out the research).

viii.   Timescale (agree with them on the duration of the work).

ix.   Deliverables (what result are they expecting from you (i.e., expected results).

x.   Budgets (Find out from them the financial implication of the project: how much are they willing to part for the work).

Xi.   Contact Details: You demand their contact details, that is the contact person(s) you will be working with or consulting in the organization.

See figure 5.1 on this.

5.6 Summary and Conclusion

In this chapter, we have learned the meaning and essence of a research brief in business, the rationale and benefits of research brief, its implications to both the student researcher, the research consultant and research-buying organizations. We also learned the basic contents of a proper research, which serves as a true asset to us in writing a research brief.

The essence of this is because, every student researcher and the research consultant needs a sound knowledge of the research brief, its implications, the rational and the benefits. Apart from knowing how to write a good research brief and the essential contents, you should also be abreast of how to defend every bit of its contents.

Exercises

i. Write a tentative research brief to any hypothetical organization of   your choice, mindful of their peculiar marketing problem(s).

ii. Defend the research brief you have written before a panel of students   and lecturers in your university.

iii. Outline and explain in details, the structures and contents of a research brief.

CHAPTER SIX

DATA COLLECTION METHODS AND THE INSTRUMENTS

6.1   Introduction

The chapter six of this book is devoted to our learning of the significant ways of collecting secondary and primary data, especially in the social sciences, including the marketing field. The strengths and weaknesses of each approach will also be explained. This is with a view to our understanding the most popular and conventional methods of data collection, when and how they are applied, and the reasons for adopting any one of them in research.

6.2 Primary Data

The Brigham Young University (2018), says when someone refers to "primary data" they are referring to data collected by the researcher himself/herself. This is data that has never been gathered before, whether in a particular way or at a specified period. Researchers tend to collect this type of data when what they want cannot be found from outside sources.

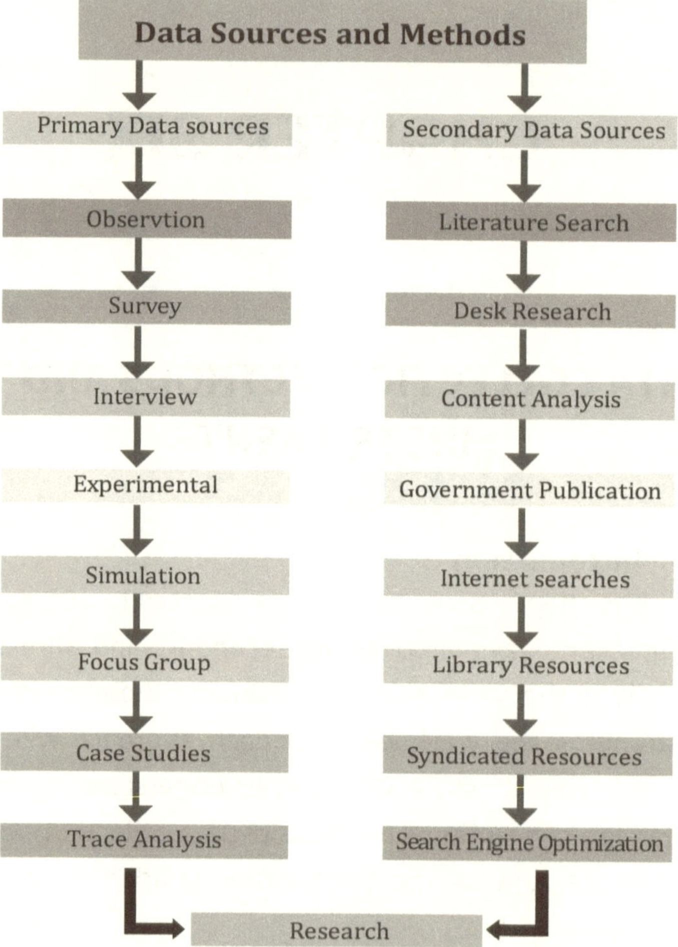

Fig. 6.1: Data collection sources and methods.

You can tailor your data questions and collection to fit the need of your research questions. If associated with a government or governmental agency, corporate organization or institute, it usually requires permission and authorization to collect such data. Issues of consent and confidentiality are of extreme importance. Primary data should come after secondary data in researches, because you ought to know what others have done in that area, before conducting more study on it. So, you have to be informed about what has already been discovered on a particular research topic, before commencing your primary data.

6.3 Secondary Data

These are data not generated directly by the researcher, but rather from previously made and documented reports or studies by others. This research approach applies when the researcher is constrained by time, other engagements, financial or human resources skills in collecting his/her data. It is also considered when the data or information sought exists or has already been done by another or others. The data, therefore, usually comes from other studies done by other individuals, organizations or institutions.

6.4   Primary Data Methods

6.4.1 Observation Method

Observation research is one of the favorite ways through which researchers collect their data. The instrument for data collection here is called observationnaire or observation guides. It is usually the researcher himself who fills each copy of the observationnaire, since, in observation research, the participants may not be aware they're on the watch. The merits include a likely reduction in respondents' biases or "reactivity," which is one of the psychological behavior people exhibit when they are aware they're under observation.

6.4.2 Merits of the Observation Method

According to the US Center for Disease Control (CDC, 2017), the merits of the observation method for data sourcing include the following:

- It enables you to collect data where and when an event or activity is occurring.
- It does not rely on people's willingness or ability to provide information.
- Observation allows you to watch peoples' behaviors and interactions directly, or watch for the results of reactions or interactions.
- When you need to know about the physical settings of a study environment, that is; seeing what the place or situation looks like, observation is the best answer.
- Observation can help increase your understanding of the event, activity, or situation you are evaluating. For example, you can observe whether a classroom or training facility is conducive to learning.
- When data collection from individuals is not a realistic option, for example, if respondents are unwilling or unable to provide data through questionnaires or interviews, observation method then comes handy.

6.4.3 Demerits of the Observation Method

The demerits of the observation method include the following:

- It is susceptible to observer bias.
- It is susceptible to the "Hawthorne effect," that is, people usually perform better when they know they are under observation, although indirect observation may decrease this problem.
- It may sometimes be more expensive and time-consuming compared to other data collection methods.

- It does not increase your understanding of why people behave as they do (CDC, 2017).

6.5 Survey

The survey is one of the most popular ways of collecting primary data in research. It usually entails the sampling of individual units from a target population. The instrument for data collection here includes the structured questionnaire, unstructured questionnaire, and the e-questionnaire, depending on the type of survey. For instance, in field research, you use paper questionnaire, in an online study you use e-questionnaire, in a mobile survey - paper or e-questionnaire, while in telephone or face-to-face interviews, again, hardcopy or e-questionnaire may be used for the recording. Hence, the Pennsylvania State University (2006), defined survey as a research method for collecting information from a selected group of people using standardized questionnaires or interviews.

In constructing the instrument, questions are usually structured into two categories: open-ended and closed questions. Open questions are questions that allow the respondents to answer the questions in their own words. The merit is to track the respondents' feelings to an issue or subject matter. While close-ended questions are questions that provide the respondents with a pre-defined set of answers, like "Yes or No," "Strongly Agree, Agree, Undecided, Disagree, Strongly Disagree," or still "Very High Extent, High Extent, Moderate Extent, Low Extent, No Extent."

6.5.1 Merits of Survey for Data Collection

The advantages of the survey as a data collection technique include the following:

- It helps to capture and describe the characteristics of a large population. No other data collection method handles large populations more than the survey.
- Survey research design and instruments are easy to develop, which is usually structured questionnaire, semi-structured questionnaire and unstructured questionnaire.
- Survey sample sizes, usually large, harbors high representatives of the characteristics of the population.
- Survey research is usually more cost-efficient compared with other data sourcing methods. This fact plays out more when data are gathered from a widely scattered geographic space. For instance, can you imagine interviewing people across continents or observing them perform some acts? But an online survey can easily handle that.
- Survey research is often more convenient for data gathering and analysis. The processing, coding, and analysis of data from surveys are usually more straightforward to handle.
- Unlike observations and interviews, survey research has little or no respondents' reactivity or personal biases.
- Survey researches often present more accurate samples and results.

6.5.2 Demerits of Survey for Data Collection

The disadvantages of the survey as a data collection technique include the following:

- Many survey research usually turns up with low response rate, especially in developing countries with high respondents' apathy.
- Survey research designs are not readily mid-stream the study. This could be a strength, as well as a weakness.

- In some survey research, there is often the shoddy construction of questionnaire by the researchers, especially student researchers.
- Survey research does not often settle disputing matters in controversial areas, like census figures or election results in developing countries.

6.5.3 Interview

Interviews are one of the primary techniques for gathering data in research.   An interview is a consented mild questioning of a person(s) on some predetermined issues and points. It is consented-to because the interviewee agrees with you before you can interview him or her, and it is mild-questioning because the style is entirely different from police interrogation. In fact, for an interview to be very successful, the questions and answers format must adopt an air of conversation between the interviewer and the interviewee.

Fig. 6.2: Telephone Interview. Source: Fieldstation.co (2018), http://fieldstation.co/telephone-interview/

6.5.3.1 Merits of Interview for Data Collection

The merits of the interview as a data collection technique include the following:

- Data gathering via interviews gives the researchers more detailed facts about respondents' feelings, opinions, perceptions, reactions, and mannerisms.
- It gives room for the researcher to generate more answers to questions arising from on-the-spot revelations to the issue at hand.
- Interviews usually result in high response rates, since everyone that has agreed to participate usually complies.
- Interviews are useful for better screening of the correctness of respondents' answers on demographic issues like age, sex, gender, occupation, race, height, etc. The respondents cannot lie to you on these, because you see it yourself.
- Interviews help researchers assess issues in an in-depth manner.
- Interviews give the researcher the opportunity to record respondents in their own words.

6.5.3.1 Demerits of Interview for Data Collection

The demerits of an interview as a data collection method include the following:

- It is difficult for large sample sizes. For instance, imagine interviewing a sample size of 300 to 1000 respondents scattered all over a State, country or even across continents.
- Because of the smallness of its sample sizes, interviews may not give a truly representative of the entire characteristics of a population.

- In interviews, respondents may give personally-biased answers or answers that are influenced and diluted by personal interests.
- Interviews are often costlier to administer. Imagine the costs in travels, hotel bills, feeding, telephone calls and more, to interview 100 to 300 respondents scattered all over a nation or cities.
- Interviews take a longer time; securing the consent of respondents, transcribing the records, coding and analyzing the data.
- It is difficult to be used for widely scattered respondents, like on global research, especially in places without telephone access or poor telephone reception, as in some developing countries.
- It may pose difficulties in data analysis due to non-standardized responses to questions.
- Problems of inconsistencies in coding and standardizing responses may reduce the reliability of results.
- Some respondents might view recording them on tapes and or videos as an invasion or infringement of their privacies.

6.5.4 Simulation Research

Simulation research is another important method of gathering data in studies. Simulation researches entail a form of role-playing, acting out, mimicking, re-performing or replaying an issue in real-life situations, while the researcher observes and records, to analyze in real terms how the target population performs a particular point of interest. For instance, this author was involved in a simulation study sponsored by UNICEF, in which they were interested in understudying the Umuada (cultural women association) system in Igboland and their dispute-resolution mechanism. In the research, different Umuada groups from different communities in Igboland, the South-East of Nigeria, were understudied on how they use their traditional alternative-dispute-resolution platforms in adjudicating on some land disputes, family disputes, and property disputes. The analysis of data here is usually both qualitative and quantitative.

For the merits and demerits of simulation research, the same things we wrote under observation research still holds sway here.

6.5.5 Experimental Research

Experimentation Research is another way of gathering data for analysis in research. It is a form of scientific test carried out in laboratories or non-laboratory settings with animate or inanimate specimens, to ascertain the reactions of the object(s) of the analysis on the issue that is being tested. The sample size like in focus group discussions is usually small. In the commercial field, experimental research is conducted to verify consumers' response, perceptions or opinions about product's taste, price, color, packaging or preferences over competitors' products. Here, the consumers are made to taste different types of disguised products and choose the best, giving their reasons for the choice. Through this, the organization will ascertain whether their demands for the product is based on company's image, company loyalty, brand loyalty or actual product taste.

For instance, in a consumer panel experiment to determine why people drink Fanta by Coca-Cola, five different kinds of orange drinks were put in different glasses. Assuming the first glass has Mirinda orange juice in it but labeled as Fanta. Now, if a majority of the consumer panelists say the drink in the first glass tastes the best and goes on to add that this is because it is Fanta. This result will show the researcher that the consumers' preference for Fanta is not based on product taste, but on brand loyalty.

6.5.5.1 Merits of Experimental Research

The merits of experimental research as a data collection method include the following:

- It usually presents strong evidence for conclusions in causal research.
- It helps to gain fresh insight into issues, matters, behavior and why they occur.
- It confers more credibility to results, since seeing-is-believing, that is, people tend to believe more what they see performed than mere opinions.
- The administration and analysis of experiments are usually faster than other research approaches.
- It gives the researcher the leeway to manipulate and controls some variables under study towards expected result(s).

6.5.5.2 Demerits of Experimental Research

The disadvantages of experimental research as a data collection method include the following:

- Experimental conditions/situations do not always represent the real cases under study, but artificial situations.
- The mood, feelings and other personal biases of the participants may influence experimental results.
- Environmental factors may influence the participants' reactions.
- It is often hindered by ethical and controversial issues like in the use of animals, human beings, human organs, use of minors, gender issues and many more.

- Sometimes, the manipulation of variables may not be seen as being entirely objective.
- Participants often behave or react in such ways as to please the researcher or research-sponsor in experiments - the he-who-pays-the-piper-dictates-the-tune effect.

6.5.6 Focus Group Discussions (FGD)

The FGD is another essential means of gathering data, especially on marketing, social, political and economic issues. It is usually a small group of people of between five to fifteen representing a population demographics, deliberately assembled to brainstorm or discuss a subject or topic under study. It is regarded as qualitative research.

6.5.6.1 Merits of Focus Group Discussions

The advantages of focus group discussion as a data collection method include the following:

- It is used to track the views of people belonging to similar market segmentation,
- It provides insights on how a target consumer perceives a company, its products or services.
- As a research approach, FGD yields faster results than surveys, interviews or observations. Hence, it saves time.
- As a research approach, FGD is also more cost-effective.
- It provides on-the-spot information regarding the issue or topic under study.
- It gives the researcher opportunity for feedback, through the moderator who can shed more lights to the discussants on any unclear issue.
- It allows the researcher opportunity to throw follow-up questions to unclear remarks from the discussants.

- o It gives the participants room to react to or build upon each other's remarks or viewpoints.

6.5.6.2 Demerits of Focus Group Discussions

The disadvantages of focus group discussion as a data collection method include the following:

- Just like in experimental researches, the mood, feelings and other personality factors of the participants may influence the flow of discussion.
- The participants may go on a band-wagon following of the train of thoughts of any member viewed as a role model.
- The researcher or moderator may experience difficulties controlling a rowdy discussion, which might veer off course. This will also pose problems in data recording and data analysis.
- Participants often behave or react in such ways as to please the researcher or research-sponsor.
- The research is not usually replicable, hence, posing reliability and validity problems.

6.5.7 Case Study Analysis

A case study is a research strategy and an empirical inquiry that investigates a phenomenon within its real-life context. Case studies are based on an in-depth investigation of a single individual, group or event to explore the causes of underlying principles. It is a descriptive and exploratory research approach. Case studies are the analysis of persons, groups, events, decisions, periods, policies, corporation or a corporate division, institutions or other systems that are studied holistically by one or more methods. It is a research strategy and an empirical inquiry that investigates a phenomenon within its real-life context (Pressacademia, 2017). It is used in generating both qualitative and quantitative data in research.

Under the academic context, Plato.acadiau (2006) defines case method of analysis as a learning tool in which students and Instructors participate in the direct discussion of a case or an issue, as opposed to the lecture method, where the Instructor speaks, and students listen and take notes. In the case method, students teach themselves, with the Instructor being an active guide, rather than just a talking head delivering content. The focus is on students learning through their joint, co-operative effort.

Students first prepare assigned cases, and this preparation forms the basis for class discussion under the direction of the Instructor. Students learn, often unconsciously, how to evaluate a problem, how to make decisions, and how to orally argue a point of view. Using this method, they also learn how to think concerning the problems faced by an administrator (Plato.acadiau, 2006), an individual, organization, institution or government. For best results, it is necessary to use a combined lecture approach and case-study approach in teaching students. An outline of the steps to be followed and the items to be contained in the subsequent students' reports must be given by the instructor, as a guide.

6.5.8 Custom Market Research Data Sources

Custom Market Research is research commissioned by an organization or individual to an external research consultancy firm. It is the outsourcing of an organization's research project to an external researcher. The advantage of this is that it is aimed at generating data and information specific to that organization's needs and problems. So, it is custom-made to the organization's directives, goals, and objectives, targeted at addressing their organizational decision-making needs.

6.6 Secondary Data

Secondary Data are data not generated directly by the researcher, but rather from previously made and documented reports or studies by others. There are many sources of secondary data which include the following:

6.6.1 Literature Search

Literature Search entails the perusing of several reports in books, journals, magazines, newspapers and even the Internet by a researcher, on issues related to his topic of study. It is a systematic, methodological, planned and organized means of searching through other published sources for information and data associated with a current research. Literature review in scholarly studies involves a comprehensive capturing, synthesizing and assessment of the key literature related to a topic under investigation; in order to learn how others did it in the past, how they did it, with what it was done, where it was done and what was found out. This is with a view to ascertaining if there is something still left undone, undiscovered or needs further studies (the gaps to be filled in your research). To do so, there are some basic rules to be strictly complied with, which includes the proper citation and referencing of all materials, ideas or opinions taken from other sources. Most times, data generated from literature search are merely qualitatively analyzed, except when they involve massive organized, reliable and analyzable quantitative data.

6.6.2 Desk Research

Desk research is a form of secondary research which does not involve fieldwork (primary research), and in which the researcher gathers all needed information and data within his office or environment in published materials and the internet.

6.6.2.1 Advantages of Literature Search and Desk Research

The advantages of desk research include the following:

- It is fast because the information and data are readily available.
- It is cost-efficient, and it helps provide a focus for future primary data.
- It is ad-hoc research that serves as a compass or launchpad for major future research.
- It gives the researcher preliminary background information and knowledge about a subject matter that needs an in-depth study.
- When there is no time, organizations can use it to acquire quick information on a problem or issue and work with that, rather than decisions based on no research at all.

6.6.2.2 Disadvantages of Desk Research

The disadvantages of desk research include the following:

- The results are viewed as secondary, so, not much valued or regarded.
- The reliability of data or information from this need to be further authenticated.
- It needs further confirmatory research, primary or experimental.
- It is usually ad-hoc and,
- The scope is typically small.

6.6.3 Content Analysis

Content Analysis is another research method for gathering data, especially in the communication and marketing communications field. It could be statistical publications, government publications, newspapers, magazines or radio comments, pictures, audio or video. It is used to assess the flow of communication, the degree of communication and the place of communications in some areas of interest. For instance, the number of times or rate at which a particular topic or issue of importance is reported in newspapers, where it appeared (editorial, front cover, inside page, back cover, etc.), in order to ascertain how topical it is or the degree of importance accorded to it by the mass media.

For it to be accepted as a research document, the study must be in a replicable and systematic manner. According to Terry College (2017), content analysis is a research technique used to make reproducible and valid inferences by interpreting and coding textual materials. By systematically evaluating texts (e.g., documents, oral communication, and graphics), qualitative data can be converted into quantitative data.

Libweb (2017) catalogs the steps in a content analysis process, with some little amendments from us, as follows:

1) You should collect and read through the materials, making brief notes in the margins when exciting or relevant information are found,
2) You should go through the records made in the margins and list the different types of information found,
3) You should read through the list and categorize each item in a way that offers a description of what it is about, which will make coding easy and possible,
4) Identify whether or not the categories can be linked anyway and list them as significant categories (or themes) and minor categories (or issues),
5) Compare and contrast the various major and minor issues raised,

6) Cross-check steps one to five for mistakes and make corrections,
7) When you have done the above with all of the transcripts, collect all of the categories or themes and examine each in detail and consider if it fits and its relevance,
8) Once all the transcript data is categorized into minor and major categories/themes, review to ensure that the information is classified as it should be,
9) Review all of the groups and ascertain whether some types can be merged or if some need to be sub-categorized,
10) Return to the original transcripts and ensure that all   the information that needs to be categorized has been   so,
11) Input the data in your coding sheet or system,
12) Analyse the data per required information.
13) Interpret and report your findings and conclusions.

6.6.3.1 Advantages of Content Analysis

The Colorado State University outlines the advantages of content analysis to researchers and organizations as follows:

- It looks directly at communication via texts or transcripts and hence gets at the central aspect of social interaction.
- It can allow for both quantitative and qualitative operations.
- It provides valuable historical/cultural insights over time through analysis of texts.
- It allows a closeness to text which can alternate between specific categories and relationships and also statistically analyzes the coded form of the report.
- It can be used to interpret texts for purposes such as the development of expert systems (since knowledge and rules can both be coded as per explicit statements about the relationships among concepts).
- It is an unobtrusive means of analyzing interactions.

- It provides insight into complex models of human thoughts and language use.
- Palmquis (2016) adds that content analysis helps the researcher to:
- It helps identify the intentions, focus or communication trends of an individual, group or institution;
- It describes people's attitudinal and behavioral responses to communications; and
- It helps determine the psychological or emotional state of persons or groups, through their conversations.

6.6.3.2 Disadvantages of Content Analysis

The University of Texas (UT iSchool, 2017) says the disadvantages of content analysis include:

- Content analysis can be extremely time-consuming;
- It is subject to increased error, particularly when a relational analysis is used to attain a higher level of interpretation;
- It is often devoid of theoretical base, or attempts too liberally to draw meaningful inferences about the relationships and impacts implied in a study;
- It is inherently reductive, especially when dealing with complex texts;
- It tends too often to consist of word counts merely;
- It often disregards the context that produced the writing, as well as the state of things after the text is presented;
- It can be difficult to automate or computerize.

6.6.4 Government Publications

Many government agencies like the Federal Office of Statistics, the National Bureau of Statistics, the Central Bank, the Ministries, the parastatals, the commissions, the institutions, and many more, usually have a data bank of published statistical reports, which scholars and industry users typically resort to, for their secondary data research.

6.6.4.1 Advantages of Government Publications

The importance of government publications includes the following among others:

- They offer you prompt and quick data resources for your ad-hoc researches and desk researches.
- They are readily available and needful when quick information is needed for decision making.
- They are viewed as authoritative, which confers a high level of source-credibility on them.
- The validity and reliability scores are equally high.

6.6.4.2 Disadvantages of Government Publications

The draw-back of government publications include the following among others:

- They are often politicized in line with State interests.
- They may be doctored to suit political or national interests.
- Access to such data is a daunting task in many developing countries.
- The government may mark some of them as officially-classified documents, thereby, inhibiting public access.

6.6.5 Internet Searches

Internet research is the browsing of the world-wide-web sources for valuable information and data related to a topic of study. The difference between Internet research and library research is that the former is based on world-wide-web resources, while the latter focuses on library-bound resources. However, the virtual libraries of today have delineated or closed-up these differences.

6.6.5.1 Advantages of Internet Searches

i.   It provides a database of unlimited global resources related to a given topic.
ii. It can provide direct access to authorities, experts and other individuals through social-media platforms, emails, online discussion forums, instant messaging, internet relay chats, teleconferencing, newsgroups, etc.
iii. It is cost-effective.
iv. It offers quick and immediate information and data for research.

6.6.5.2 Disadvantages of Internet Research

i.   It poses difficulties, sometimes, in verifying an author's qualifications, therefore, raising doubts about the accuracy of the information/data obtained.
ii. Researchers, need sufficient skill to make meanings or draw meaningful results from the abundance of materials available on the Internet (Hargittai, 2002).
iii. The mass of resources may not suit a researcher's need; hence, the researcher needs to wade through them to sieve the ones relevant to the topic at hand.
iv. Library research has organized search tactics and strategies which students/researchers could follow, but the Internet doesn't offer this opportunity.

6.6.6 Library Data Resources

Library Data Resources involves the use of library materials like books, journals, newspapers, magazines, technical papers and many more. It is a vital source for students and researchers in conducting their literature reviews and secondary research. Today, there are virtual libraries in almost all universities and public libraries with a massive repository of electronic materials via the world-wide-web and local organizational data banks.

For the advantages and disadvantages of library resources, see the advantages and disadvantages of literature search in unit 6.1 of this module.

6.6.7 Syndicated Market Research Data Sources

For the fact that data acquisition and analysis (research) is not an easy and cheap task, some specialized research consultancy firms undertake this task for others. When they are commissioned by an organization to offer such service to them, it is called custom marketing research, but when these research firms sell their research-generated data or information to the general market or anyone that demands it, it is called syndicated research. Hence, Market Research Knowledge Base (2017), defines syndicated study as a research study which is conducted and funded by a market research firm but not for any specific client. The result of such research is often provided in the form of reports, presentations, raw data, etc. and is made available in the open market for anyone to purchase. Every commercial and even non-commercial organization needs market and marketing research to know and understand their customers or target publics better and how to deal more effectively with them. However, only a few organizations can afford the resources to commission a custom market research study, hence, the resort to syndicated market research firms and data sources.

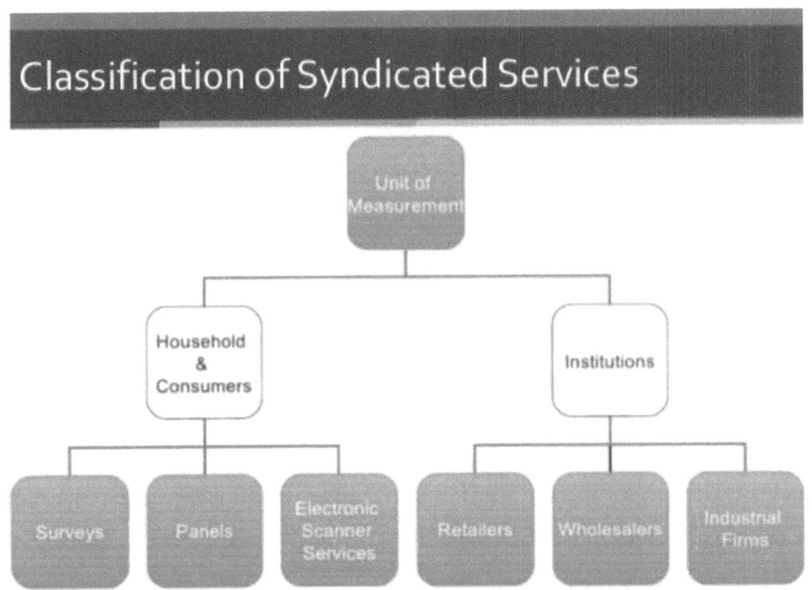

Fig. 6.3: Types of syndicated research and the consumers of such services. Source: https://www.slideshare.net/velibahceci/syndicated-sources-of-secondary-data

6.6.8 Search Engines Research Data Sources

Search engines are programs that index and then search documents for specified keywords. A list of matching records is returned to the user. Using search engines effectively is now an essential skill for both corporate, institutional and students' researchers. In addition to searching text, search engines will also let you search for graphics, sounds and other kinds of files. Search engines will also explore through the latest news stories from recently released press releases to news stories in national newspapers which are very useful if you are looking for the absolute most recent information on your search topic. Search engines can also be used to search newsgroup postings, online and offline events and perform services such as chat, instant messaging and product searches for online shopping. Search engines also provide search access to databases of third parties which allow you to search through corporate reports, telephone listings, yellow pages, zip codes and numerous other information databases (Knollenberg, 1998).

For the search engine to give you accurate results, you must type your spellings correctly, be more specific and use the right keywords. For example, if you're conducting research on 'the Queen of England,' and you type 'Queen,' on a search engine, it will shoot up for you, the definitions, classifications, histories, and names of all the queens the world has had. However, if you type 'Queen of England,' the search engine will now narrow its search and more specifically to information bordering on the 'Queen of England.'

Experts in various fields of your interest can also be reached via search engines and vital information solicited from them on diverse or specific subjects on the World Wide Web. There are many search engines and internet directories, which include: Google, Infoseek, Yahoo, Excite, HotBot, AltaVista, Lycos, and LookSmart.

6.9 Summary and Conclusion

In this chapter, we have learned what data collection in researches is all about, and some of the famous data collection methods. We also gained insight into when and how they are applied, and the justifications for adopting any one of them in a study. We also learned the instrument for data collection in each of the research design chosen. The strengths and weaknesses of each of them were even highlighted.

This is because data collection is an intrinsic part of most research designs. Hence, every student and research consultant must be abreast of it. For you to come up with a good project, thesis or dissertation, a sound knowledge of data collection and data collection methods is inevitable. This chapter is, therefore, designed to arm us with explanations on the significant ways of collecting secondary and primary data in research.

Exercises

1. List and explain the differences and similarities between primary data and secondary data.
2. The Vice-Chancellor of your university has directed you to do a quick study to ascertain students' school fees payment patterns and the reasons for that. Would you use primary data or secondary data for this study? Justify your choice.
3. List the merits and demerits of: (i) the observation method for sourcing data. (ii). The survey method for data collection; and (iii). The interview method as a data collection tool.

REFERENCES

Brigham Young University (2018), Data Types and Sources. FHSS Research Support Center, Provo, UT 84604.
https://fhssrsc.byu.edu/Pages/Data.aspx

Hargittai, E. (April 2002). "Second-Level Digital Divide: Differences in People's Online Skills". Retrieved January 20, 2018.

Knollenberg, Greg (1998), Effective Use of Search Engines. The Internet Writing Journal, May 1998, p1.

Library Web 92017), Introduction to Research.
http://libweb.surrey.ac.uk/library/skills/Introduction%20to%2

0Research%20and%20Managing%20Information%20Leicester/page_74.htm

Market Research Knowledge Base (2017), What is syndicated research. http://whatismarketresearch.com/market-research-types/what-is-syndicated-research/

Pennsylvania State University (2006), Using Surveys for Data Collection in Continuous Improvement: Innovation Insight Series Number 14. http://www.virginia.edu/processsimplification/resources/PennState%20Surveys.pdf

Plato.acadiau (2006), Introduction to Business: An Approach to Case Analysis Winter 2006. http://plato.acadiau.ca/courses/Busi/IntroBus/CaseMethod.html.

Pressacademia (2017), Definition of Case Study. https://www.pressacademia.org/case-studies/definition-of-case-study

Terry College (2017), Content Analysis Methodology & Prominent Scholars. https://www.terry.uga.edu/management/contentanalysis/research/

UT iSchool (2017), Disadvantages of Content Analysis. https://www.ischool.utexas.edu/~palmquis/courses/content.html

CHAPTER SEVEN

RESEARCH METHODOLOGY AND DESIGNS

7.1 Introduction

This chapter is devoted to our learning of research methodology and designs, with emphasis on their meanings, format, types, and components. It treats in details, the meaning of research methodology, that of research design, the research design format, and elements. The differences between research methodology, research design and research method are also examined here. Then, the various types of research designs are also discussed. The essence is to make you more conversant with research methodology and designs.

7.2 What is Research Methodology

A research method is a scientifically systematic plan for conducting research. It is a brief statement identifying the approach, strategy, and methods to be undertaken in doing a research. Hence, the methodology must point out the way, means, and modes for the study's problem identification, research design, data collection, data analysis, interpretation of result and conclusions. According to Labaree (2009), as cited by the University of Southern Carlifornia (2017), library research guide, research methodology describes actions to be taken to investigate a research problem and the rationale for the application of specific procedures or techniques used to identify, select, process, and analyze information applied to understanding the problem, thereby, allowing the reader to evaluate a study's overall validity and reliability critically. The methodology section of a research paper answers two central questions: How was the data collected or generated? Then, how was it analyzed? The writing should be direct and precise and always written in the past tense.

7.3   Importance of a Good Methodology

A University of Southern California (2017), library research guide, catalogs seven-points importance of research methodology with some amendments from us, as follows:

- Research methodology confers' credibility on a study from readers, who are interested in knowing how the data was obtained and analyzed, because the method you chose affects the findings and, by extension, how you interpreted them.
- An unreliable methodology produces unreliable results and, as a consequence undermines the value of your interpretations of the findings.
- The methodology section of your research articulates the reasons and justifications for choosing that particular procedure or technique.

- The methodology shows the reader that the data was collected and analyzed in a way that is consistent with accepted scientific practice.

- The method must be appropriate to fulfilling the overall aims of the study. For example, you need to ensure that you have a large enough sample size to be able to generalize and make recommendations based on the findings.
- The methodology should discuss the problems that were anticipated and the steps you took to prevent them from occurring. For any issues that do arise, you must describe how they were minimized or why these problems do not impact in any meaningful way your interpretation of the findings.
- In the social and behavioral sciences, it is crucial always to provide sufficient information to allow other researchers to adopt or replicate your methodology. This information is particularly relevant when a new method has been developed, or innovative use of an existing process is utilized.

- We also wish to add that apart from the above-stated merits, other benefits of research methodology include the following:
- It acts as the mirror of research and the compass that shows whether it is headed the right way or wrong way.

- Once set out, the methodology makes a study more manageable for the researcher and also shows him when he/she has veered off-course.

- The methodology serves as a benchmark for a researcher's evaluation of where he/she got it right, where he/she got it wrong, to make appropriate amendments in a study.

7.4   What is Research Design

A research design is the master plan or blueprint for the collection, processing, analysis, and interpretation of data. Labaree (2009) defines research design as the overall strategy adopted to integrate the different components of a study coherently and logically, thereby, ensuring the research problem is effectively addressed. It constitutes the blueprint for the collection, measurement, and analysis of data in a study. See figure 7.1 on this. From our figure 7.1 you could see clearly that the research design is kick-started by a research idea or problem, which must be clearly defined. Then, must follow a literature search to ascertain what information already exist on this, which will now lead to your coming up with an informed research objective(s), research questions and hypotheses. Meanwhile, the nature of the objectives, research questions and hypotheses will determine the research approach and design to be adopted. Then, follows the study population, sample size, and sampling technique. See figure 7.1 for an enlarged scope of research design.

Fig 7.1: Research Design

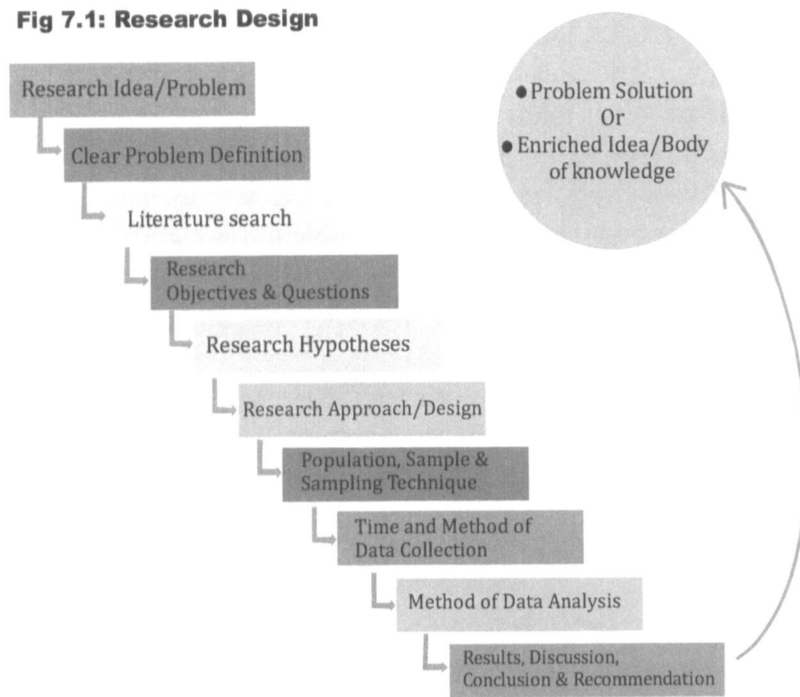

According to the New York University (2017), the function of a research design is to ensure that the evidence obtained enables us to answer the initial question as unambiguously as possible. Obtaining relevant evidence entails specifying the type of evidence needed to answer the research question, to test a theory, to evaluate a programme or to describe some phenomenon accurately. In other words, when designing research, we need to ask the questions: given this research question (or theory), what type of evidence is required in order to answer the question (or test the hypothesis) convincingly? The way in which researchers develop research designs is fundamentally affected by whether the research question is descriptive or explanatory. This also affects what information is collected.

7.4.1 Importance of Research Design

New York University (2017), itemizes the importance of research design as follows:

- o It helps us to minimize the chance of drawing incorrect causal inferences from data.
- o The research design is a logical task undertaken to ensure that the evidence collected enables us to answer questions or to test theories as unambiguously as possible.
- o It helps others to identify the type of research we conducted and to identify the type
- o of evidence required to answer the research question(s) convincingly.

7.5 Differences Between Research Methodology, Research Design and Research Method

In many works of literature, students are being confused with the interchangeable uses of Research Methodology, Research Design, and Research Method, as though they mean the same thing. This is fundamentally wrong. The three are intrinsically different in meaning and actions. A research design is not the same as research methodology, while research methodology is not the same as a research method. Research methodology means the un-detailed statement of the type of research to be conducted, the research approach, and the justification for that. Research design, on the other hand, is a detailed roadmap, master plan or blueprint for conducting that type of research chosen. By research method, we are referring only to the process by which data are collected and analyzed. The New York University (2017), observes that it is not uncommon to see research design treated as a mode of data collection rather than as a logical structure of the inquiry, and warns that failing to distinguish between design and method leads to poor evaluations in research.

7.6   Types of Research Designs

The University of Southern California Libraries (2016), outlined and explained with some modifications from us, eleven types of research designs that can be adopted by researchers and students, depending on their types of research and the research approaches as follows:

7.6.1 Case Study Research Design

Case study research design is usually an in-depth study of a particular issue or problem rather than a sweeping statistical survey or comprehensive comparative inquiry. The case study research design is useful for testing whether a specific theory and model applies to phenomena in the real world. It is a valuable design when much is not known about an issue or event.

7.6.2 Causal Research Design

This type of research is used to measure what impact a specific change will have on existing norms and assumptions. Most social scientists seek causal explanations that reflect tests of hypotheses. The causal effect occurs when variation in one phenomenon, an independent variable, leads to or results, on average, in changes in another phenomenon, the dependent variable.

7.6.3 Cohort Research Design

A cohort study refers to a survey conducted over a period involving members of a population which the subject or representative member comes from, and who are united by some commonality or similarity. It is often used in the medical sciences but also found in the applied social sciences. It uses a quantitative method to make notes of statistical occurrence within a specialized subgroup, united by same or similar characteristics that are relevant to the research problem being investigated, rather than studying statistical occurrence within the general population. Then, using a qualitative framework, cohort studies also gather and analyze data through observation.

7.6.4 Cross-Sectional Research Design

Cross-sectional research designs have three distinctive features: no time dimension; a reliance on existing differences rather than change following intervention; and, groups are selected based on existing differences rather than random allocation. The cross-sectional design can only measure differences between or from among a variety of people, subjects, or phenomena rather than a process of change. As such, researchers using this design can only employ a relatively passive approach to making causal inferences based on findings (University of Southern California Libraries, 2016).

7.6.5 Descriptive Research Design

The descriptive research design is a type of research design that answers to the questions: who, what, when, where, and how associated with a particular research problem. However, it does not conclusively provide answers to the question: why. Descriptive research is used to obtain information concerning the current status of the phenomena and to describe "what exists" concerning variables or conditions in a situation.

7.6.5 Experimental Research Design

The experimental research design is a type of research design that enables the researcher to maintain control over the variables that may affect the result of the experiment (an experimental group and a control group). This form of research is often used where there is time priority in a causal relationship (cause precedes effect), there is consistency in a causal relationship (a cause will always lead to the same result), and the magnitude of the correlation is enormous. The independent variable is administered to the experimental group and not to the control group, and both groups are measured on the same dependent variable. The right experiments usually have control randomization and manipulation.

7.6.6 Exploratory Research Design

The exploratory research design is a form of research design that is conducted on a research problem when there are few or no earlier studies to refer to or rely upon to predict an outcome. The focus is on gaining fresh insights or more profound insights and familiarity for later investigation or undertaken when research problems are in a preliminary stage of an investigation. It is first-line research that can be used to show the way on how best to proceed in studying an issue or what methodology would efficiently apply to gathering information about the problem.

7.6.7 Historical Research Design

The historical research design is a form of research design that involves the collection, verification, and synthesizing of an issue or problem from the past to establish facts that confirm or refute a hypothesis or some hypotheses on it. It uses secondary sources and a variety of primary documentary evidence, such as diaries, official records, reports, archives, and non-textual information (maps, pictures, audio and visual recordings). For the research to be acceptable, however, the data sources must be both authentic and valid.

7.6.8 Longitudinal Research Design

The longitudinal research design is a type of research design in which the study sample is followed over time by repeated observations. That is to say, in this type of research design, the same group of people is interviewed at regular intervals, enabling researchers to track changes over time and to relate them to variables that might explain why the changes occur. For instance, it could be used to study consumers' reaction or demand pattern to price changes, products' tastes, sizes, quality, color, packaging changes, etc., over time. It can also be used to assess the effect of an increase in taxes, inflation, etc., on schools' enrolment in the country. The researcher here observes and records the variables under study and their patterns of changes on two, three or four occasions, to establish the direction and magnitude of causal relationships.

7.6.9 Meta-Analysis Research Design

Meta-analysis is an analytical methodology designed to systematically evaluate and summarize the results from some individual studies, thereby, increasing the overall sample size and the ability of the researcher to study effects of interest. The purpose is not to merely summarize existing knowledge, but to develop a new understanding of a research problem using synoptic reasoning. The primary objectives of meta-analysis are to analyze differences in the results among studies and increase the precision by which effects are estimated. A well-designed meta-analysis depends upon strict adherence to the criteria used for selecting studies and the availability of information in each study to analyze their findings properly.

7.6.10 Observational Design

The observational design is a type of research design in which the researcher keeps the study elements under open or discreet observation to draw some conclusions. In it, the researcher usually has no control over the study elements. There are two types of observational designs: Direct and Indirect observations. On direct observations, people know that you are watching them. In indirect observations, individuals do not realize they are under scrutiny.

7.6.11 Ex-Post Facto Design

The ex-post facto research, also known as 'causal comparative research' is a kind of research in which the researcher predicts the possible causes behind an effect that has already occurred. It is an empirically based investigation which does not involve the researchers' direct control over the independent variables because they have already led to effects which can no more be manipulated. It focuses on the event or the phenomena that has already occurred. For example, if there has been a continued drop in a country's standard of education or quality of education, then in order to find the basic reason behind this drop, a researcher would try to find out the remote and immediate causes from past events that have occurred and the degree of their contributions to the problem. The expected hypothetical possibilities may include: low budgetary allocations to education over the years; poor educational facilities in schools; aggregate drop in number of qualified teachers in schools; lack of quality text-books, lack of discipline at schools; poor parental counselling, poor monitoring and supervision by relevant agencies, and many more.

For another example, supposing there has been a dramatic increase in the rate of road accidents in a particular road in your country. Now, as research consultant the government contracts you to investigate the reason behind this. There is practically no way you can study the actual accidents because they are past and gone. You cannot also play the video to critically examine a replay of the accidents to find out what really happened, except where that exists. However, you can study the statistics, examine the accident spots, examine reports of charges or penalties handed down to erring drivers by police or traffic authorities, interview surviving victims of the accidents and witnesses. A critically analysis of all these will give you some possible informed determinants of the accident. These may include: drunk driving, excessive speed, sleeping on steering, answering phone-calls while driving, poor road conditions, poor maintenance of vehicles, influence of drugs or alcohol and so on. Based on these, you can formulate hypotheses on the likely causes and test them to determine the actual causes, upon which your conclusions and recommendations will be made.

In all the two examples above, the researcher tries to find the cause(s) based on analysis of existing data or another controlled effect, since he/she cannot do anything on the effect which has already taken place on the basis of the independent variable(s) or the cause(s). The results or conclusions regarding the relationship between the variables are derived without intervening or varying the independent or dependent variable. The ex-post facto is therefore targeted at determining the pre-existing causal conditions between the independent and dependent variable or a situation and its cause(s). Meanwhile, the ex-post facto design is a quasi-experimental study because the participants are not randomly assigned by the researcher, since the event has already occurred and the participants may not be reached anymore. In true experiments, participants are randomly assigned, which means all the elements in the population under study have equal chance of being selected in the experimental or control group.

7.6.12 When to use the Ex-Post Facto Design

The ex-post facto design can be used where a real experimental design is not possible; when the researcher is unable to select, control and manipulate the variables necessary to study cause and effect relationships in a study directly, and when control variables may be unrealistic in a study. In most cases, ex-post facto research uses data already collected, but not really for the study.

7.7 Summary and Conclusion

This chapter has tried to acquaint us with the meaning of research methodology, the definition of research design, the research design format, and components. It has also taught us the differences between research methodology, research design and research method. The various types of research designs were examined, to equip us well for our research work in future. This is because for any student researcher or research consultant to carry out his/her research well, knowledge of research methodology and designs is very crucial.

Exercises

1. State the research methodology and design for a tentative study of your choice, and list ten merits and five demerits in the method chosen.
2. With clear, practical examples outline and explain the differences between research methodology, research design and research method.
3. List and explain at least eight types of research designs that can be adopted by researchers?
4. What is research design and what are the necessities for research designs?
5. What do you understand by research methodology, and why is it important?

REFERENCES

Labaree R.V. (2009), The Methodology - Organizing Your Social Sciences Research.
libguides.usc.edu/writingguide/methodology.

New York University (2017), What Is Research Design?
https://www.nyu.edu/classes/bkg/methods/005847ch1.pdf

University of Southern California Libraries (2016). Organizing Your Social Sciences Research Paper: Types of Research Designs.
http://libguides.usc.edu/content.php?pid=83009&sid=818072

CHAPTER EIGHT

SAMPLE SIZE DETERMINATION AND SAMPLING TECHNIQUES

8.1 Introduction

The chapter introduces us to another very crucial area in research – population, sample size determination, and sampling techniques, their purposes, their types, when to use each of them and the reasons for the usage. This is designed to make us master the meaning and purposes of study populations and sample sizes in research, the various ways of determining sample sizes and when to use them. We will also learn the meaning of sampling techniques and when it comes up in research, the two major classifications of sampling techniques - non-probability sampling techniques and probability sampling techniques. The advantages and disadvantages of each one of them are also examined here. The chapter also sheds some light on sampling and non-sampling errors among other things.

8.2   What is a Study Population

By study population which is also called the universe of interest, we mean the total number of all elements of interest or concern in research, from which the sample size will be drawn. A study population is entirely different from a geographic population. For instance, the geographic population of Lagos may be 15,000,000. However, in a study to ascertain reasons for consumers' preferences of beer in Lagos, the study population here will not be the 15,000,000 entire residents of Lagos, but instead, only consumers of beer in Lagos, which could be merely 1,000,000 or even 500,000. Many students make the mistake of confusing the two, and some supervisors don't point this out to them. For the fact that your study is in Calabar, New York, London, Paris, Cairo, etc., never means the entire residents of any of these cities are your study population. Hardly can you find any study where the whole residents in a city are concerned, except in some health matters or government policies. But even at that, it is rare.

Again, students make the mistake of using obsolete populations in their studies, especially in developing countries, due to the shortage of current census figures. They will tell you they used the year 2000, 2006, 2010 or thereabout census figures; they got from one census authority or the other. This is wrong because the population must have naturally changed over the years. In fact, any population figure older than three years, renders the result(s) of your study technically wrong. Even if there is no current census figure of that year from official sources, this is no excuse to use old and obsolete populations. You should use the obsolete population you've gotten to compute a projected population of the current year or the year of the study. We will see and learn how to compute projected populations in subsequent chapters of this book.

8.3   What is a Sample Size

The sample size is a demographically selected part of a population that must reflect the general attributes in that population to help a researcher draw conclusions about the population. It is necessary because, conducting research in most studies with the entire population is not feasible, time-consuming and expensive. Hence, using an appropriate sample size that is truly representative of the population to make inferences about the population becomes the norm. According to Sagepub (2011), the sample size of a survey most typically refers to the number of units that were chosen from which data were gathered. However, sample size can be defined in various ways. There is the designated sample size, which is the number of sample units selected for contact or data collection.

On the other hand, Omniconvert (2017), defines sample size as the number of subjects included in a sample, which is a group of items that is selected from the general population and is considered a representative of the entire population for that specific study. It is believed in the scientific world that large sample sizes produce better results and leads to increased precision in estimates of various properties of the population.

8.4 Importance of Sample Size in Research

The importance of sample size in studies include:
- The appropriate sample size is required for validity. If the sample size is too small, it will not yield valid results.
- Appropriate sample size can produce an accuracy of results.

- The results from small sample sizes are often questionable.
- A sample size that is too large will result in wasting money and time.
- It is also unethical to choose too large a sample size in research.
- A truly representativeness sample size allows the researcher to generalize his/her findings to the broader population.

8.5   How to Determine Sample Sizes

There are four major approaches used in determining the sample size of a study. Students should adopt anyone that is approved by their schools or supervisors, while research consultants should take anyone that is recommended by their clients. These four approaches include:

Using an entire population for small population figures,
Adopting the sample size of similar a study(ies),
Using published sample size tables, and
Applying formulas to compute a sample size.

8.5.1 Using an Entire Population

Where the population or universe of interest in a study is 500 or below, it is most appropriate or proper to use the entire population as your sample size. Students are, however, advised not to be on any collision course with their supervisors on this. The merit of this approach is that it eliminates sampling error, by providing data on all the elements in the population. It helps achieve a high level of precision since virtually the entire population would have to be sampled.

8.5.2 Adopting the Sample Size of Similar Study(ies)

Where there is a credible recent study similar in context with the one at hand, and with the same population of interest, you may adopt the sample size used in that very study, especially in commercial research and when you're running out of time. However, this may not be acceptable in academic or students' research, because, we're not only testing the accuracy of your study but also concerned with knowing whether you've mastered how to do it.

The merits of this approach are that it saves time and costs. However, the demerit is that you may repeat the errors that were made in determining the sample size in that very study.

8.5.3 Using Published Sample Size Tables

Some research organizations or individuals, using globally-certified research formulas have also come up with some ready-made sample sizes, computed from hypothetical populations, which you may use in your studies, especially when the time is of the essence. However, students should confirm the acceptability of this or not from their universities or supervisors. See one of such computed sample size tables from populations by Surveysystem.com (2006) in table 8.1 below:

Required Sample Size[†]

Population Size	Confidence = 95%				Confidence = 99%			
	Margin of Error				Margin of Error			
	5.0%	3.5%	2.5%	1.0%	5.0%	3.5%	2.5%	1.0%
10	10	10	10	10	10	10	10	10
20	19	20	20	20	19	20	20	20
30	28	29	29	30	29	29	30	30
50	44	47	48	50	47	48	49	50
75	63	69	72	74	67	71	73	75
100	80	89	94	99	87	93	96	99
150	108	126	137	148	122	135	142	149
200	132	160	177	196	154	174	186	198
250	152	190	215	244	182	211	229	246
300	169	217	251	291	207	246	270	295
400	196	265	318	384	250	309	348	391
500	217	306	377	475	285	365	421	485
600	234	340	432	565	315	416	490	579
700	248	370	481	653	341	462	554	672
800	260	396	526	739	363	503	615	763
1,000	278	440	606	906	399	575	727	943
1,200	291	474	674	1067	427	636	827	1119
1,500	306	515	759	1297	460	712	959	1376
2,000	322	563	869	1655	498	808	1141	1785
2,500	333	597	952	1984	524	879	1288	2173
3,500	346	641	1068	2565	558	977	1510	2890
5,000	357	678	1176	3288	586	1066	1734	3842
7,500	365	710	1275	4211	610	1147	1960	5165
10,000	370	727	1332	4899	622	1193	2098	6239
25,000	378	760	1448	6939	646	1285	2399	9972
50,000	381	772	1491	8056	655	1318	2520	12455
75,000	382	776	1506	8514	658	1330	2563	13583
100,000	383	778	1513	8762	659	1336	2585	14227
250,000	384	782	1527	9248	662	1347	2626	15555
500,000	384	783	1532	9423	663	1350	2640	16055
1,000,000	384	783	1534	9512	663	1352	2647	16317
2,500,000	384	784	1536	9567	663	1353	2651	16478
10,000,000	384	784	1536	9594	663	1354	2653	16560
100,000,000	384	784	1537	9603	663	1354	2654	16584
300,000,000	384	784	1537	9603	663	1354	2654	16586

Table 8.1: Population and Sample Size Table (From surveysystem.com)

From table 8.1 you could see the various population figures and their accruing sample sizes at different confidence levels. You can see that the data displayed on this table obeyed the rule of "the smaller the population, the use of all the elements as the sample size." For instance, when the population is 10, the sample sizes at 5%, 3.5%, 2.5% and 1% margin of error respectively were the same 10, both at 95% confidence level and 99% confidence level.

Again, notice that the larger the sample size, the smaller the margin of error. For instance, the population of 75 gives a sample size of 74 at 95% confidence level and 75 at 99% confidence level. Likewise, the population of 5,000 gives sample sizes of 357 at 5% margin of error, 678bat 3.5%, 1176 at 2.5% and 3288 at 1% margin of errors respectively, all at the 95% confidence level.

Notice also that at the 99% confidence level, the sample sizes at 5%, 3.5%, 2.5% and 1% margin of error for the same 5,000 population, were higher. These facts authenticate the veracity of all we have told you here, earlier. Compare determined sample size table 8.1 from Surveysystem.com with that of Taro Yamane (1967) on table 8.2.

Size of Population	Sample Size (n) for Precision (e) of:			
	±3%	±5%	±7%	±10%
500	a	222	145	83
600	a	240	152	86
700	a	255	158	88
800	a	267	163	89
900	a	277	166	90
1,000	a	286	169	91
2,000	714	333	185	95
3,000	811	353	191	97
4,000	870	364	194	98
5,000	909	370	196	98
6,000	938	375	197	98
7,000	959	378	198	99
8,000	976	381	199	99
9,000	989	383	200	99
10,000	1,000	385	200	99
15,000	1,034	390	201	99
20,000	1,053	392	204	100
25,000	1,064	394	204	100
50,000	1,087	397	204	100
100,000	1,099	398	204	100
>100,000	1,111	400	204	100
a = Assumption of normal population is poor (Yamane, 1967). The entire population should be sampled.				

Table 8.2: Taro Yamane (1967) Population and Sample Size Table. a = Assumption of normal population is poor (Yamane, 1967). Hence, the entire population should be sampled.

From table 8.2, you could see that the Taro Yamane's sample size table is advising that when the population is between 500 to 1000, you should adopt it all as the sample size, at 3% margin of error. However, at 5%, 7% and 10% margins of error respectively, the tabular sample sizes were given. Table 8.1 from Surveysystem.com (2006) agrees to a large extent with the Taro Yamane's own population and sample sizes table at ±3%, ±5%, ±7%, and ±10%, where Confidence Level is 95% and P =.5.

8.5.3.1 Explaining the Confidence Level and Margin of Error

The confidence level, used in computing sample sizes from known populations, tells the reader how sure we can be of your study. It is expressed as a percentage and represents how often the actual percentage of the population who would pick an answer, lies within the confidence interval (Surveysystem.com, 2006). The 95% confidence level means you can be 95% certain; the 99% confidence level means you can be 99% certain. Most researchers use the 95% confidence level. The margin of error expresses the degree to which the study and its outcome may be short of precision. It is the difference between 100% and your level of confidence. That is to say, when Confidence Level is 95%, Margin of Error will be 5%, and when your Confidence Level is 99%, Margin of Error will be 1%. Remember, that in research as in every other thing in life, practice-makes-perfect. See figure 8.1 for the level of confidence distribution table.

This means that if a 95% confidence level is selected, 95 out of 100 samples will have the true population value within the range of 95% precision. There is always a chance that the sample you obtain does not represent the real population value.

The shaded areas in figure 8.1 represent such samples with extreme values. The shaded regions of figure 8.1 represent such examples with absolute values. This risk is reduced for 99% confidence levels and increased by 90% (or lower) confidence levels (Israel, 1992).

Again, the level of confidence we require concerning the actual value of a mean or proportion. This is closely connected with the level of significance for statistical tests, such as a t-test. For example, we can be '95% confident' that the true mean value lies somewhere within a valid 95% confidence interval, and this corresponds to significance testing at the 5% level (P < 0.05) of significance. Likewise, we can be '99% confident' that the true mean value lies somewhere within a valid 99% confidence interval (which is a bit wider), and this corresponds to significance testing at the 1% level (P < 0.01) of significance.

8.5.3.2 Applying Formulas to Compute a Sample Size

There are many different formulas for computing sample sizes of finite or known populations and infinite or unknown populations. When in doubt, students are advised to seek their supervisor(s)' advise on the appropriate one to use. Here, as a matter of guide, we will treat only one sample size formula for finite populations (the Taro Yamane formula), and one sample size formula for infinite populations.

Taro Yamane Sample Size Determination Formula

As earlier stated, this is one the most popular formulas for determining sample sizes from finite or known populations. The Yamane's formula is as follows:

$$n = \frac{N}{1 + N(e)^2}$$

Where;   n = Sample Size
          N = Population
          e = Margin of Error.

Let us compute this with a hypothetical question:

Question 1: The World Bank worried by the level of unemployment in Africa and its influence on the global migration crisis in which thousands of African youths, women, and children trying to cross into Europe die daily, wants to conduct a survey on the level of acceptability of a proposed micro-credit loans to Graduates from Nigerian universities, as a take-off for an Africa-wide poverty alleviation program. The Nigerian National Bureau of Statistics gave them the population of graduates in the country to be 4,185,000. Using this population figure, compute for the World Bank what the sample size for the survey will be at a 6% margin of error and 94% level of confidence, using a sample size formula for finite (known) populations.

Answer:

Applying the Taro Yamane's formula, which is = =

$$n = \frac{N}{1+N(e)^2}$$

Hence, computing at a 6% margin of error of 6% and 94% level of confidence, we have:

n = $\underline{4,185,000}$
    1 + 4,185,000 (0.06)²

n = $\underline{4,185,000}$
    1 + 4,185,000 (0.0036)

n = $\dfrac{4,185,000}{1 + 15,066}$

n = $\dfrac{4,185,000}{15,066}$

n = 277.78

n = 278 approx.

So, the sample size for the study will be 278 graduates.

Question 2: Now assuming the Nigerian authorities have no recorded data of the number of graduates in the country; still compute the study's sample size for the World Bank, at a 95% confidence level and 5% margin of error, using the results of a pilot survey of 20 graduates in which 16 persons responded positively, while 4 persons declined.

Answer:

Applying the Freund and Williams sample size formulae for unknown (infinite) populations:

n = $\dfrac{Z^2.PR}{e^2}$

Where:

Z = Level of Confidence Table Statistical Value = (95% = 1.96).

P = Rate of Response = (16 translates to 80% or 0.8)

R = Rate of Non-response = (4 translates to 20% or 0.2)

e = Margin of Error = (5% or 0.05)

Now computing, we have:

$$n = \frac{1.96^2 \times (0.80 \times 0.20)}{(0.05)^2}$$

$$n = \frac{3.8416 \times (0.16)}{0.0025}$$

$$n = \frac{0.614656}{0.0025}$$

$$n = 245.86$$

So, the sample size for the survey will be 246 graduates.

8.6 Sampling Techniques

Sampling or sampling technique means the way and manner or the method(s) that will be employed in generating data from the respondents. It can also be explained as the method a researcher uses in selecting the study elements that will be included in a sample, and even the technique used in distributing the chosen sample amongst the study population. It is classified into two broad categories: probability and non-probability sampling techniques.

8.7 Non-Probability Sampling Techniques

Under the non-probability sampling techniques, the study elements in the population that will be included in a sample have no known chance of being selected. That is to say, the likelihood of anyone being chosen as a participant or amongst the sample size in the study is a matter of chance. There are five types of non-probability sampling techniques. They are:

8.7.1 Purposive or Judgmental Sampling Technique

Crossman (2013), says purposive sample, also commonly called a judgmental sample, is a non-probability technique in which the sample elements are selected based on the researcher's knowledge of a population and the purpose of the study. The subjects are selected because of some stated specific characteristic. Explorable.com (2009) adds that judgmental sampling is a non-probability sampling technique where the researcher selects units to be sampled based on his/her knowledge and professional judgment. This type of sampling technique is also known as purposive sampling and authoritative sampling. The process involves the researcher purposely picking individuals from the population based on his/her knowledge and judgment. Dudovskiy (2014), points out that in judgment sampling, the researcher relies on his or her judgment when choosing members of a population to participate in the study. Black (2010), also observes that judgment sampling is a non-probability sampling method and it occurs when elements selected for the sample are chosen based on the informed judgment of the researcher. He mentioned the advantages of this sampling technique to include low costs and less time needed to select perspective sampling group members compared to many other alternative methods.

We must add here, however, that for any researcher to adopt this technique in his/her study, he/she must have lived or schooled or worked and had ample knowledge of members of the study population distribution, to make an informed judgment about those qualified to be selected for the study. You cannot use it for a people you know a little.

8.7.2 Convenience Sampling Technique

This is a non-probability sampling technique done at the researcher convenience or beck and call, without any predetermined benchmark to follow. The probability of anyone being selected for the study is zero, and purely a game of chance. Hence, the validity of the outcome or result is unsatisfactory. For instance, supposing the Vice Chancellor of your University wants to test students' response to a 50% increase in school fees and has given you the assignment to survey students' opinion on this.

Now, you adopted a sample size of 300 students, and staying in your hostel or lecture hall, you constructed a questionnaire on this, and by 8 a.m. the next morning, you went and positioned yourself at the University's main gate, and administered the questionnaire copies to the first 300 students to come into or go out of the gate that morning, within one hour. After this, you smiled back to your hostel that you have accomplished the task. However, the shortcomings in the convenience sampling you did include:

It is possible that probably law students of the University have an 8.00 O'clock lecture that morning, so, all the 300 students you surveyed are law students. Hence, your survey does not serve a truly representative sample of the students' population. You cannot beat your chest that you surveyed students of the university, you only surveyed one faculty, law students. Their views, may not represent the views of the entire students.

The survey did not accommodate any gender balance.
The survey did not take into account students' age distribution balance.
The survey did not take into account students' income distribution balance, based on their parentage or home background. There is every likelihood that all the 300 students surveyed came from elitist backgrounds.

8.7.3 Quota Sampling Technique

This is a non-probability sampling technique in which the researcher shares out the sample frame amongst the population on a quota basis. It is just a step ahead of the convenience sampling technique. For example, supposing that our student friend who was charged by the Vice-Chancellor of our University to survey what will be students' likely reaction to a 50% increase in school fees, now decides that he will accommodate all the Departments in the university.

Now, assuming the University has a total of 30 Departments, and our friend decides to use a quota sampling technique to share the 300 samples to the students in these Department on an equal proportion basis. Based on this, each Department will receive ten copies. Meanwhile, even though students of the whole Departments in the University are accommodated in this study, there is still some drawback in this format, which includes:

- It failed to tell us whether students of all levels in each of the Departments were surveyed.

- When he enters any class, does he distribute the ten copies to people sitting in the front row, or did he use any formula to make it go around on equitable grounds?
- The survey may not have accommodated gender balance.
- The survey may not have taken into account students' age distribution balance.
- The survey may not have taken into account students' income distribution balance, based on their parentage or home background.

8.7.4 Accidental Sampling Technique

This is a non-probability sampling technique. In the accidental sampling technique, there are no set rules for selecting the sample elements. The sampling procedure is merely set to match the research objective. It is regarded as one of the worst sampling methods because there is no guarantee that the sample elements selected can truly possess all typical characteristics of the population.

8.7.5 Snow-Ball Sampling Technique

This is another non-probability sampling technique. Under the Snowball Sampling technique, each of the sampling unit, mainly a person, is randomly selected from the population. Then that person will suggest to the researcher the next sample or person that will be selected. The researcher will continue to repeat this process until the total sample size of the study is secured. The shortcomings of this method, again, is that so much reliance is placed on judgments of the sample elements rather than on any scientific or statistical technique. Hence, most of the time, the people chosen will not give a truly representative sample of the population.

8.8 Probability Sampling Techniques

These are a range of sampling techniques in which all members of the population have a known chance of being selected or included in the sample. There are five major types of probability sampling techniques. These are simple random sampling, systematic random stratified random sampling, systematic random sampling technique, cluster sampling technique and disproportionate sampling technique.

8.8.1 Simple Random Sampling

This is a probability sampling technique in which each element in the population has an equal chance of being selected, based on chance or luck. For instance, supposing the World Bank has donated 500 free laptops to your university for students in social sciences and demanded from the Vice-Chancellor that it must be shared out to the students on a purely simple random sampling technique so that there will be no allegations of favoritism tomorrow. Assuming there is a population of 10,000 social sciences students in your university, your Vice-Chancellor took the following simple random sampling approach to convince the World Bank of his impartiality and integrity:

In the presence of the World Bank officials, he asks his computer operator to type and print and tear out pieces of papers, a bold 'LAPTOP' written on 500, and 'NO LAPTOP' written on the remaining 9,500. This gives a total of 10,000, the total population of social sciences students.

He directs the Public Relations or Publicity Department of the University to put up an advert/announcement in all the University's communication media, summoning all students in social sciences for a mandatory briefing-meeting by the Vice Chancellor, tomorrow morning by 10 a.m., at the University's auditorium.

Before 9 a.m. tomorrow morning, all the 10,000 students have taken their seats, and by 10 a.m., the Vice-Chancellor arrived with the World Bank officials and addressed the students on their mission, and the process to be followed.

Now, they empty the entire 10,000 pieces of paper in a large bowl and shuffle it thoroughly before every one. Then, ask the students to go in turn and pick one piece of each.

Those who picked 'NO LAPTOP' were asked to quietly go back to their classes or hostels, while the 500 who picked 'LAPTOP' were asked to march to the Vice Chancellor's office to sign and collect their free laptops.

Now, you can agree with us that no one will accuse the VC or World Bank officials of favoring anyone. Even if three of the VC's children are in social sciences, their chances of picking a 'LAPTOP' is purely a matter of luck, just like everyone else. The entire social sciences students in the university were given equal chances of winning or losing. That's a typical example of simple random sampling technique also called independent random sampling. The probability of a person picking a 'LAPTOP' in the 500-sample size was independent of the identity of the other people selected.

However, some people believe that simple random sampling, although technically valid, still have some shortcomings.

8.8.2 Systematic Random Sampling

This is a probability sampling technique in which every study element in the population is systematically given a chance of being selected, using a fixed sampling interval, after the first individual is picked using a random number table. Now, assuming that in the World Bank's 500 free laptops competition to social sciences students in your university, the Vice-Chancellor decided to adopt systematic random sampling technique, so that there will still be no allegations of favoritism tomorrow. To get this 500 sample size from the population of 10,000 social sciences students, using systematic random sampling approach, he will do the following:

Determine the sampling interval's' by dividing the population 'N' (10,000) with the sample size 'n' (500). This gives him 20, which means that as soon as he enters that auditorium with the World Bank officials, every student sitting from a count of 20 will be picked out for a laptop.

However, to convince the World Bank officials that he has not licked the information to anyone to sit at a count of 20, they have to jointly agree and select 'a seed point' or 'starting point,' called 'r' which must be a number lying between 1 and 20. Assuming they jointly and secretly agreed on the number 11.

As soon as they enter that hall, the student sitting in the eleventh seat will be picked out as the random number. From 11 to the next 20, that 31, then 51, then 71, then 91, then 111...., until the 500-sample size is got or the entire 10,000 population exhausted.

That is systematic random sampling method for you. However, the researcher must be careful to ensure there is no gender-bias or racial bias or social-bias in the students' sitting arrangement.

8.8.3 Stratified Random Sampling

This is a probability sampling technique which involves the breaking of the population into strata, based on some demographic, sociographic, psychographic, economic or other criteria. It ensures that all the inherent features or characteristics of the population are captured in each stratum and are represented in the sampling process. Now, assuming that in the World Bank's 500 free laptops competition to social sciences students in your university, the Vice-Chancellor and the World Bank are gender-sensitive. So, they decided to adopt a stratified random sampling technique, in which 250 of the laptops must go to females, and the remaining 250 laptops to males. To get this 500-sample size from the population of 10,000 social sciences students, using stratified random sampling approach, he will do the following:

The students must be divided into two strata based on gender-balance criterion.
He will then apply either simple random sampling techniques or systematic random sampling techniques to select the 250 winners from each of the two strata.

This would ensure that the final sampling frame of 500 winners of the laptops is genuinely representative of the gender structure in the university's social sciences students' population.

8.8.4 Cluster (Multistage) Sampling

This is a probability sampling technique which allows individuals or the sample elements to be divided into clusters and selected especially in geographic basis. Every cluster must, however, be an assemblage of its heterogeneous members and their distinct features, to be a true representative of that population. There should also be no bias in the designation. That is to say; every cluster must be as homogeneous as the other. For instance, assuming that in the World Bank's 500 free laptops competition to social sciences students in your university, the Vice-Chancellor and the World Bank officials mindful of the fact that your country is a multi-ethnic nation didn't want to be accused of ethnic bias in the sharing of the laptop tomorrow. So, they decided that the laptops must be distributed equitably to students from all the ethnic groups in your country. If there are five ethnic groups in the country, to get the 500 sample size from the population of 10,000 social sciences students, using cluster sampling approach, they will do the following:

Divide the nation into the five ethnic groups to get 5 clusters.

Divide the 500-sample size by 5 to get 100 per cluster.
Divide the population of 10,000 social sciences students by 5, to get 2000 for each ethnic group.
Then use either simple random sampling techniques or systematic random sampling techniques to administer 100 (laptops) sample size on each of the 2000 ethnic population.

However, the drawback in this technique is that qualifications, merit or even numerical strength may be compromised or sacrificed on the altar of ethnic balancing. For example, people in some ethnic group may be more qualified or have a dominant population, while others may be in the minority. In fact, there are chances that an ethnic group may not fill up their quota of 2,000 students in that university. So, there is need to accommodate these factors in the sampling criteria.

8.8.5 Disproportionate Sampling Technique

To solve the problem of inequities mentioned in the cluster and stratified sampling techniques aforementioned above, researchers use the disproportionate sampling technique. Disproportionate sampling is, therefore, a probability sampling technique where the size of the sample drawn from each stratum is not usually proportional to the size of the stratum, but based on other informed criteria. It is used to address some of the difficulties researchers encounter with stratified populations of different features.

In proportional sampling, each of the cluster or stratum has the same sampling fraction, as we allotted to the five ethnic groups when discussing cluster sampling above, but in disproportional sampling, each of the five ethnic groups making up the University's social sciences students; may be allotted a sample size based on factors like the percentage of students they have in the 10,000 population, the percentage of students offering computer-based courses, students' performance in the last five years, majority versus minority ethnic groups, poor versus affluent students, and many more. The essence is to achieve equity and fairness in the exercise.

According to Fox, Hunn, and Mathers (2007), the critical thing to note here about disproportionate sampling is that sampling is still taking place within each stratum or category. So, we would use systematic or simple random selection to select a sample from the 'majority' group and the same process to select samples from the minority groups.

8.10 Sampling Error and Non-Sampling Errors

Sampling error refers to the level of precision to which a sample statistic is close to the population characteristics. According to Odo (2016), it measures the closeness or otherwise of the statistic to the population parameters that are being estimated. Israel (2016), adds that the level of precision, sometimes called sampling error, is the range in which the actual value of the population is estimated to be. This range is often expressed in percentage points (e.g., ±5 percent) in the same way that results for political campaign polls are reported by the media. Thus, if a researcher finds that 60% of farmers in the sample have adopted a recommended practice with a precision rate of ±5%, then he or she can conclude that between 55% and 65% of farmers in the population have adopted the practice. It helps determine the level of confidence to be placed on a given study's result. Regarding this, probability samplings are held to be more superior to non-probability sampling techniques.

On the other hand, non-sampling errors are errors not emanating directly from the sampling technique used. These may include situational and operational errors, concept-related errors, interview-induced errors, respondents' errors, data processing errors, and many more. To enhance the validity and reliability of their research results, researchers must try to avoid or drastically minimize these errors.

8.11 Degree of Variability

The degree of variability in the attributes being measured, refers to the distribution of characteristics in the population. It holds that the more heterogeneous a population, the larger the sample size required to obtain a given level of precision. The less variable (more homogeneous) a population, the smaller the sample size. For instance, a proportion of 50% indicates a higher level of variability than either 20% or 80%. This is because 20% and 80% suggest that a vast majority do not or do, respectively, have the attribute of interest. Because a proportion of 0.5 shows the maximum variability in a population, it is often used in determining more conservative sample size, that is, the sample size may be larger than if the actual variability of the population attribute were used (Israel, 1992).

8.12 Summary and Conclusion

In this module, we have learned what study populations and sample sizes mean in research, various ways of determining sample sizes and when to use each of them including the justifications for that. We also learned the meaning of sampling techniques, when it comes up in research, the two major classifications of sampling techniques - non-probability sampling techniques and probability sampling techniques. The advantages and disadvantages of using probability sampling techniques and non-probability sampling techniques were also highlighted, together with sampling and non-sampling errors.

We cannot talk about research without talking about sample and sampling techniques. It is an area, students and researchers must be well-tutored on, to conduct their studies very well.

Exercises

1. What is a Study Population? List and explain five basic criteria you could use to select a truly representative sample size of a population.
2. The President of your country wants to research to test farmers' acceptability of a micro-credit loans' scheme in the country. Assuming the 2017 farmers' population in the country is 7,300,000. (a) Using a sample size formula for finite (known) populations, compute the sample size for the survey at a 5% margin of error and 95% level of confidence. (b) Assuming the population of the farmers is unknown, still compute the sample size for the study, using a sample size formula for unknown (infinite) populations at a 5% margin of error and 95% level of confidence, and the result of a pilot study you did.

References

Black, K. (2010), "Business Statistics: Contemporary Decision Making" 6th edition, New Jersey: John Wiley & Sons

Crossman, Ashley (2013), "Judgemental Sampling," 2013, At:http://sociology.about.com/od/Types-of-Samples/a/Purposive-Sample.htm.

Dudovskiy, John (2014), E-book: "The Ultimate Guide to Writing a Dissertation in Business Studies: a step by step approach," At

http://research-methodology.net/sampling/judgement-
sampling/

Explorable.com (Sep 13, 2009), "Judgmental Sampling," Retrieved Mar
12, 2015, from https://explorable.com/judgmental-sampling.

Fox N., Hunn A., and Mathers N. (2007), Sampling and sample size
calculation
The NIHR RDS for the East Midlands / Yorkshire & the Humber, p4-36.

Fox NJ, Mathers NJ. (1997) 'Empowering your research: statistical
power in general
http://methods.sagepub.com/reference/encyclopedia-of-
survey-research methods/n507.xml

Israel, Glenn D. (1992), Sampling the Evidence of Extension Program
Impact. Program Evaluation and Organizational Development,
IFAS, University of Florida. POD-5. October.

Odo, C. O. (2011), Essentials of Marketing Research. Enugu: Benak
Ventures

Omniconvert (2017), What is Sample Size? Practice research'. Family
Practice 14 (4): 324-329.

Sagepub (2017), Sample Size - SAGE Research Methods

Statistics Solutions (2018), Sample Size Formula.
http://www.statisticssolutions.com/sample-size-formula/

Surveysystem.com (2006), Sample Size Calculator Terms: Confidence
Interval & Confidence Level
http://www.surveysystem.com/sscalc.htm.

Yamane, Taro (1967), Statistics: An Introductory Analysis, 2nd Ed., New
York: Harper and Row.

CHAPTER NINE

DATA PRESENTATION AND ANALYSIS

9.1 Introduction

In this chapter, we will learn what data presentation and analysis means, the steps and processes in doing them, and the various tools and techniques used. We will also learn when to use each of them and the justifications for that. These will include the meaning and purposes of data preparation, data collation, data sorting, data editing, data coding and data reduction, frequency tabulation and cross tabulation. The uses of graphs, proportions, diagrams, polygons, etc. in data presentations will be treated. We will also look into some data analysis mechanisms and tools like percentage frequencies, Likert 5-points scale, chi-square (X2), correlation analysis, regression analysis, one-way and two-way analysis of variance (ANOVA).

Finally, the use of computers in data processing (especially the SPSS) will be treated.

9.2 What is Data Presentation and Analysis

By data presentation and analysis, we mean the way and manner including the means employed by a researcher in treating, processing and analyzing data he/she gathered in research. These include activities like data collation, data preparation, data sorting, data editing, data coding and data reduction. It is done in a predetermined and systematic manner targeted at addressing the research objectives, aid in answering the research questions and testing the research hypotheses.

9.2.1 Data Collation

Data collation entails the accumulation together and recording of all the data administered by a researcher from all sources and respondents to help in facilitating our analysis.

9.2.2 Data Preparation

Data preparation involves the arrangement, formatting, cleaning, checking, consolidating and organizing of data procured in research, before the data coding and analysis.

9.2.3 Data Sorting

Data sorting involves the re-arrangement and grouping of data into their homogenous sets and the removal of invalid, empty or wrongly-filled ones from the total number of data collected by a researcher, before the data analysis.

9.2.3 Data Editing

Data editing entails the checking of data collected for errors and or omissions, then review and adjustment of the data by a researcher in a study, with the aim of vetting the quality and correctness of the data collected. Data editing could be done manually or with a computer. Some researchers combine both the manual and the computer-aided methods.

9.2.4 Data Coding

Data coding is an analytical process that involves the categorization of data from quantitative or qualitative research into discrete numbers or "codes" to facilitate analysis. It is also the assignment of numerical and or non-numerical values to a response in a study, for further analysis. In computer-aided analysis like the SPSS, it is the transformation of responses or data into explained numerical figures and non-numerical values that the software can interpret. It is inevitable in all computer-aided analysis.

9.2.5 Data Reduction

Data reduction is a preliminary data analysis activity that involves the transformation of digitally numerical and or alphabetical information, empirically or experimentally derived into a vetted, edited, corrected, ordered, coded, summarized and simplified form, discarding irrelevant data, to aid data analysis.

9.3 Frequency Tabulation and Cross-Tabulation

Frequency tabulation is the aggregation and presentation of numeric and or non-numeric data in a summarized, condensed, organized and manageable form, without any loss of information. It is usually reflected in percentage frequencies, numerical frequencies, graphical frequencies, mean, media or modes. It is the recording of the unique values or features in the data and the number of times each occurred on a scale of measurement.

On the other hand, frequency cross-tabulation records the interactions between and betwixt the variables in the data under analysis. For instance, how does age affect the number of times people go for a medical check-up in a city; or how does gender influence the buying behavior of people in an environment. You also have a high-frequency and low-frequency coupling in some studies, to ascertain the compromise point. Table 9.1 gives us an example of frequency tabulation in percentage frequencies.

Table 9.1: Media through which respondents got information about immunization in Nigeria.

Options	Frequen	Percent
Radio	231	34.68%
Television	183	27.48%
newspapers/magazines	63	9.46%
friends/relations	99	14.86%
govt./health workers	81	12.16%
Others	9	1.35%

*** Multiple Response. Source: Odigbo, Benedict (2016), Social public relations (SPR) for enhanced immunization campaigns. Germany: Lambert Academic Publishing, p.114.**

From table 9.1 above, 34.68% of the respondents heard the message via radio, 27.48% via televisions, 9.46% read it in the print media, 14.86% heard of it from friends or relations, while 12.16% heard it from health workers'/government workshops. Figure 9.1 gives us an example of data presentation in graphical frequencies (Odigbo, 2016).

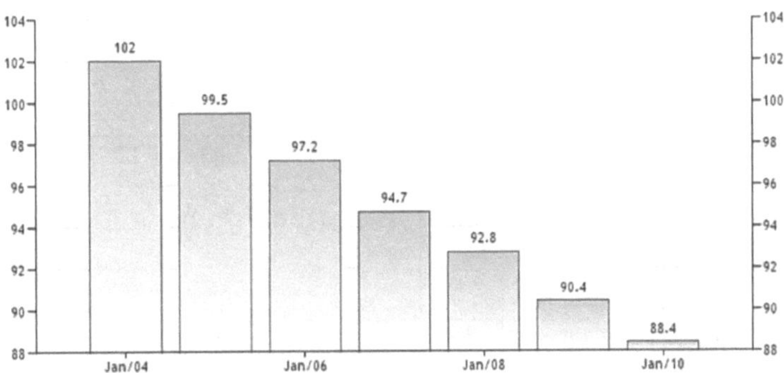

Fig. 9.1: Nigeria's Infant Mortality Rates, 2004–2010. Source: World Bank Indicators (2011),
http://data.worldbank.org/indicator/SP.DYN.IMRT.IN. Cited in: Odigbo, Benedict (2016), Social public relations (SPR) for enhanced immunization campaigns. Germany: Lambert Academic Publishing, p.61.

Figure 9.1 above shows a continuous drop in infant mortality rate in Nigeria between 2004 to 2010. From a 102 per thousandth in 2004, the mortality rate dropped to around 85 per thousandth in January 2010. However, this is still considered high in certain circles where the value of life is held sacrosanct, especially innocent children (Odigbo, 2016). See also table 9.2 for a frequency presentation of data in scales (Likert 5-points scale).

S/N	Issues	Strongly Agree	Agree	Indifferent	Disagree	Strongly Disagree	Mean	Std. Dev.
1	The opinions of the target beneficiaries are accommodated in formulating immunizations policies and strategies in Nigeria	13 (8.8)	27 (18.4)	19 (12.9)	76 (51.7)	12 (8.2)	31 97	1. 13
2	The social marketing products are also packaged in harmony with the socio- cultural and religious norms of the target publics	21 (14.3)	27 (18.4)	24 (16.3)	72 (49.0)	3 (2.0)	3. 06	1. 15
3	The products, services and messages employed in the health promotion campaigns are made easily reachable and accessible to their target beneficiaries	23 (15.6)	47 (32.0)	22 (15.0)	43 (29.3)	12 (8.2)	2. 82	1. 24
4	Both the rural and urban target publics of the immunizations campaigns in Nigeria are adequately accommodated in the programs distribution policies	19 (12.9)	22 (15.0)	25 (17.0)	73 (49.7)	8 (5.4)	3. 20	1. 16
5	Institutional framework for adequate project-monitoring is instituted in the health-promotion campaigns	25 (17.0)	58 (39.5)	26 (17.7)	30 (20.4)	8 (5.4)	2. 58	1. 15
6	The vaccines and other social-health marketing products are made easily/readily available to the target publics	22 (15.0)	62 (42.2)	15 (10.2)	41 (27.9)	7 (4.8)	2. 65	1. 17
7	Social-marketing messages that are religious friendly are used in the health marketing messages	11 (7.5)	16 (10.9)	53 (36.1)	48 (32.7)	19 (12.9)	3. 32	1. 07

Source: Odigbo, Benedict (2016), Social public relations (SPR) for enhanced immunization campaigns. Germany: Lambert Academic Publishing, p.104.

Table 9.2: Respondents views on the implementation of the immunization programme in Nigeria, presented in Likert's 5-points Likert Scale

9.4 Use of Graphs in Data Presentations

For ease of readers' comprehension, understanding and appreciation, it is often advisable to present research data and results in graphic formats which include the use of graphs, proportions, diagrams, polygons, and many more.

9.4.1 Graphs

A graph is a visual symbol or diagram showing the relationship between two or more variable quantities, measured along two axes (the horizontal and vertical angles), at right angles to each other. It could be represented by dots, lines, line segments, areas, curves, bars, pies, etc. It is sometimes a mathematical symbol and often describes the relationships between some lines and points. They come in the form of bar graphs, pie graphs, histograms, line graphs, scatter charts, stemplots, Venn diagrams, population pyramid graphs and many more. See figures 9.3 to 9.6 for some examples of graphs.

9.4.2: Line Graphs

According to Samantha (2018), line charts, or line graphs, are powerful visual tools that illustrate trends in data over a period or a particular correlation. For example, one axis of the graph might represent a variable value, while the other axis often displays a timeline. Each value is plotted on the chart, and then the points are connected to display a trend over the compared time span. Multiple directions can be distinguished by plotting lines of various colors or patterns. For example, figure 9.3 shows the popularity of different social media networks over the course of a year.

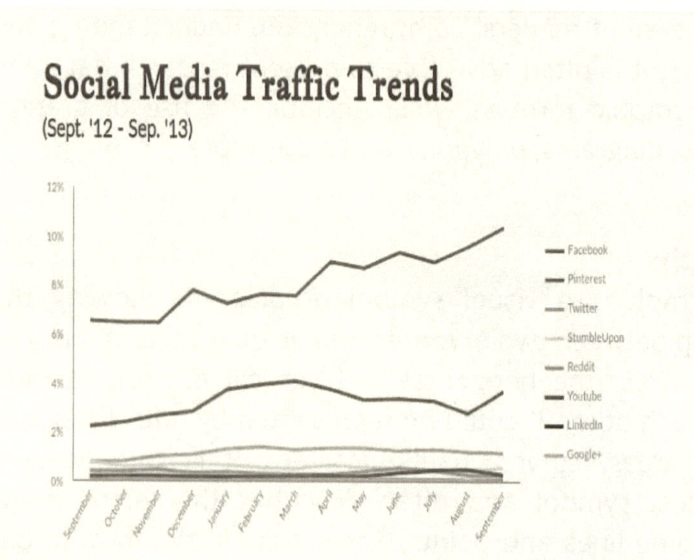

Fig. 9.3: Line graphs of social media traffic. Source: Samantha Lile (2018), 44 Types of Graphs Perfect for Every Top Industry. http://blog.visme.co/types-of-graphs/

9.3.3 Population Pyramid Graph

Population pyramid graph is a form of pyramidal visual representation of two groups in a population. The chart classically takes on the shape of a pyramid when a population is healthy and growing — the most abundant groups are the youngest, and each gender dwindles somewhat equally as the population ages, leaving the smallest groups at the top of the graph (Samantha, 2018).

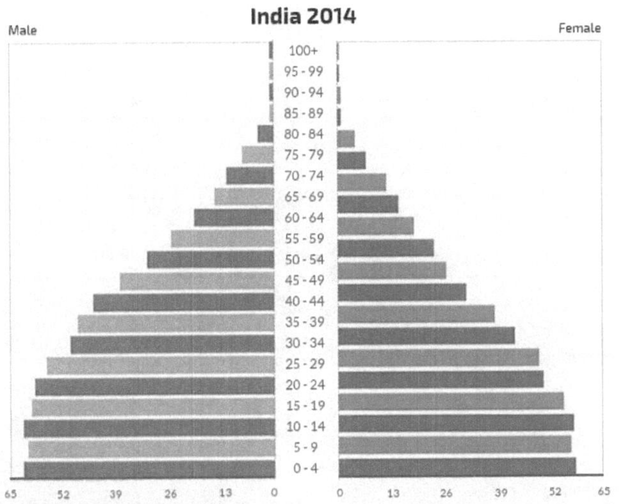

Fig. 9.4: Population pyramid graph. Source: Samantha Lile (2018), 44 Types of Graphs Perfect for Every Top Industry. image: http://blog.visme.co/wp-content/uploads/2017/07/

Figure 9.4 gives a pictorial view of the population trend in India, between males and females, in 2014. Organizations and marketers could use it in their products' production and distribution decision-making.

9.4.4 Scatter Plots

A scatter graph also known as a scattergram is a form of figure that is made up of two axes, each representing a set of data. One axis might represent the numbers of miles driven by a vehicle, while the second axis displays the total gallons of gasoline or fuel used.

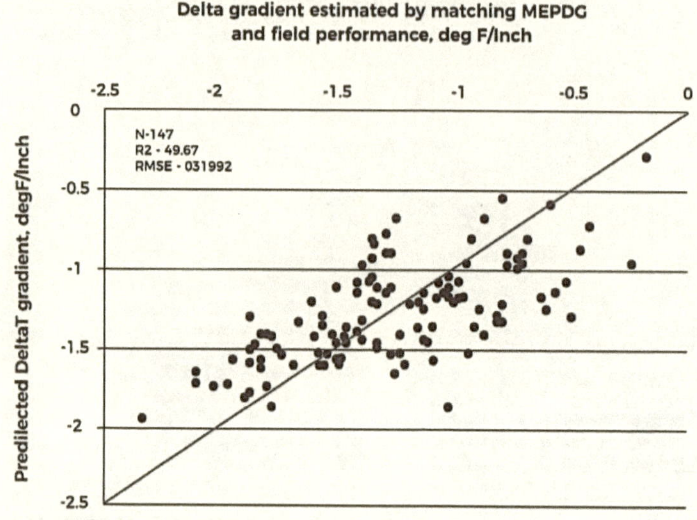

Fig. 9.5: A scatter graph. Source: Samantha Lile (2018), 44 Types of Graphs Perfect for Every Top Industry. image: http://blog.visme.co/wp-content/uploads/2017/07/Engineering-and-Technology-Scatter-Plots.jpg

For each car examined, the miles-per-gallon reading is shown by dots plotted on a graph. When multiple dots are plotted, the trends can be marked out, and the samples then can be compared, based on how many colors are seen in the chart (Samantha, 2018).

9.5 Some Data Analysis Tools

Hundreds of statistical tools are employed in data analysis. Students should find out from their supervisor's or the school authority which ones are approved for them. Meanwhile, we are going to look into some of the most popular ones amongst students as follows: Chi-square (X2), Spearman's Correlation Analysis, Tests of Proportion, Regression Analysis,

One-Way and Two-Way Analysis of Variance (ANOVA), and the use of computers in data processing (the SPSS).

9.5.1 Chi-square (X²) Test

The chi-square statistic commonly represented by 'X²' is a statistical technique used to determine the extent to which two categorical variables' distributions differ from one another. It is used to determine the level of relationship between two nominal numerical, categorical variables. According to the Jonh Hopkins University and Dernier (2008), the chi-square statistic may be used to test the hypothesis of association or no association between two or more variables, populations, or criteria where observed frequencies are compared to expected frequencies.

Fisher and Yates (2014), observe that Chi-square is a statistical test used to compare observed data frequencies with the one we expect to obtain according to a specific hypothesis. While Statistics Solution (2017), posits that the Chi-Square statistic is most commonly used to evaluate Tests of Independence when utilizing a cross-tabulation. This is often called a bivariate table. Crosstabulation usually shows the distributions of two categorical variables simultaneously, with the intersections of the categories of the variables appearing in the cells of the table. The Chi-Square Test assesses the degree of association between the two variables by comparing the observed frequencies or responses in the cells to the expected frequencies should the variables be truly independent of each other. Computing the Chi-Square statistic and comparing it against a critical value from the Chi-Square distribution allows the researcher to assess whether the observed cell counts are significantly different from the expected cell counts (Statistics Solution, 2017).

To compute the Chi-Square demands the following steps:
Present the data table(s) to be used, displaying the observed frequency, which is your collated data.
Work out the Expected Frequencies from the data table(s).
Compute and determine the degree of freedom.
Compute the Chi-Square result.
Interpret your result.

In the Chi-Square calculation, the formula is:
$$X^2 = \sum \frac{O - E}{E}$$
Where, O = Observed Frequency (the observed counts in the cells).

E = Expected Frequency if no relationship exists between the variables.

Others use the notations: $X^2 = \frac{(f_o - f_e)^2}{f_e}$

Where, fo = Observed Frequency (the observed counts in the cells).

fe = Expected Frequency if no relationship exists between the variables.

Whichever notation you use is still right, what matters is the correctness of the computations.
To compute the expected frequency, the formula is:
$$\frac{(Row\ Total\ X\ Column\ Total)}{Overall\ total}$$

However, for one table, you may use the formula:

Expected Frequency = $\frac{\sum \text{Observed Frequency}}{\text{Number of Observations}}$

Whatever result you get, could be used to trace the degree of freedom from a chi-square statistical table, based on study's margin of error. Let us now see one worked example:

Table 9.3: Respondents' views on whether the use of ICT media resources would have significant positive effect as a tool for check-mating electoral violence in Nigeria

Options	Frequency	Percent
Strongly Agree	127	33.60%
Agree	137	36.24%
Undecided	33	8.73%
Disagree	41	10.85%
Strongly Disagree	40	10.58%
Total	378	100%

Data on table 9.3 reveal that 33.60% of the respondents strongly agreed that the use of ICT media resources in the country would have significant positive effect as a tool for check-mating electoral violence in Nigeria. 36.24% of the respondents equally agreed with that; 8.73% were undecided; 10.85% disagreed, while 10.58% strongly disagreed with the point. See figure 9.6 for a pictorial graph of this result.

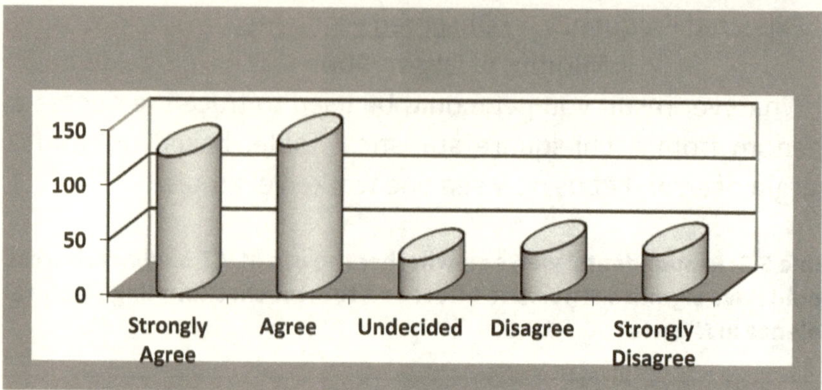

Fig. 9.6: Respondents' views on whether the use of ICT media resources would have significant positive effect on check-mating electoral violence in Nigeria.

Test of Hypothesis

Ho: The use of ICT media resources would not have significant positive effect as a tool for check-mating electoral violence in Nigeria.

Hi: The use of ICT media resources would have significant positive effect as a tool for check-mating electoral violence in Nigeria.

Test Statistics = Chi-Square (X^2)

$$X^2 = \frac{\sum O - E}{E}$$

Expected Frequency = $\frac{\sum \text{Observed Frequency}}{\text{Number of Observations}}$

$$= \frac{127 + 137 + 33 + 41 + 40}{5} = 75.\,6 = 76. \text{ approximately}$$

Degree of Freedom = 4. Hence, Critical Chi-Square at 5% Margin of Error = 9.49

$$X^2 = \frac{(127-76)^2}{76} + \frac{(137-76)^2}{76} + \frac{(33-76)^2}{76} + \frac{(41-76)^2}{76} + \frac{(40-76)^2}{76}$$

$$= 34.22 + 48.96 + 24.33 + 16.12 + 17.05$$

$$= 140.68$$

Decision

Since the calculated chi-square (= 140.68, $p < 0.05$) is greater than the critical chi-square (9.49), we hereby reject the Ho and accept the Hi which says that "The use of ICT media resources would have significant positive effect as a tool for check-mating electoral violence in Nigeria."

Note: That 'Ho' means null-hypothesis, while the 'Hi' means alternative hypothesis.

9.5.2 Correlation Analysis

These are a range of statistical analysis that measures bivariate variables, to test the degree of association between the two variables and the direction of the relationship. In computing the strength of the relationship, the correlation coefficient is valued between +1 and -1. There are two major types of the correlation analysis: Pearson correlation coefficient (that measures only linear relationships), and the Spearman correlation coefficient (that measures only monotonic relationships). Researchers can also measure other relationships. There is also the Kendall correlation coefficient.

9.5.2.1 Pearson Product Moment Correlation

The Pearson correlation evaluates the linear relationship between two continuous variables. A relationship is linear when a change in one variable is associated with a proportional change in the other variable (Minitab, 2017). For example, you can use a Pearson correlation to evaluate the extent increases in a product's quantity, price, volume, etc., is correlated with consumers' brand switch to another product.

9.5.2.2 Spearman Rank-Order Correlation

The Spearman correlation analyzes the single relationship that exists between two continuous or ordinal variables. In the single correlation, the variables usually change together, but not necessarily at the same rate. Hence, the Spearman correlation coefficient follows the ranked values for each variable rather than the raw data (Minitab, 2017). Let us now see one worked example with Spearman correlation analysis.

Table 9.4: Assessment of whether there is a significant degree of correlation between the pre-election comments of politicians and electoral violence in Nigeria. **Source:** Odigbo, Ben; Ugwu-Ogbu, Silk & Odigbo, Rose Adannia (2014), The Correlation between Social Violence and the Comments of Nigerian Politicians during Electioneering Campaigns: A Political Marketing Study. Journal of Law, Policy and Globalization, Vol.26, p.1-12.

Options	Frequency	Percent
Strongly Agree (SA)	134	33.58%
Agree (A)	187	46.87%
Undecided (Und)	29	7.27%
Disagree (D)	25	6.27%
Strongly Disagree (SD)	24	6.02%
Total	399	100%

A graphic display of this result is shown in figure 9.7 below:

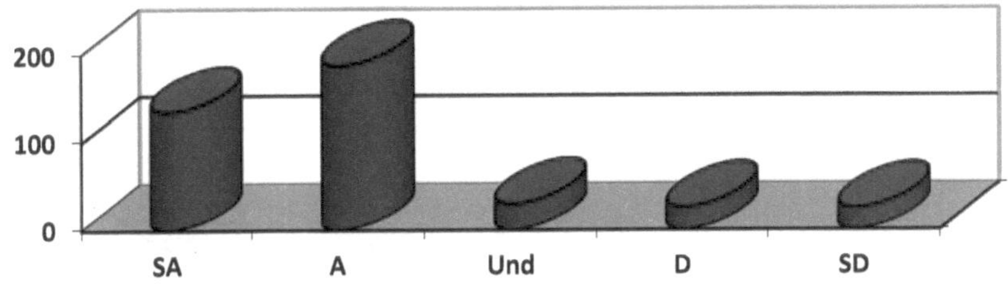

Fig. 9.7: Assessment of the correlation between the pre-election comments of politicians and electoral violence in Nigeria. Source: Odigbo, Ben; Ugwu-Ogbu, Silk & Odigbo, Rose Adannia (2014), The Correlation between Social Violence and the Comments of Nigerian Politicians during Electioneering Campaigns: A Political Marketing Study. Journal of Law, Policy, and Globalization, Vol.26, p.1-12.

Table 9.5: Assessment of the strength of political marketing tools to provide a significant panacea for the problem of electoral violence in Nigeria.

Options	Frequency	Percent
Strongly Agree (SA)	133	33.33%
Agree (A)	147	36.84%
Undecided (Und)	33	8.27%
Disagree (D)	27	6.77%
Strongly Disagree (SD)	59	14.79%
Total	399	100%

Source: Odigbo, Ben; Ugwu-Ogbu, Silk & Odigbo, Rose Adannia (2014), The Correlation between Social Violence and the Comments of Nigerian Politicians during Electioneering Campaigns: A Political Marketing Study. Journal of Law, Policy, and Globalization, Vol.26, p.1-12.

See a graphic display of this result in figure 9.8 below:

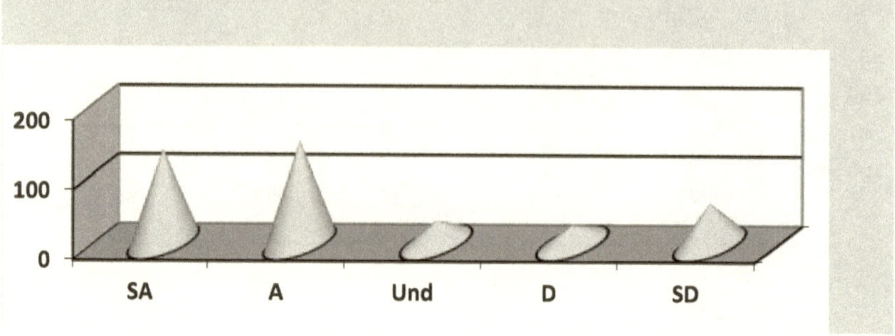

Fig. 9.8: On whether political marketing tools could provide a significant panacea for electoral violence in Nigeria. Source: Odigbo, Ben; Ugwu-Ogbu, Silk & Odigbo, Rose Adannia (2014), The Correlation between Social Violence and the Comments of Nigerian Politicians during Electioneering Campaigns: A Political Marketing Study. Journal of Law, Policy, and Globalization, Vol.26, p.1-12.

Test of Hypothesis

Ho: There is no significant correlation between the pre-election comments of politicians and electoral violence in Nigeria.

Hi: There is a significant correlation between the pre-election comments of politicians and electoral violence in Nigeria.

Test Statistics = Spearman Correlation Coefficient (r^s)

Table 9.6: **Statistical Test of Hypothesis 1**

Options	Data 1	Data 2	Rank 1	Rank 2	D	d^2
Strongly Agree	134	133	4	4	0	0
Agree	187	147	5	5	0	0
Undecided	29	33	3	2	1	1
Disagree	25	27	2	1	1	1

Strongly Disagree	24	59	1	3	-2	4

Analyzed with data from tables 9.4 and 9.5. Source: Odigbo, Ben; Ugwu-Ogbu, Silk & Odigbo, Rose Adannia (2014), The Correlation between Social Violence and the Comments of Nigerian Politicians during Electioneering Campaigns: A Political Marketing Study. Journal of Law, Policy and Globalization, Vol.26, p.1-12.

$\Sigma d2 = 0 + 0 + 1 + 1 + 4 = 6$

So $r^s = \underline{1- 2 \times \Sigma d2}$

$n(n2-1)$

$r^s = \underline{1- (2 \times 6)}$

$\quad n(n2-1)$

$r^s = \underline{1- 2 \times 6}$

$\quad 5(52 - 1)$

$rs = \underline{1- 12}$

$\quad 124$

$rs = 1- 0.096$

$rs = 0.904$

Fig. 9.9: Interpretation of the Result of the Spearman Correlation Coefficient

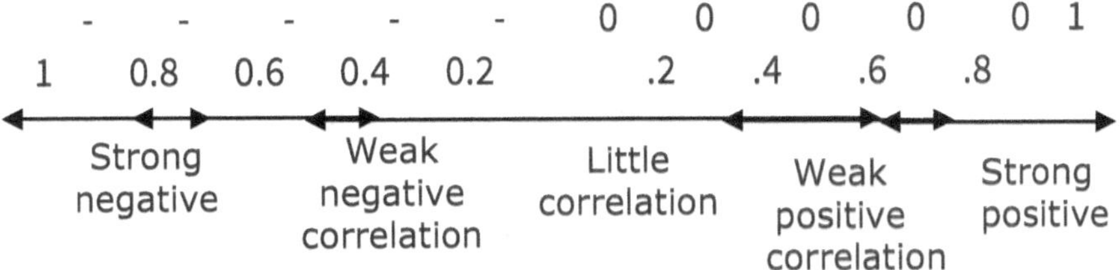

Decision

Since the result of the Spearman Correlation Coefficient (rs = 0.904), indicates a strong positive correlation, we hereby reject the Ho and accept the Hi which says that "there is significant correlation between the pre-election negative comments of some politicians and the violence that followed the 2011 presidential election in Nigeria (Odigbo, Ugwu-Ogbu & Odigbo, 2014)."

9.5.3 Test of Proportion

This is a statistical technique for comparing two populations when the variable is categorical (for example, males/females, beer drinkers/non-alcohol drinkers, supporters/non-supporters of a political party, and so on) when we are interested in the proportion of individuals on one side or the other and their characteristic.

To make this comparison, two independent (separate) random samples need to be selected, one from each population. The null hypothesis (Ho) is that the two population proportions are the same; in other words, that their difference is equal to 0. The notation for the null hypothesis is Ho: p1 = p2, where p1 is the proportion of the first population, and p2 is the proportion of the second population (Rumsey, 2018).

To calculate the test statistic, do the following:
You compute the sample proportions for each of the observed data samples,
Compute the difference between the two sample proportions,
Calculate the overall sample proportion,
Compute the standard error,
Then, divide the result from Step 2 by the result from Step 4.

Let us now work one example for better understanding of the subject matter.

Table 9.7: Respondents' views on whether the country's electoral laws are adequately potent enough for enforcing ethical communication behavior during electioneering in Nigeria

Options	Frequency	Percent
Strongly Agree	122	32.28%
Agree	141	37.30%
Undecided	37	9.79%
Disagree	35	9.26%
Strongly Disagree	43	11.38%
Total	378	100%

Data on table 9.7 gives the information that 32.28% of the respondents strongly agreed that the country's electoral laws are adequately potent enough for enforcing ethical communication behavior amongst Nigerian politicians during electioneering. 37.30% of the respondents equally agreed with that; 9.79% were undecided; 9.26% disagreed, while 11.38% strongly disagreed with the point.

Test of Hypothesis

Ho: Nigeria's electoral laws are not adequately potent for enforcing ethical communication behavior during electioneering in the country.

Hi: Nigeria's electoral laws are adequately potent for enforcing ethical communication behavior during electioneering in the country.

Test Statistics = Tests of Proportions (using data from table 9.7).

With the formula:

$$\hat{P} = P\big/SE$$

Where

$\hat{P}$ = observed proportion

P = hypothesised proportion (40%)

SE = Standard Error of proportion which is $\sqrt{\dfrac{P(1-P)}{N}}$

Since P, and N are known, the value of SE is determined as follows:

$$\sqrt{\dfrac{0.4\,(0.6)}{400}} = 0.0245$$

P_e = Pr expected. Since N > 30, normal distribution is assumed, hence, at 5% level of significance for a two-tail test, the P_e value is 1.96.

Based on these conditions, decisions on the propositions suggested in table 4 are determined as follows:

Testing hypothesis 3 with propositions on Table 4:

1. $122\big/378 = 0.322$

$$P_o = \dfrac{0.322 - 0.4}{0.0245} = -3.18, \qquad P_o = 3.18 > P_e = 1.96$$

2. $141\big/378 = 0.373$

$$P_o = \dfrac{0.373 - 0.4}{0.0245} = -1.102, \qquad P_o = 1.102 < P_e = 1.96$$

3. $37\big/378 = 0.098$

$$P_o = \dfrac{0.098 - 0.4}{0.0245} = -12.33. \qquad P_o = 12.33 > P_e = 1.96$$

4. $\dfrac{35}{378} = 0.093$

$$P_o = \frac{0.093 - 0.4}{0.0245} = 12.55. \qquad P_o = 12.55 > P_e = 1.96$$

5. $\dfrac{43}{378} = 0.645$

$$P_o = \frac{0.645 - 0.4}{0.0245} = -11.68. \quad P_o = 11.68 > P_e = 1.96$$

Result Interpretation

Question 1 with the result Po = 3.18 > Pe = 1.96, indicates agreement from the respondents that the country's electoral laws are adequately potent for enforcing ethical communication behavior during electioneering in the country. Question 2 gave a result of Po = 1.102 < Pe = 1.96, indicating that some Nigerians are doubtful of the capabilities of the existing electoral laws to checkmate the problem. Question 3 resulted in a score of Po = 12.33 > Pe = 1.96 again indicating strong agreement from the respondents that the country's electoral laws are adequately potent for addressing the problem. So also did question 4 with the result Po = 12.55 > Pe = 1.96, and question 5 with the result Po = 11.68 > Pe = 1.96. All these cumulatively signify a rejection of the Ho and acceptance of the Hi that the country's electoral laws are adequately potent for enforcing ethical communication behavior amongst Nigerian politicians during electioneering in the country.

9.5.4 Independent T-test

This is a parametric test which compares the means of two independent groups to determine the extent of statistical evidence that the associated population means are significantly different. The independent t-test, which is also referred to as two sample t-test, independent-samples t-test or student's t-test, is regarded to be an inferential statistical test used to determines whether there is a statistically significant difference between the means in two unrelated groups, on the same continuous, dependent variable. Statistics solutions (2017), adds that the independent samples t-test can only compare two groups (if your independent variable defines more than two groups, you either would need to run multiple t-tests or an ANOVA with post hoc tests). Let us now see a worked example from tables 9.8 to 9.10.

Table 9.8: Assessment of marketing communication for malaria awareness, prevention, and control in Nigeria

S/N	QUESTIONS	RESPONSES	
		Agree	Disagree
1.	Marketing communications has increased my awareness on malaria prevention and control policies and measures in the country	63	21
2.	Messages on ways of preventing and controlling malaria have helped me in sleeping with insecticide treated mosquito nets	63	21
3.	The awareness gained has helped reduce the rate at which my family members are infected with malaria	53	29

Source: Odigbo, Ben; Samaila, Mande & Effiong, Etim Okon (2017), Assessment of Marketing Communications for the Prevention and Control of Malaria in Nigeria. Journal of Biology, Agriculture and Healthcare Vol. 7, No. 14, p.14-21.

The data analysis in table 9.8 shows that 63 respondents or 75% agreed that marketing communication increased their awareness on malaria prevention and control measures and policies. Similarly, the same percentage of respondents agreed that messages on ways of preventing and controlling malaria informed their decisions to sleep with insecticide-treated mosquito nets. More so, 53 respondents or 65% reported that the malaria prevention and control awareness they gained, helped reduce the rate at which their family members are infected by malaria.

Table 9.9: The relationship between the marketing communication-mix used and the reduction in the rate of malaria morbidity and mortality in Nigeria

S/N	QUESTIONS	RESPONSES	
		Agree	Disagree
4.	Do you believe that malaria causes death both in infants and adults	71	13
5.	The knowledge of the malaria prevention and control measures has reduced the rate at which people die from malaria in my area	61	23
6.	Messages on how to keep clean environment, use mosquitoe nets, what to do when infected by malaria and the right place to go for treatment have reduced deaths from malaria in my area	61	23

Source: Odigbo, Ben; Samaila, Mande & Effiong, Etim Okon (2017), Assessment of Marketing Communications for the Prevention and Control of Malaria in Nigeria. Journal of Biology, Agriculture and Healthcare Vol. 7, No. 14, p.14-21.

Data displayed in table 9.9 reveal that 71 respondents, representing 85% believed that malaria causes death in both infants and adults, while 13 or 15% of respondents disagreed with that. 61 or 73% agreed that their knowledge of malaria prevention and control measures had reduced the rate of malaria morbidity and mortality in their communities, while 23 or 27% disagreed. Similarly, the same number of respondents believed that messages on hygiene, use of mosquito-nets and effective treatment of malaria disease has helped reduce death caused by the infection in their areas, while 23 or 27% of respondents did not queue behind this position.

Test of Hypothesis

Ho: Marketing communications' tools did not create significant awareness for the malaria prevention and control in Nigeria.
Hi: Marketing communications' tools created significant awareness for the malaria prevention and control in Nigeria.

Test Statistics: Independent T-Test.
Independent variable: Marketing Communications
Dependent variable: Malaria awareness, prevention, and control.

Table 9.10: Result of independent t-test showing whether the use of marketing communication helped in creating awareness on the malaria prevention and control in Nigeria

Variables	N	X	SD	t-value
Marketing communications	6 3	48 .3	8. 9	9.868
No marketing communications	2 1	25 .8	9. 1	

df = 82, critical t = 1.98; calculated t = 9.868; < 05 significant.

In the table 9.10, since the calculated t-value (i.e. 9.868), is greater than critical t-value (i.e. 1.980) at 0.05 level of significance, and 82 degrees of freedom, the null-hypothesis one is rejected and the alternative upheld, which says that: "Marketing communications' tools created significant awareness for the malaria prevention and control in Nigeria."

9.5.5 Regression Analysis

Regression analysis (RA) is a statistical approach for forecasting change in a dependent variable also called a response variable (e.g., sales volume) and changes in one or more independent variables also called predictor variables (e.g., product price, product taste, product packaging, product quantity or size, etc.). It is, therefore, a statistical tool for determining the relationship between a dependent variable and an independent variable(s). It is also used to ascertain which among the independent variables are related to the dependent variable, and to determine the forms of these relationships.

There are three types of regression analysis methods: linear regression, multiple regression, and non-linear regression analysis. Linear regression uses one independent variable 'X' to explain or predict the outcome of one dependent variable 'Y.'

Multiple regression analysis uses one dependent variable (e.g., sales volume) to explain or predict the outcome and changes in multiple independent variables (like increase in product price + alterations in product taste + modification in product packaging + reduction in product quantity). While non-linear regression analysis is used for the testing of more complicated data and their analysis.

Regression analysis is one of the reliable and favorite statistical tools, the student should, therefore, be abreast of it. You can see the book Mastering Research or other proper research or statistical text-books on this.

9.5.6 One-Way and Two-Way Analysis of Variance (ANOVA)

Analysis of Variances (ANOVA) is a statistical analysis of the relationship between two groups - the independent variable and dependent variable. There are two major types of the ANOA test – one-way ANOVA and two-way ANOVA.

9.5.6.1 One-way ANOVA

The one-way ANOVA is statistical that examines the extent of influence of two different categorical independent variables on one continuous dependent variable. It is used to determine whether there are any statistically significant differences between the means of the two or more independent variables that are unrelated groups. That is to say; the one-way ANOVA statistically compares the factors between the two groups of study to determine the extent their means are statistically significantly different from each other.

Conventionally, one-way and two-way ANOVA test the null hypothesis: where μ = group mean and k = number of groups. When the one-way ANOVA returns a statistically significant result, we accept the alternative hypothesis (HA), which is that there is at least two group means that are statistically significantly different from each other.

The shortcomings in the one-way ANOVA is that this test statistic can only tell us that at least two groups were significantly different from each other, but cannot tell us which among the two groups is more statistically considerably different than the other. To do that, however, we need to use a post hoc test.

9.5.6.2 Two-way ANOVA

Two-way analysis of variance (ANOVA) is an extension of the one-way ANOVA. A two-way ANOVA usually has two or more independent variables (factors) and one dependent variable. It is a statistical tool for comparing more than two groups – independent variable (e.g., students' health status: A). Visit a hospital in 1 week, B) Visit to the hospital in 2 weeks, C) Visit to the hospital in 3 weeks, D) Visit to the hospital in 1 month, E) No Visit to the hospital in 1 year). Here, the independent variable compares students' state of health in one year, through the rate they visited the university's hospital or health center.

On the other hand, the dependent variable will analyze: the type of medication received - A) Mere routine checks, B) Outpatients, C) Admissions. Here, the dependent variable is concerned with determining how many of the students that visited the hospital within the period under review were not really sick. How many went for routine medical checks, how many were ill, but not so severe that they were treated as out-patients, and how many were seriously sick and went on medical admissions within the period.

9.5.6.3 Differences Between One-Way ANOVA and Two-way ANOVA

The fundamental difference between One-Way ANOVA and Two-way ANOVA is that One-Way ANOVA has one ndependent variable (1 factor), while the Two-way analysis of variance (ANOVA) has two independent variables (factors), with usually multiple conditions.

9.5.6.4 When to use One-Way ANOVA

You are advised to use One-way ANOVA when you have a single independent variable with more than two conditions to tests. For example, studying consumers' perception of three types of pain relievers: paracetamol vs. panadol vs. ibuprofen.

9.5.6.5 When to use Two-Way ANOVA

You are advised to use Two-way ANOVA: you have more than one independent variables (factors) to test. For example, studying consumers' perception of three types of pain relievers, based on opinion and their purchase patterns of the drugs. Factor 'A' here will be Pain reliever (paracetamol vs. panadol vs. ibuprofen). While the Factor 'B' will be: Purchase patterns (regularly vs. sometimes vs. always).

9.6 Use of Computers in Data Processing and Analysis (the SPSS)

The use of computers in data processing and analysis is gaining wider popularity by the day. Data processing with a computer includes the coding, input and conversion of raw data to a machine-readable form, flow of data through the CPU and memory to output devices, and formatting or transformation of the output in ways that could be easily understood by concerned readers. On the other hand, the use of computers in data analysis also referred to an analysis of data or data analytics, entails any computer-assisted data processing and analysis method or technique employed by a researcher in his/her data analysis. The processes in data analysis include data inspection, data cleansing, data transformation, finally data analysis or data modeling, to find answers to hypotheses or problems in research.

The exploratory data analysis (EDA), focuses on discovering new features in the data, the confirmatory data analysis (CDA) focuses on confirming or falsifying existing hypotheses, while the Predictive data analytics focuses on the application of statistical models for predicting or forecasting future trends. There are varieties of computer-aided data analysis techniques today which include the statistical package for the social sciences (SPSS), Analysis of Moment statistics (AMOS), Minitab, and many more.

9.6.1 SPSS Data Analysis

The software named Statistical Package for the Social Sciences (SPSS) is a data processing, management, and statistical analysis tool. It has a very versatile data analysis capability. The inputting, processing, management and analysis of your data in SPSS, depends much upon the kind of data you have and the type of analysis you wish to conduct. The steps in SPSS data analysis are as follows:
- Data coding and classifications,
- Data input in parametric and or non-parametric forms,
- Variable definitions,
- Data and variables checking for errors,
- Data analysis and
- Data interpretations.

Students are advised to undertake a short training course on the SPSS, to master this versatile data analysis technique, that is desirable in research today.

9.7 Summary and Conclusion

In this chapter, we have learned the meaning and purposes of data preparation, data collation, data sorting, data editing, data coding and data reduction, frequency tabulation, and cross-tabulation. The uses of graphs, proportions, diagrams, polygons, etc. in data presentations and how to do them were also treated with a highlight of some examples. We also presented worked examples with some data analysis tools like percentage frequencies, Likert 5-points scale, chi-square (X^2), correlation analysis, regression analysis, one-way and two-way analysis of variance (ANOVA), computer-aided analysis and the SPSS. Try as much as possible to master these, when to use each of them and the justifications, as the knowledge will be an asset to you during your research project, thesis or dissertation.

Data presentation and analysis is a very crucial part of a research, without which your project, thesis or dissertation will be incomplete. Hence, the emphasis we have given to this chapter.

Exercises

1. List and explain the various systematic activities for treating and processing data before analysis in empirical research.
2. Give practical examples of data presentations in percentage frequencies, mean, and five types of graphs.
3. List and explain four primary statistical tools for data analysis in your university. Explain their uses and importance in research.

4. With some practical examples, explain the uses of computer in data processing and analysis.
5. What do you understand by SPSS analysis? What are its primary steps and benefits in research?

References

Chekanov, S. (2016) Numeric Computation and Statistical Data Analysis on the Java Platform, Springer. ISBN 978-3-319-28531-3

Fisher, R.A., and Yates, F. (2014), Statistical Tables for Biological Agricultural and Medical Research, 6th ed., Table IV, Edinburgh: Oliver & Boyd, Ltd.

Hair, Joseph (2008). Marketing Research 4th ed. McGraw Hill. Data Analysis: Testing for Association ISBN 0-07-340470-5

Johns Hopkins University and Diener-West, Marie (2008), Use of the Chi-Square Statistic. Johns Hopkins University School of Public Health.

Minitab (2017), A comparison of the Pearson and Spearman correlation methods.

http://support.minitab.com/en-us/minitab-express/1/help-and-how-to/modeling-statistics/regression/supporting-topics/basics/a-comparison-of-the-pearson-and-spearman-correlation-methods/

Odigbo, Ben; Samaila, Mande & Effiong, Etim Okon (2017), Assessment of Marketing Communications for the Prevention and Control of Malaria in Nigeria. Journal of Biology, Agriculture and Healthcare Vol. 7, No. 14, p.14-21.

Odigbo, Ben; Ugwu-Ogbu, Silk & Odigbo, Rose Adannia (2014), The Correlation between Social Violence and the Comments of Nigerian Politicians during Electioneering Campaigns: A

Political Marketing Study. Journal of Law, Policy, and Globalization, Vol.26, p.1-12.

Odigbo, Benedict (2016), Social public relations (SPR) for enhanced immunization campaigns. Germany: Lambert Academic Publishing.

Rumsey, Deborah J. (2018). How to compare two population proportions. http://www.dummies.com/education/math/statistics/how-to-compare-two-population-proportions/

Samantha Lile (2018), 44 Types of Graphs Perfect for Every Top Industry. http://blog.visme.co/types-of-graphs/

Slideplayer (2017), "Graphing- 3 Types of Graphs -Bar Graphs, Line Graphs & Pie Charts."— Presentation Transcript. http://slideplayer.com/slide/9604713/

Statistics Solutions (2017), Using Chi-Square Statistic in Research -

http://www.statisticssolutions.com/using-chi-square-statistic-in-research/

Tabachnick, B.G.; Fidell, L.S. (2007). Using Multivariate Statistics, 5th Edition. Boston:

CHAPTER TEN

MEASUREMENT SCALES IN RESEARCH

10.1 Introduction

This chapter dwells on the various measurement scales that are applied in research and statistical analysis, their properties, differences, and usages. It is designed to make us understand the meaning and purposes of measurement scales in research and statistical analysis, the various measurement scales commonly used, their properties, their differences, when to use each one and the justification(s) for the usages.

10.2 What are Measurement Scales in Research

Measurement Scale also called levels of measurement in research, and statistical analysis is the art of assigning numerical values to the items you want to measure, in line with the type of measurement.

10.3 Types of Measurement Scales in Research

Figure 10.1 from SlidePlayer (2017), gives us a pictorial view of the measurement scales and their characteristics.

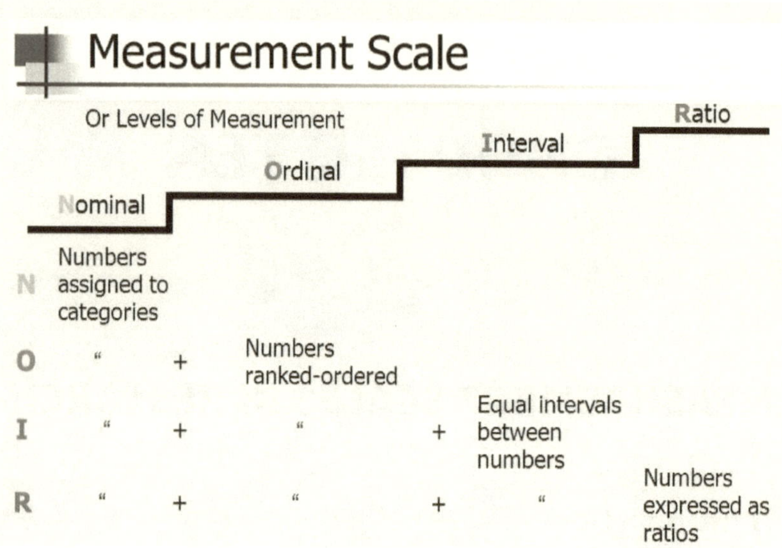

Fig. 10.1: Properties of the Measurement Scales. Source: SlidePlayer (2017), Quantitative Research Methods. http://slideplayer.com/slide/3822815/

10.3.1 Nominal Scale

This satisfies name only, that is, it is descriptive and only satisfies identity with no numerical values like gender, religion, the town of residence, occupation, educational qualification, etc. In the SPSS, nominal data may be coded as numbers, but the numbers will have no real meaning, no default or natural order, but just a label.

10.3.2 Ordinal Scale

Satisfies with identity and magnitude, e.g., strongly agree, agree, disagree and strongly disagree. To a great extent moderate extent, low extent, not at all. High, low, not at all.

10.3.3 Interval Scale

Have properties of identity, magnitude and equal intervals in scales, e.g., measuring a country's GDP growth rate, thermometer, Fahrenheit (used in measuring weather condition). Garth (2008), adds that these are numerical data where the distances between numbers have meaning, but the zero has no real meaning. With interval data, it is not always true to say that one measurement is double the other. It might not still be true if the units were changed. Example: Temperature measured in Centigrade, a cup of coffee at 80°c isn't twice as hot a one at 40°c. See figure 10.2 for an example of the interval scale.

Fig. 10.2: Visualdictionary (2017), An example of the interval scale. Source: http://visualdictionary.com

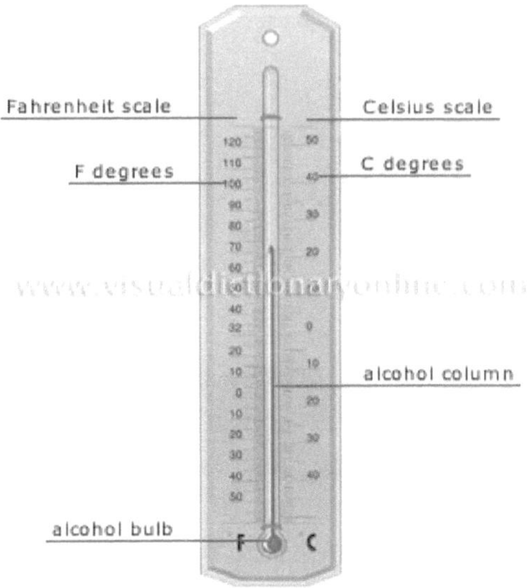

10.3.4 Ratio Scale

Have the three earlier properties plus absolute zero as the starting point. Garth (2008), observes that these are numerical data where the distances between data and the zero point have real meaning. With such data, it is correct to say that one value is twice as much as another, and this would still be right if the units changes. Examples: Heights, Weights, Salaries, Ages. If someone is twice as heavy as someone else in pounds, this will still be true in kilograms.

10.4 A Summary of The Measurement Scales Properties

Nominal Scale - Satisfies only identity, name only.
Ordinal Scale - Satisfies identity and has magnitude.
Equal Interval - Satisfies identity, magnitude and equal interval scale.
Absolute Zero - Satisfies identity, magnitude, equal interval scale and ratio scale.

10.5 Explanation of the Four characteristics of the Measurement Scales

10.5.1 Identity:

Means that this measuring scale assigns only the property value of meaning or identity to the items you want to measure. Examples include the property age, sex, gender, educational qualification, etc, as shown in tables 10.1 and 10.2 regarding the age and educational qualifications demographic characteristics of respondents in a study to ascertain the effectiveness of the marketing communications strategies employed for the prevention and control of malaria in Nigeria (Odigbo, Samaila & Effiong, 2017).

Table 10.1: Respondents' AGE Distribution

		Frequency	Percent	Valid Percent	Cumulative Percent
Valid	<18	9	10.71	10.71	10.71
	18-29	27	32.14	32.14	32.14
	30-39	28	33.33	33.33	33.33
	40-49	12	14.29	14.29	14.29
	>50	8	9.52	9.52	9.52
	Total	84	100.0	100.0	

Source: Odigbo, Ben; Samaila, Mande & Effiong, Etim Okon (2017), Assessment of Marketing Communications for the Prevention and Control of Malaria in Nigeria. Journal of Biology, Agriculture and Healthcare Vol. 7, No. 14, p.14-21.

Table 10.1 gives the age range of respondents as follows: those below 18 years were 9 (10.71 percent); those between 18 to 29 years were 27 (32.14 percent); those in the age bracket of 30 to 39 years accounted for 28 (33.33 percent), respondents within 40 to 49 years were 12 (14.29 percent), while those above 50 years were 8 (9.52 percent). This is a good example of nominal scale (age – identity, and name only).

Table 10.2: Respondents' Educational Qualification

		Frequency	Percent	Valid Percent	Cumulative Percent
Valid	PRIMARY	8	9.52	9.52	9.52
	SECONDARY	27	32.14	32.14	32.14
	TERTIARY	49	58.33	58.33	58.33
	Total	84	100.0	100.0	100.0

Source: Odigbo, Ben; Samaila, Mande & Effiong, Etim Okon (2017), Assessment of Marketing Communications for the Prevention and Control of Malaria in Nigeria. Journal of Biology, Agriculture and Healthcare Vol. 7, No. 14, p.14-21.

Table 10.2 reveals that 8 (9.52 percent) of the respondents had only primary school education; 27 (32.14 percent) had secondary school education, while the remaining 49 (58.33 percent) had tertiary schools' education. This is another good example of nominal scale (educational qualification – identity and name only).

10.5.2 Magnitude:

Means that this measurement scale assigns not only meaning or identity but also degrees or magnitude to it. For example, the Likert's scales strongly agree, agree, undecided, disagree and strongly disagree, as can be seen in tables 10.3 and figure 10.1 on a study of the correlation between the public relations crisis management techniques of the IOCs and the level of mutual understanding between them and their host communities (Odigbo, Samaila & Okonkwo, 2017).

Table 10.3: Respondents' views on whether there is a significant correlation between the public relations crisis management tools of the IOCs and the level of mutual understanding between them and their host communities

Options	Frequency	Percent
Strongly Agree	102	26.58%
Agree	163	42.63%
Undecided	28	7.10%
Disagree	42	10.79%
Strongly Disagree	50	12.89%
Total	385	100%

Source: Odigbo, Ben E., Samaila, Mande & Okonkwo, Raphael V. (2017), Assessment of public relations strategies employed by major international oil companies for crisis management in Nigeria. Developing Country Studies, Vol.7, No.7, p.1-11.

Data displayed on table 10.3 show that 102 (26.58%) of the respondents strongly agreed that there is a significant relationship in the public relations crisis management techniques of the IOCs and the level of mutual cordiality between them and their host communities. 163 (42.63%) of the respondents equally agreed with that; 28 (7.10%) were not quite sure; 42 (10.79%) somehow disagreed, while the remaining 50 (12.89%) disagreed with the point. See figure 10.3 below for a graphic picture of this result (Odigbo, Samaila & Okonkwo, 2017).

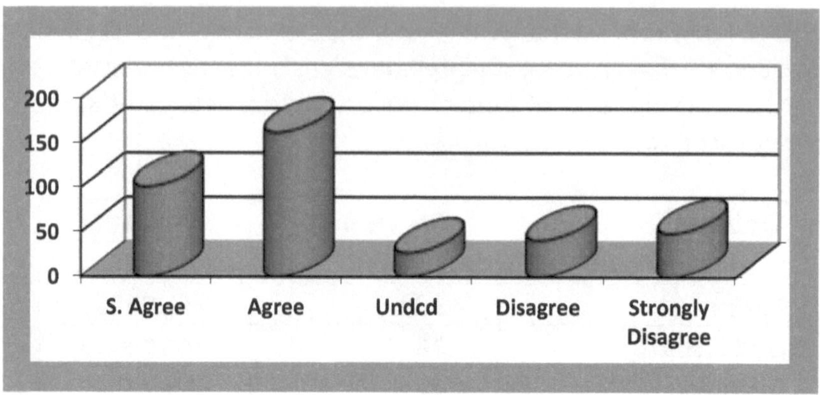

Fig. 10.3: A test of the correlation between the public relations crisis management tools of the IOCs in Nigeria and the level of mutual understanding between them and their host communities. Source: Odigbo, Ben E., Samaila, Mande & Okonkwo, Raphael V. (2017), Assessment of public relations strategies employed by major international oil companies for crisis management in Nigeria. Developing Country Studies, Vol.7, No.7, p.1-11.

10.5.3 Equal Interval:

Is when the measurement scale has identity, magnitude and equal intervals in its measuring range like the thermometer for measuring temperature.

10.5.4 Absolute zero:

This has all the other three properties above, plus an absolute zero, which makes it the highest measuring scale.

10.6 Summary and Conclusion

Measurement scales are valuable tools in research and statistical analysis. They are the various measuring tools used in data presentation and statistical analysis part of a study. This chapter has carefully explained the different measurement scales, their properties, differences and usages in research.

Exercises

1. Diagrammatically outline and explain the four types of measurement scales in research and statistical analysis.
2. State the measurement scale(s) you will be using in a possible research topic of your choice, and give the justifications for the option.
3. List and explain the properties and characteristics of the four measurement scales in research and statistical analysis.

References

Garth, Andrew (2008), Analysing data using SPSS. Sheffield: Sheffield Hallam University.

Odigbo, Ben E., Samaila, Mande & Okonkwo, Raphael V. (2017), Assessment of public relations strategies employed by major international oil companies for crisis management in Nigeria. Developing Country Studies, Vol.7, No.7, p.1-11.

Odigbo, Ben; Samaila, Mande & Effiong, Etim Okon (2017), Assessment of Marketing Communications for the Prevention and Control of Malaria in Nigeria. Journal of Biology, Agriculture and Healthcare Vol. 7, No. 14, p.14-21.

SlidePlayer (2017), Quantitative Research Methods. http://slideplayer.com/slide/3822815/

Visualdictionary (2017), An example of the interval scale. Source: http://visualdictionary.co

CHAPTER ELEVEN

RESEARCH REPORT WRITING

11.1 Introduction

This chapter introduces research report writing to us, its uses, consideration, organization, presentation and also, how to do your oral presentation, effectively. It is meant to let us understand appreciably the ways and how of writing our research reports very well, so that students will be at home with this, since it is a very crucial requirement for graduation. We will also try to master the intricacies of research presentations, to gain confidence for that.

11.2 What is Research Report Writing

Research report writing is the documentation or electronic recording of research, encompassing all its ramifications and dimensions. It is meant to let others read and grab needed information from the findings of the study, as well as assess the quality and the rightness of the method and means used in conducting it.

11.3 Uses of Research Reports

Research reports have numerous benefits which include the following:

- Research reports are used to communicate research-ascertained information to individuals and organizations for enhanced decision-making.
- Research reports can be tailored to communicate or transmit information with a clear purpose to a specific audience(s).
- In the academic settings, a research report demonstrates a student's level of scholarship, knowledge, and ability to undertake research in all its ramifications and dimensions, and an appreciation of its significance.
- Research reports are invaluable resources for future references for knowledge, further researches, and decision-making.
- The written report and the oral defense are typically the only aspects of the study that your supervisor, the client or business executives are exposed. Consequently, the overall evaluation of the research work rests on how well this information is communicated (FAO, 201`7).
- For research, a consultant, the quality, effectiveness, and usefulness of your research report to a large extent determine whether the client will still consult you tomorrow and whether they will recommend you to others.
- For student research, the quality and significance of your research report determine the score that will be awarded to you by your supervisor, on the one hand, the external examiner and the various panel of examiners on the other side.

11.4 Considerations for Your Research Report Writing

Before writing your research report, the following considerations have to be observed:

The report should not be too technical ambigous with a lot of jargons. This is a particular difficulty when reporting the results of statistical analysis where there is a high probability that few of the target audience, have knowledge of statistical concepts. Hence, for example, there is a need to translate such terms as standard deviation, significance level, confidence interval, etc. into everyday language (FAO, 2017).

Be mindful of your target audience and write in a language that suits their educational levels. That is to say, the same way you write a report that will be presented in defense to professors is not the same language you might use to write to a marketing manager.

Every industry group has their technical languages, try as much as possible to accommodate this by following the target audience's functional languages. For example, the word 'product' may mean one thing to the banking sector, and quite a different thing to the manufacturing industry.

Don't be too verbose or use too much big-vocabularies or high-sounding words. The emphasis should be more in communicating than in grammatical displays.
While being concise and precise, your report must, however, be complete in contents and context, so as not to call for additional clarifications.

For a research consultant, be mindful of the fact that your report will be judged by the contribution it makes towards solving the identified organizational or marketing problem that motivated the study in the first place and not by your displays in packaging or research methodology.

For student research, be mindful of the fact that your report will be judged by the extent you adhered to your university's format, grammatical quality, and the quality of your research design, methodology, and implementation.

11.5 Organization/Structure of Your Research Report Writing

Some universities and colleges have already-made house-styles or research reporting format for their students to follow in their projects, thesis or dissertations. My advice here is that you do not disobey your school's guideline because research obeys and follow conventionally agreed scientific footsteps. The differences come only in the organizational structure of the work. So, if you look critically, you will see that what is one format is also on the other, only that it could be located in a different chapter or sub-title.

However, we're going to give to you, here, a research-reporting format that will be in line with global scientific order and best practices in research, and which you can adapt to your own supervisor's or university's format.

11.6 Guides for Successful Oral Presentation of Your Research Report

Many universities demand that students at both undergraduate, Masters and doctoral levels must undergo oral defense of their projects, thesis or dissertations. This is aimed at ascertaining the student's proof of ownership of the work in one hand and understanding of it on the other hand. The score awarded to the student during such defenses, by the defense committee or panel or the external examiner, usually overrides the rating assigned to the student by his/her supervisor. Thus, the essence of oral research presentation, as a skill any student must master. By oral research presentation, we mean a student's or a research consultant's physical defense of his/her research work/report before his/her supervisor, client, external examiner or a committee or panel.

Often, Oral research presentations in some universities are done with presentation software like slides or PowerPoint. The presentation time may range between twenty minutes to one hour, before the questions-and-answers session, hence, it cannot cover all the contents of the report, but must cover all the essential technical details.

The University of Virginia (2018), gave some tips for your successful oral research presentation with some little modifications from us as follows:

Timing: Find out how long your defense will be. As you decide what to present, keep in mind that a ten-minute speech is very different from a 45-minute lecture. If you only have ten minutes, then, focus on the most important points. With more time, you'll still need to focus on those points, but you'll be able to present additional supporting details. Time yourself per the time given to you. It is okay to end a few minutes earlier, because shooting overtime may show your lack of preparation.

Know Your Audience: Find out what sort of audience will listen to your talk. Specialists in the field of your study will shoot more in-depth and probing questions at you than a general audience.

However, with a broad audience, you need to ask yourself what educated people, not in your field will know, define unfamiliar terms to them, and make an effort to explain the significance of your study in clear languages the audience are likely to understand.

Contents Delivery: Dwell only on the primary technical points like: What the study is all about. What motivated your interest. What are the research objectives? What are the research hypotheses? What are the scope, limitations, and significance of the study? Then, a summary of your research methodology/design, area of study, population, how sample size and the sampling were arrived at, the instrument, its validation and reliability, the data analysis tools used and the justifications for all these. Followed by how data were processed and analyzed, the results obtained, the implications and your recommendations, including the area for further studies.

Organization of Your Presentation: Your talk must have a beginning, middle, and end. You need to (1) introduce yourself; (2) present your research question and why it matters; (3) describe how you conducted your research, (4) explain your findings and the implications; and (5) conclude with a summary of your main points. Do not even think of opening the PowerPoint until you have organized your ideas and decided on your main points.

PowerPoint Usage: You should treat PowerPoint as a useful tool. You can use it to input figures, pictures, charts and other images into your presentation, to emphasize important points, and to carry along your audience. Don't present too much information on the slides. Try to explain to your audience what each chart or graph means. Use the charts and graphs to convey information clearly, not merely to show that you did the work.

Appearance, Tone & Manners: It is best to approach your prepared talk as a somewhat formal occasion. Treat your audience—and your topic—with respect. Even if you know everyone in the room, introduce yourself.   Don't address audience members as "you guys." Dress neatly. Most of all, exhibit your enthusiasm for the subject matter.

Practice: Practice speaking audibly and clearly, but don't shout. If you want to emphasize an important point, try to repeat it, bearing in mind the saying that 'practice makes perfect.' You can practice delivering the talk to a small group of your classmates, family members or friends, within a time-frame, and let them critique your performance. On no account should you read your talk, it might give the impression the work is not yours, and you have not internalized it.

Other authorities (University of Southern California & Labaree, 2009; University of North Carolina, 2016; University of Toronto & Perret, 2017; Ohio Wesleyan University & Peoples, 2017; Peery, 2011; University of Canberra, 2017; Lucas, 2008; Colorado State University; Kelly, 2017; Colorado State University, 2017), added the following guidelines with little amendments from us, to be followed in your oral research presentation:

- **Capture Your Listeners' Attention At The First Shot:** You can do this by starting with a question, an amusing story, a provocative statement, or anything that will engage your audience and make them think, after greeting them.

- **Be mindful that your audience has just one chance to hear your talk;** they can't "re-read" your words if they get confused. So, focus on being audible and clear.

- **Make small notes in bold typeface, to refer to as you speak;** so as not to run the risk of conjecturing during your defense. This is because having no notes increases the chance you'll lose your train of thought and begin relying on reading from the book or presentation slides, which is not acceptable. Master the critical points in your notes, because, nothing is more distracting to an audience than the speaker fumbling around with records as he/she tries to speak. It gives the impression you are disorganized and unprepared.

- **Jot down notes and or observations from the audience/panelist during your presentation,** in response to their questions and comments. That gives them the impression you have regards and respect for them.

- **Practice to spell-out challenging words;** like foreign names, technical or scientific terminology, or words in a foreign language, phonetically and practice saying them ahead of time.

- **Remember to summarize your work,** into crucial points to write on your presentation slides and note cards or handout.

- **Remember that the aim is to communicate, not to show off:** Using complex words or phrases increases the chance of stumbling over a word and losing your train of thought. So, keep it simple and straight (KISS).

- **Use your body language well to communicate by standing straight and comfortably:** Do not slouch, shuffle about, appear bored or uninterested in what you're talking. Wear something comfortable, not an itchy wool sweater or high heels for the first time. Hold your head up. Look boldly into the eyes of the audience to gain psychological confidence. Do not look at your supervisor or your notes the whole time! Looking up at your audience brings them into the conversation. If you don't include the audience, they won't listen to you.

- **Don't turn your back on the audience and don't fidget!** Practice to make yourself comfortable. Even when pointing to a slide, don't turn your back; stand at the side and turn your head towards the audience.

- **Keep your hands out of your pocket, as you speak:** This might give the impression you are proud, too relaxed, too casual or in some cultures disrespectful to elders around.

- **Be mindful of how your audience is reacting to your presentation:** Are they interested or bored? Try to carry them along all the time.

- **Be open to questions:** If someone asks a question in the middle of your talk, answer it. If it disrupts your train of thought momentarily, that's human, so, don't border much about that. Questions show that the audience is listening with interest and should not be regarded as an attack on you.

11.7 Ethical Considerations in Research

Ethics are broadly the set of rules, written and unwritten, thatgovern the expectations of our own and other peoples' behavior (SkillsYouNeed, 2018). For any research report, academic or business, to be acceptable, it must observe and adhere to a round of conventionally agreed ethical codes. This includes reporting your research, the methods employed, the implementation, the data, the data analysis and the results honestly. You must also affirm whether the work has been previously published, in part or full, and any other author's work taken in part or full.

Dudovskiy (2009), observes that ethical considerations can be specified as one of the most crucial parts of your research. This is because your project, thesis or dissertations may even be doomed to failure if this part is neglected. Based on these facts, Bryman and Bell (2007), itemized the following ten points as the essential ethical elements to be considered in your project, thesis or dissertation:

1. Research participants should not be exposed to harm in whatsoever form or guise.
2. Respect for the dignity of research participants should be prioritized.
3. Full consent should be obtained from the participants prior to the study.
4. The protection of the privacy of research participants has to be ensured.
5. An adequate level of confidentiality of the research data should be ensured.

6.   The anonymity of individuals and organizations participating in the research has to be respected.
7.   Any deception or exaggeration about the aims and objectives of the research must be avoided.
8.   Affiliations in any forms, sources of funding, as well as any possible conflicts of interests have to be declared.
9.   Any communication concerning the research should be done with honesty and transparency.
10.   Any misleading information, as well as representation of primary data findings in a biased way, must be avoided.

Dudovskiy (2009) adds that to address ethical considerations aspect of your project, thesis or dissertation in an effective manner, the following points have to be adhered to:

i.   Voluntary participation of respondents in the research is essential. Moreover, participants have rights to withdraw from the study at any stage if they wish to do so.

ii.   Respondents should participate on the basis of informed consent. The principle of informed consent involves researchers providing sufficient information and assurances about taking part, to allow individuals to understand the implications of participation and to reach a fully informed, considered and freely given decision about whether or not to do so, without the exercise of any pressure or coercion (Bryman & Bell, 2007).

iii. The use of offensive, discriminatory, or other unacceptable language needs to be avoided in the formulation of Questionnaire/Interview/Focus group questions.

iv. Privacy and anonymity of respondents are of paramount importance.

v. Acknowledgment of works of other authors used in any part of the project, thesis or dissertation based on the citation/referencing style approved by your university.

vi. Ensure there is a maintenance of the highest level of objectivity in discussions and analyses throughout the research.

vii. Adherence to Data Protection Act (1998), if you are studying in the UK or other countries where that applies.

Most universities have their own code of ethics in research. It is advisable for you to thoroughly adhere to this code in every aspect of your research and declare your adherence to ethical considerations part of your project, thesis or dissertation.

11.8 Types of Project, Thesis or Dissertation Writings

There are five major types of project, thesis or dissertation writings. You are right to follow any of this but must stick to it. The five categories are as follows:

Analytical Paper: This type of research report breaks down the issue or motivating problem for the study into its parts, evaluates the issue or idea and presents this breakdown and evaluation to the audience.

An Expository Paper: This type of research report emphasizes the explanation of the issue or motivating problem for the study to the audience.

An Argumentative Paper: This type of research report tries to provide convincing evidence or justifications for the subject matter or topic. The target of an argumentative research report is to convince the audience that the thesis or claims of the study are valid based on the convincing evidence provided.

Historical Paper: This type of research report gives a historical rendition of the problem that motivated the study, to convince the audience that the research is worth it.

Perspectival Paper: This type of research report presents in perspectives how the issue or problem that motivated the study has been playing out, and its adverse effects, hence, the justification for the study.

For examples of these and a project, thesis or dissertation format, you may see the next chapter.

Exercises

1. With a 10-points argument, defend or debunk the claim that every research project is not complete or useful until it is reported.

2. Outline and defend the fundamental considerations necessary for effective research reporting.
3. Give and defend 12-points conditions for a successful oral presentation of a research report.
4. What are the inevitable ethical considerations you must observe in research?

References

Bryman, A. & Bell, E. (2007), "Business Research Methods," 2nd edition. Oxford University Press.

Colorado State University (2017), Creating and Using Overheads. http://www.writing.colostate.edu/guides/guide.cfm?guid eid=35

Dich, L., McKee, H. A., & Porter, J. E. (2013), Ethical Issues in Online Course Design: Negotiating Identity, Privacy, and Ownership. Selected Papers of Internet Research, 3.

Dudovskiy, John (2009), The Ultimate Guide to Writing a Dissertation in Business Studies: a step by step assistance. http://research-methodology.net/about-us/e-book/

FAO (2017), Research Reporting process. http://www.fao.org/docrep/W3241E/w3241e0b.htm

Grand Canyon University (2017), Ethical Considerations. Center for Innovation in Research and Teaching.

Kelly, Christine (2017), Mastering the Art of Presenting. Inside Higher Education Career Advice. http://www.insidehighered.com/advice/2017/02/06/

Lucas, Stephen (2008), The Art of Public Speaking. 10th edition. Boston, MA: McGraw-Hill Higher Education.

Mazur, D. J. (2007), Evaluating the science and ethics of research on humans: a guide for IRB members.

Ohio Wesleyan University & Peoples, Deborah Carter (2017), Guidelines for Oral Presentations. Ohio Wesleyan University Libraries. http://go.owu.edu./-dapeople/ggpresent.html

Peery, Angela B. (2011), Creating Effective Presentations: Staff Development with Impact. Lanham, MD: Rowman and Littlefield Education.

SkillsYouNeed (2018), Ethical Issues in Research. https://www.skillsyouneed.com/learn/research-ethics.html

University of Canberra (2017), Giving an Oral Presentation. Academic Skills Centre.

University of North Carolina (2016), Speeches. The Writing Center. http://writingcenter.unc.edu/handouts/speeches/

University of Southern Carlifornia & Labaree, R.V. (2009), Giving an Oral Presentation - Organizing Your Social Sciences. http://libguides.usc.edu/writingguide/oralpresentation

University of Toronto & Perret, Nellie (2017), Oral Presentations. The Lab Report. University College Writing Centre. University of Toronto publication.

University of Virginia (2018), How to Make an Oral Presentation of Your Research. Virginia: University of Virginia publication. http://www.virginia.edu/cue/presentationtips.html

CHAPTER TWELVE

PRACTICAL GUIDELINES FOR PROJECT, THESIS AND DISSERTATION WRITING

12.1 Introduction

This chapter dwells on a chapter-by-chapter guideline for project, thesis and dissertation writing, based on popular demands from students. We will use a project-writing format on this since there are no significant differences between the three.

12.2 Research Project Format

While some universities adopt a five-chapter format for their undergraduates' projects, others go for a four-chapter format, while others settle for a six-chapter format. But if you study all the three critically, you will see that they contain the same things in contents and context. Hence, we are going to dwell on the five-chapter style, which is the most popular for undergraduate projects in most universities around the world. For it to be scientifically acceptable in the academic setting, however, a good five-chapter project should contain the following items, subject to some amendments in line with your university's guidelines:

12.3 Project Preliminary Pages Format

Cover Page: You must follow your University's approved format, look at previous projects done in your department or college and work in the same line.

Title Page: This should also be in line with your University's approved format, with your supervisor's name. Search for it and follow suit. When in doubt, confirm from your supervisor, college or Department.

Dedication (When Necessary): It is usually better to dedicate to one person, than multiples of persons, especially when dedicating to God. Many supervisors believe that He is Almighty, so, should not share or compete a place with another.

Certification: It is the student or researcher that should certify the ownership and originality of the work, not the supervisor. Many students make the mistake of putting their supervisor's and other authorities' names here and compelling them to sign "the originality" of a work the students' did. This is legally wrong; it's like asking them to sign their death warrant. That is solely the researcher/author's responsibility. The supervisor should not be held legally responsible if there is plagiarism or other ethical breaches in the report but may answer to administrative charges for the negligence of duty in pointing out to their supervisee.

Approval Page: This is where the supervisor's and other authorized signatories names should appear. They have to approve the work, when it meets the University's minimum standards, and not to sign to the originality of the work.

Acknowledgments: Students should acknowledge their supervisor and other teachers first, followed by their parents, sponsors, and others that have touched their lives in meaningful ways.

Abstract: Your abstract must contain only six essential technical items:
- A short statement of what the study/paper is all about,
- A concise statement of the issues or problems that motivated it,
- A summary of the objectives,
- A tight summary of the methodology/design,
- A summary of the results, and
- A summary of the recommendations.

Some students make the mistake of writing another literature review in the abstract. Some even go to the extent of inputting citations there. This is wrong. When in doubt, please contact your supervisor or other authorities on these.

Table of Contents: This must be in line with your Department's, College's or University's approved style. However, it must capture all the major headings and sub-headings in your work.

Many universities around the world, however, follow the under-listed project contents format:

12.4 Project Chapter by Chapter Format
CHAPTER ONE: INTRODUCTION

1.1 Background of the Study: There are four types of background of the study – historical, analytical, perspectival, and expository.

1.1.1 Types of Background of the Study:
Historical Background of the Study

The historical background of the study tries to give a historical account or rendition of the issues that prompted a study, to convince the audience that the research is worth it. For instance, a doctoral seminar paper by Basil (2017), which followed the historical approach went as follows:

"There have been perennial incidences of fuel adulteration in Nigeria, causing deaths, deformities, and incalculable damages to consumers of the petroleum products in the country, due to the harmful practices of some marketers, according to a 2014 report by the Department of Petroleum Resources (DPR). For instance, records show that the first significant kerosene explosion in Nigeria occurred in March 1984 in Lagos due to adulteration of kerosene with fuel (Emewu, 2001). Emewu (2001) and Sanni (2001), also report that a significant kerosene explosion disaster occurred in the oil-producing area of Ondo State, Nigeria in October 2001, due to petroleum products' adulteration. One hundred and twenty-five burn patients were treated at the Lagos State University Teaching Hospital from that incident. All but two of the patients sustained fire/flame burns resulting from hurricane lantern and cooking stove explosions in the home or enclosed environments. In a scene reminiscent of petrol bomb explosions, most injuries were extensive, covering the face, chest, and abdomen. The burns were relatively thick because the clothing was usually perfused with the splashed fuel. Severity was higher in females than males, as they were more in contact with lamps and cooking stoves in the household.

In 2003, another fuel explosion occurred in Delta State, Nigeria, where ten persons died, and 30 others were seriously injured. The blasts occurred in their homes from adulterated kerosene, the local press reported. Several homes in Warri and Effurun in the oil-producing state were affected by the explosions, which occurred as the victims tried to light their cooking stoves or lanterns, which had been filled with the adulterated kerosene. The 30 injured persons, most of whom suffered first and second-degree burns, were treated at the Warri General Hospital, where medical personnel was overwhelmed with the sheer number of those affected and the magnitude of the wounds. Among the victims were a nursing mother and her eight-week-old baby, both of whom were severely burnt after the family's cooking stove exploded (NAN, 2012).

In 2007, following the reduction of the pump price of petrol to N65, while the street price of kerosene dangled between N140 to N150, many unscrupulous marketers, started mixing kerosene with gasoline, leading to kerosene explosion in many parts of the country, as witnessed in PortHarcourt, Potiskum, Lagos, Lokoja, Delta, Kano, Abuja and Abia State respectively. In the process, many Nigerians met their untimely deaths, while hundreds sustained permanent injuries (Gistmania, 2007).

In 2009, six members of a family in Kano State were hospitalized at the Murtala Mohammed Specialist Hospital over explosion from adulterated kerosene. One of them died immediately after admission (Ogun, 2010).

Then, in 2011 kerosene explosions occurred almost at the same time in Rivers and Edo states of the south-south zone of Nigeria. The blasts killed many and either incapacitated or disfigured other permanently (NAN, 2011). There were controversies over the sources of the contamination, as blames were traded between the Nigerian National Petroleum Corporation, NNPC, the Petroleum Products Marketing Company (PPMC) and the independent marketers with each body passing the bulk. In their investigations, the Petroleum and Natural Gas Senior Staff Association of Nigeria (PENGASSAN) reported that some marketers adulterated products in their tank farms (Ogun, 2010). Kerosene was also contaminated through the deliberate addition of water to increase its volume by unscrupulous marketers (NAN, 2011).

Again in 2012, Badejo (2012), reports that kerosene explosions occurred in both Delta and Edo States between February 1 and March 14, which claimed the lives of eleven persons, while several people were hospitalized for severe degrees of burns. Nine of the victims later died at the University of Benin Teaching Hospital (UBTH). Two others died in other hospitals. The explosions were said to have occurred in boundary villages between Edo and Delta while others happened in Warri and Irrua. Some of the victims said the explosion occurred when they attempted to pour kerosene into their lanterns (Badejo, 2012).

Recently, in August 2015, nine children were rushed to Warri Central Hospital following severe burns they got in the explosions caused by suspected adulterated kerosene in Warri

South and Udu local government areas of Delta State. The victims were said to have suffered between 50 to 90 degrees of burns. The incidents occurred on August 15 and 16 when the children attempted to fuel lit lanterns, while others said the explosions happened while they were pouring kerosene into a lamp.

All these motivated this study for a critical appraisal of unethical marketing practices by independent petroleum marketers in Nigeria, with particular emphasis on the manipulations of prices and products adulteration by dealers and the consequent effect on motorists and cars/vehicles' engines damages in the country."

You could see that the above is a masterpiece example of the historical background of a study, giving a moving and touchy picture of unethical practices in the marketing of petroleum products in Nigeria, and the negative consequences on citizens between 1984 to 2015, as the motivation for going into a study on this.

Analytical Background of the Study

An analytical background of the study tries to break down the issue or motivating problem for the research into its parts, evaluates the issue or idea and presents this breakdown and evaluation to the audience. It follows the approach of critical analysis because in it, a researcher critique what other researchers or reports hold or say on an issue, and tries to locate a gap or missing element, which his/her study is seeking to fill.

Eleje (2019) observes that a critical analysis is subjective writing because it expresses the writer's opinion or evaluation of a text or texts. Writing a critical paper requires two steps: essential reading and critical writing. Wiki (2014), also reports that a critical analysis examines an article or other work to determine how effective the piece makes an argument or point.

Perspectival Background of the Study

This entails the presentation of your background of the study, not really in a historical fashion, but perspective by perspective. It paints a picture to the reader(s) of different aspects of how the issue or problem that motivated the study has been playing out, and its adverse effects, hence, the justification for the study. An example of this type of background of the study is found in Odigbo (2014) doctoral thesis, published in 2016, which goes as follows:

"Before 2007, national coverage in Nigeria for full immunization was less than 13%, one of the lowest rates in the world, with some states like Jigawa even recording as low as 1% (GAVI, 2008). According to the 2003 National Immunization Schedule, the percentage of fully immunized infants on the States targeted was less than 1% in Jigawa, 1.5% in Yobe, 1.6% in Zamfara and 8.3% in Katsina. The consequences of all these were the persistent high rate of infant and maternal mortality in Nigeria from vaccines preventable diseases (VPDs).

A negative rumor occasioned the low immunization rate, widely spread and accepted mainly in the Northern parts of the country that the immunization vaccines were laced with hazardous substances that could render men impotent and women infertile by alleged international conspirators bent on reducing the population of the country. The perpetrators of this hot rumor thus made sure that the programme never saw the light of the day. The story even became so bad, culminating in the banning of immunization personnel from some villages and communities in the North, under the allegations that they also had plans to inject their vaccines into public wells and other drinking-water sources (Shekarau, 2011).

This resulted in the persistent high rate of infant and maternal mortality mainly in Northern Nigeria from vaccines preventable diseases (VPDs) like polio, measles, tetanus, diphtheria, cholera, tuberculosis, yellow-fever, cerebra-spinal meningitis (CSM), most of which are endemic in the area. The problem thus posed a severe marketing communications challenge.

In the South-West, South-East, and South-South of the country, the immunization programme is also beset by mainly the problem of poor awareness amongst the populace. Even amongst needy parents that are aware of the exercise, accessing the services for their babies became a daunting task. This was due to the poor distribution of primary healthcare centers within the populace, while available ones, especially in the rural areas, seem to have been turned to playgrounds for rodents, snakes and mosquitoes, (Babasola and Aina, 2004: 5). This informed the appraisal of the effectiveness of the social public relations strategies being employed in the public health campaigns or immunization in the country, as a way of addressing the identified social, psychological, and cultural marketing communications problems."

From the above, the author presented his background of the study in two perspectives. In the first perspective, the unfortunate immunization problem in the Northern part of Nigeria was caused by a bad rumor, while in the second perspectives, the immunization programme was beset by poor awareness problem in the South-West, South-East and South-South parts of the country. All of these, he said, called for a critical examination of the marketing communications strategies employed, hence, the motivation for the study.

An Expository Background of the Study

In this type of background of the study, the author tries to marshal many points and defend them intelligently as the justification for the study. He/she emphasizes the explanation of the issues or motivating problems pointed out, for the audience to see and convinced that the investigation is worth the time, effort and resources to be invested in it.

1.2 Statement of the Problem

While the background of the study highlights the issues that informed research, the statement of the problem is emphatic in explaining the problems that justify the study. It tries to convince the reader that there is indeed a problem and that the consequences of the issue on the study population are worthy of the proposed research. According to the University of Southern California (2016), a research problem is a definite or explicit statement about an area of concern. It may include a condition to be improved upon, a difficulty to be eliminated, or a troubling question that exists in scholarly literature, in theory, or within existing practice that points to a need for meaningful understanding and careful investigation. It does not state how to do the problem.

Datt and Datt (2016) cite (Saunders et al. 2009) observe that a problem statement is a brief overview of the issues or problems existing in the concerned area selected for the research. It is an explanation of the issues prevalent in a particular sector which drives the researcher to take an interest in that sector for in-depth study and analysis, to understand and solve them.

University of Southern California (2016), states that the purpose of a problem statement is to: convince the reader to the importance of the topic being studied. It also anchors the research questions, hypotheses, or assumptions to follow, place the issue into a particular context that defines the parameters of what is to be investigated. It provides the framework for reporting the results and indicates what is probably necessary to conduct the study and explain how the findings will present this information. To do these effectively, the problem statement should possess the following attributes:

- Clarity and precision [a well-written account of the problem does not make sweeping generalizations and irresponsible pronouncements; it also does include unspecific determinates like "very" or "giant"],
- Demonstrate a researchable topic or issue [i.e., the feasibility of conducting the study is based upon access to information that can be acquired efficiently, gathered, interpreted, synthesized, and understood],
- Identification of what would be studied, while avoiding the use of value-laden words and terms,
- Identification of an overarching question or small set of questions accompanied by crucial factors or variables,
- The identification of fundamental concepts and terms,
- The articulation of the study's boundaries or parameters or limitations,
- Some generalizability in regards to applicability and bringing results into general use,

- Conveyance of the study's importance, benefits, and justification [i.e., regardless of the type of research, it is essential to demonstrate that the study is not trivial],
- Does not have unnecessary jargon or overly complex sentence constructions; and,
- Conveyance of more than the mere gathering of descriptive data providing only a snapshot of the issue or phenomenon under investigation.

Examples of suitable problem statements are as follows:

Example 1: (Quantitative Study) From Odigbo (2016):

"Although global immunization coverage has increased during the past decade to levels of around 78% for diphtheria–tetanus–pertussis-3 (DTP-3), the African Region has consistently fallen behind, reaching only 69% DTP-3 coverage by 2004. Studies rate Nigeria's performance on its immunizations management low, in spite of substantial financial resources being sunk into the programme (UNODC, 2003; WHO, 2014; GAVI, 2014). A catalog of this problem from GAVI (2003) records that national coverage in Nigeria for full immunization is less than 13%, one of the lowest rates in the world.

Situations in the northern parts of Nigeria are even worse, with some states recording coverage rates below 1%, and the average for the whole North West Zone about 4%, reports GAVI (2003:5). Both the Nigeria Demographic and Health Survey (NDHS, 2003), conducted by the National Population Commission, and the Nigeria Immunization Coverage Survey (NICS, 2003), conducted by the National Programme on Immunization (NPI), provide the same irrefutable evidence.

Precisely in 2013 and 2014, survey reports indicate the story has not changed significantly (WHO, 2014; GAVI, 2014)). Some of the reasons for such low rates of vaccination include dangerous anti-immunization rumors, lack of confidence and trust by the public in the vaccines administered, especially in the predominantly religious-sensitive northern parts of the country. These problems have been exacerbated again by a lack of understanding of the value of the vaccines by the public (Transaid, 2007: 2; WHO, 2013, Rainey et al., 2011). The study is focused, therefore, on a critical assessment of the social public relations (SPR) media employed by the health marketers in the immunization exercise."

Example one above obeyed the rules of good problem statement by starting from the general Africa picture, down to Nigeria, then specifically to a part of Nigeria. It is also compelling, has statistical proofs and supported by other studies.

Example 2: (Quantitative Study) From Datt and Datt (2016):

A Brief Overview of the problem: The high attrition rate in the manufacturing organization is creating anxiety and fear among the employees and thus affecting the productivity of the organization as a whole.

Here you need to refer to previous research done in the past in the manufacturing sector to determine the key reasons for high attrition rate. It should stimulate the reader to read further.

Anchor: This must include a statistical value to magnify and elucidates the problem.

Here you can present the attrition percentage within the manufacturing industry and compare it with the case company.
General Problem: The general business problem is to determine the financial loss to the organization.
The general business problem needs to outline the problem.

Specific Problem: Since high attrition rate is affecting the overall productivity of the employees it is in turn affecting the performance of the organization. To do so, one needs to determine the relationship between employee productivity and organizational performance.

This is narrower in scope than the general business problem and focused on the need for the study which allows a smooth transition to Need of the Study.

Example 3: (Qualitative Study) From Datt and Datt (2016):

A Brief Overview of the Problem: There has been an increase in workplace deaths of miners from 2010 to 2011 (Cite here).
Anchor: Study conducted by XYZ (Year) indicates that 7 out of 10 deaths in the mining industry are due to ABC reasons.
General Problem: The cost of workplace deaths negatively influences profitability to the business workers.
Specific Problem: There is little information on what measures can be undertaken to reduce the workplace death toll.
These three examples will guide you sufficiently in writing your problem statement. However, there could be modifications from your supervisor, based on your topic or type of research.

1.3 Objectives of the Study

You should state your broad or general objective first, before the specific objectives. An example from Odigbo (2016) is as follows:

Broad or Major Objective and Specific Objectives Examples

The principal objective of the study was a situation analysis of the applications of social public relations (SPR) in the immunization campaigns in Nigeria. The specific objectives were as follows:

- To examine the extent right beneficiaries were significantly targeted in the social public relations' communications' campaigns.
- To ascertain the extent the programs' executors/managers employed pre-and post-project public relations research and monitoring in the campaigns.
- To determine the degree of accessibility of the media employed in the campaigns to the target publics, and
- To evaluate the compatibility of the social public relations messages engaged in the campaigns to the cultural-sensibility of the target publics.

1.4 Research Questions

The research questions must be in accord with the research objectives, and each research question must be in line with its matching research objectives. That is research question one, must be saying what objective one is saying, but in a question format. The same goes for research questions two, three, four, etc. Going by this, the objectives above will now be stated as follows:

- Were the right beneficiaries significantly targeted in the social public relations' communications' campaigns for the immunization?
- To what extent did the programs' executors/managers employ pre-and post-project public relations research and monitoring in the campaigns?
- Were the media employed in the immunization significantly accessible to the target publics?
- What is the level of compatibility of the social public relations messages employed in the campaigns to the cultural sensibilities of the target publics?

1.5 Research Hypotheses

There are two classes of tests for hypotheses; the parametric tests and non-parametric tests.

Parametric Tests: These are tests whose data are generally derived from interval and ratio measurements. Hence, they are more powerful statistical tools. Examples of parametric tests include: The Z-test and the t-test. The Z-test is a parametric test used to determine the statistical significance between a sample distribution mean and a population parameter. The t-test is also a parametric test used to determine the statistical significance between a sample distribution mean and a population parameter.

Non-Parametric Tests: These are tests whose data are usually generated from nominal and ordinal measurements. A good example of this is the chi-square, which is also the most widely used non-parametric test of significance. The chi-square is used especially in testing bivariate hypothesis, that is, hypothesis with two variables only, but can also be used for other higher measurements if the situation demands.

In formulating hypotheses, students must ensure that each of the research hypotheses must be in accord with the matching research objectives and research question. That is, number one must be saying what objective one and research question one is answering. The same goes for hypothesis two, three, four, etc. You should state your hypotheses either in the null forms only, or state both the null and alternative hypotheses. However, whichever option you choose, must be explicitly stated. For example, the null-hypotheses emanating from the research questions and objectives above will be stated as follows:

The following null hypotheses were tested in the aforementioned study:

Ho1: The right beneficiaries were not significantly targeted in the social public relations' communications' campaigns for the immunization.

Ho2: The programs' executors/managers did not significantly employ pre- and post-project public relations research and monitoring in the campaigns.

Ho3: The media employed in the immunization were not significantly accessible to the target publics.

Ho4: The level of compatibility of the social public relations messages employed in the campaigns to the cultural sensibilities of the target publics were not significant.

1.6 The significance of the Study

Your significance of the study should cover three primary areas:

- The relevance to the organizational group or industry group to which the study organization (s) represent.

- The significance to the community, state, society or country's economic, social or political development.
- The significance to the body of knowledge: the academia, scholars, other researchers, and so on.

1.7 The scope of the Study

The scope of the study should also cover three technical areas:

The subject scope: That is, the scope of the issue(s) included in the topic.

The geographic scope: That is, the geographic area(s) to be covered in the study population.

The sampling scope: That is, the select groups to be sampled amongst the study population.

1.8 Limitations of the Study

The limitations of the study should encompass only factors that hindered the research and not what the researcher anticipates will impair the research. They must also be limited to issues related to the study's design, data gathering and or data analysis. Problems like difficulty in sourcing secondary data or information from relevant authorities, poor library resources in the researcher's environment, poor internet facilities, respondents' apathy, shortage of data analysis tools/software, and others. Some students make the mistake of including financial constraints, time constraints, and such other things. These are requirements for accomplishing the task and not limitations.

1.9 History of the Organization (where applicable).

Some universities require this, while others don't. Our advice is, follow your university's format on this.

1.10 Conceptual/Operational Definition of Terms

Many universities go for the operational definition of terms, which tells you only what the researcher/author mean by those terms, without citations. Others go for the conceptual definition, which shows you the meanings as exist in literature with citations. Others go for both. Again, our advice is, follow your university's format on this.

CHAPTER TWO: LITERATURE REVIEW

Some universities require students to kick-off their chapter two and indeed every other chapter with a short introduction, while others don't. There is nothing wrong with either of the two formats; it's a matter of writing style. So, adhere to your university's adopted style.

Literature review in scholarly studies, involves a comprehensive capturing, synthesizing and assessment of the critical concepts in literature related to a topic under investigation, in order to learn what others know, think and have written about it; what other researchers did about it in the past, how they did it, with what they did it, where they did it and what they found out, with a view to ascertaining if there is something still left undone, undiscovered or needs further studies. Other necessary contents of a literature review, include:

2.1 Theoretical Framework

You should start here by introducing the theories you wish to use to explain your research topic and the main issues surrounding it. Then, followed by a listing and explanation of those theories. It must be a theory from the body of knowledge or field where the research topic or critical variables under investigation falls.

Meanwhile, a theoretical framework is the introduction and description of a theory or theories that are related to research under study and explains why the research phenomenon or problem exists. It is the groundwork that holds or supports a research study. In practice, students should come up with a collection of a few interrelated theories that explain and defend their research topic and also guides it. This is because, theoretical Framework acts as a guide to your research, by pointing the way and proving that there exist already, other tested and proven concepts explaining the reasons for a phenomenon or phenomena. A good theoretical framework gives a robust scientific research base for a study and provides support for a project, thesis or dissertation. It often serves as the lens through which a research problem and research questions will be evaluated.

2.1.1 Theory of this or that: Here you table and expound on your theory number one.

2.1.2 The Theory of this or that: Here you present and expound on your theory number two.

2.2 Application of the Theories to the Work: Here, you explain how the theory or theories apply to the research.

2.3 Conceptual Framework

The conceptual framework of a study is a collection of ideas, concepts, opinions, assumptions, beliefs, and theories that are related a topic under study. It captures and gives all the literature direction of a research project, thesis or dissertation. It marshals out the key variables under study and explains how they are related to each other. A good conceptual framework must give an organized bird-eye-view of the theoretical side and or secondary data angles of a study. According to the Business Dictionary (2017), conceptual framework provides the theoretical structure of assumptions, principles, and rules that hold together the ideas encompassed in a study. Mae-Nalzaro (2012), outlines the purposes of conceptual framework as follows:

To clarify concepts and propose relationships among the ideas in a study.

To provide a context for interpreting the study findings.

To explain observations, and

To encourage theory development that is useful to practice.

The differences between conceptual framework and theoretical framework stem from the fact that while the conceptual framework is ideas contained in literature covering all areas of research, the theoretical structure is based on theories related to the topic, its problems or questions that have been developed, tested and proven over time, with a long history.

2.3.1 – 2.3 (Infinity): From here comes the listing and explanation (literature review) of all the concepts related to the study. That is, as other authors see them, records, authorities, and researchers.

2.4 Empirical Review: This entails a review of similar or other related studies by other researchers in the past.

2.5 Conceptual model of the Study: While this is compulsory in some universities, it is optional in others. Whichever one applies, adhere to your university's, college or departmental format.

2.6 Summary of and Gap in Literature: Students are advised to summarize their literature review at the end, pointing out the gap(s) identified, which their study intends to fill.

Note: Table titles must be sequentially numbered and labeled on top, while figures are to be sequentially numbered and marked below. Sources of tables and figures must be fully referenced. Some universities adopt the chapter-by-chapter sequential numbering, while others follow the whole-work sequential numbering. Whichever one applies, is still good. It's a matter of style.

Again, you must follow your University's approved citation and reference style in your research reporting. Students are advised to study and be conversant with the major citations and referencing formats like the Harvard style, APA style, Oxford style, and others.

CHAPTER THREE: RESEARCH METHODOLOGY AND DESIGN

The principal contents of a standard chapter three in a five-chapter project format include:

Research Methodology

See chapter seven and specifically sub-topic 7.2 on this.

Research Design

See chapter seven and specifically sub-topic 7.4 on this.

Area of the Study

This encompasses the actual geographical area(s) to be covered by the study.

Population of the Study

Certainly not everybody in the area will be surveyed in the research. This means only the people or study elements of interest or concern in a study, not the entire population of people or elements in the area. For more on this, see chapter eight of this book.

3.5 **Sample Size Determination**

3.6 Sampling Technique (either probability or non-probability technique).

3.7 Sources and Method(s) of Data Collection

3.8 Instrument for Data Collection

3.9 Validity of the Instrument

3.10 Reliability of the Instrument

3.11 Data Analysis Techniques

When at a loss with any of these, students should consult their supervisors for proper guidance. All of these are already explained in preceding chapters of this book. See particularly, chapter seven on research methodology and designs and chapter eight on sample size determination and sampling techniques for these.

CHAPTER FOUR: DATA PRESENTATION AND ANALYSIS

Your data analysis could be quantitatively or qualitatively or a combination of both, depending on your research methodology and design. It should be done either manually or computer-aided, like with the statistical package for the social sciences (SPSS), if you're conversant with it and if your university demands that. If you're not conversant with any of the computer-aided data analysis techniques when your university wants that, you can outsource the services; it is allowed. However, you must know what the data analyst did, sufficient enough because you are the one that will defend every bit of it, not him or her. Meanwhile, the primary contents of a good chapter four in a five-chapter' project format include:

4.1 Data Presentation in percentage frequencies, mean, median, mode, Likert's scale and or other styles, followed with their interpretations.

4.2 Tests of Hypotheses

4.3 Results Interpretations

4.4 Discussion of Findings (in line with the research objectives and previous research findings on the subject matter.

CHAPTER FIVE: SUMMARY OF FINDINGS, CONCLUSION, AND RECOMMENDATIONS

The principal contents of a good chapter five in a five-chapter' project format include:

5.1 Summary of Findings: The findings should be itemized. The essay format is not clear enough, and not acceptable to most people.

5.2 Conclusion: This should follow the essay format.

5.3 Recommendations: The recommendations should be itemized.

5.4 Area for Further Studies: You should identify and point out any area you feel the study might need further research on by others in future, for enhanced human knowledge and benefits.

5.5 Contribution to Knowledge: Some universities require you to mention here what your study has contributed to the body of knowledge.

References: Chapter five References.

Bibliography: This must contain a full aggregation of all the references from chapter one to five. Follow your university's adopted style.

Appendices: If any.

NOTE: Some universities adopt end-of-chapter references for all the chapters (where applicable), while others don't. Find out which applies to your university and follow it. Where end-of-chapter references are the style, there must be bibliography that will sum up all, at the end of the work. But where there are no end-of-chapter references, then, there must be references at the end of the work, that will capture all the citations from chapter one to five. The first, however, is more acceptable, because experience has shown that when students are asked not to do the end-of-chapter references, they usually leave out a large chunk of their cited works unreferenced at the end.

12.5 Seminar Papers

12.5.1 Journal Article Format (Empirical Study)

First comes the preliminary pages, which is usually the cover page, the title page, and the Abstract, in most universities' formats.

Cover Page: This must be in line with your university's approved format.

Title Page: Also adhere to your university's approved format.

Abstract: This must contain: A summary of what the study/paper is all about, the issues or problems that motivated it, the objectives, methodology, results, and recommendations.

Keyword: Some universities might demand you put a few keywords following the area(s) or critical subject matters covered by the study or paper. This practice is also in line with international standards for journal articles published. Students, especially at postgraduate levels are advised to publish their seminar papers, thesis or dissertations. This is compulsory in some universities.

Then follows the body text of the paper, containing:
Background of the Study
Statement of the Problem
Objectives of the Study
    Research Questions
    Research Hypotheses
    The significance of the Study
    The scope of the Study
    Limitations of the Study

1.9 Review of Related Literature: This must contain among other things the theoretical framework, conceptual framework, other related concepts and empirical evaluation of other similar studies.

1.10 Methodology: This should contain a summary of the research design, area of the study, the population of the study, sample size, sampling technique, sources of data, the instrument for data collection, validity and reliability of the instrument and data analysis tools, all in two or three paragraphs.

1.11 Data Presentation and Analysis: Here, you present and analyze your data, including hypotheses tests and results' interpretation.

1.12   Summary of Results: Here, an itemized summary of your results should be highlighted.

1.13 Discussion of Results: The results should be exhaustively discussed at this point.

1.14 Conclusion: This entails a tight summary and implication of the work.

1.15 Recommendations: The recommendations should be itemized and must be strictly related to the study and its findings.

-References: All the works/authors cited in the body text must be referenced here.

Seminar Paper Format 2: Mini-Thesis Format

This is usually in the chapter by chapter style, but not more than three or four chapters, depending on the university. In most universities, it comes in the following way:

Cover Page: Follow your University's Format.

Title Page: In line with your University's Format.

Table of Contents

Abstract (Must contain: A summary of what the study/paper is all about, the issues or problems that motivated it, the objectives, methodology, results, and recommendations).

CHAPTER ONE: Introduction

1.1 Background of the Study

1.2 Statement of the Problem

1.3 Objectives of the Study

1.4 Research Questions

1.5 Research Hypotheses

1.6 The significance of the Study
1.7 The scope of the Study

CHAPTER TWO: LITERATURE REVIEW

2.1 Theoretical Framework
2.1.1 Theory of …
2.1.2 The Theory of …
2.2 Application of the Theories to the Work (How the theories apply to the research).
2.3 Conceptual Framework.
2.3.1 – 2.3…(Infinity) Other Concepts of your choice related to the study.
2.4 Empirical Review (of other similar studies)
2.5 Conceptual model of the research
2.6 Summary of and Gap in Literature

Note: Table titles must be labeled on top, while figures are to be labeled below. Sources of tables and figures must be fully referenced in APA style.

CHAPTER THREE: RESEARCH METHODOLOGY

3.1 Research Design
3.2 Area of the Study
3.3 Population of the Study
3.4 Sample Size Determination
3.5 Sampling Technique (either probability or non-probability technique).
3.6 Sources and Method(s) of Data Collection
3.7 Instrument for Data Collection
3.8 Validity of the Instrument
3.9 Reliability of the Instrument
3.10 Data Analysis Techniques

CHAPTER FOUR: DATA PRESENTATION AND ANALYSIS

4.1 Data Presentation and Interpretation

4.2 Data Analysis

4.3 Tests of Hypotheses (where applicable)

4.4 Summary of Findings

4.5 Discussion of Findings (in line with the research objectives).

4.6 Conclusion

4.7 Recommendations

Exercises

1. What is research project format? Outline and explain your university's project preliminary pages format?
2. List and explain with practical examples the four major types of a background of the study?
3. Write a broad objective and four specific objectives of a tentative research topic of your choice.
4. From the four specific objectives in item (iii) above, produce four research questions and four hypotheses.
5. Write the significance of the study of the hypothetical topic in item (iii) above.
6. What are the differences and similarities between a conceptual and operational definition of terms?
7. What are the differences and similarities between theoretical, conceptual framework and empirical review?
8. Outline and explain the major contents of a standard chapter three research methodology and design.

References

Basil, Glory (2017), Unethical marketing practices by independent petroleum marketers in Nigeria. A Ph.D. Seminar paper presented to the Department of Marketing, University of Calabar.

Businessdictionary (2017), What is a conceptual framework: Definition and meaning. https://www.businessdictionary.com/definition/conceptual-framework.html

Datt, Sudeshna & Datt, Shrutti (2016), How to write the problem statement in a research paper? https://www.projectguru.in/publications/write-problem-statement-research-paper/

Eleje, U. (2009), Critical Writing, http://www2.southeastern.edu/Academics/Faculty/elejeune/critique.htm

Mae-Nalzaro, Ludy (2012), Chapter 6-Theoretical & Conceptual Framework. https://www.slideshare.net/ludymae/chapter-6theoretical-conceptual-framework

Saunders, M., Lewis, P. & Thornhill, A. (2009) Research methods for business students, 5th ed., Harlow, Pearson Education.

University of Southern Carlifornia (2016), Organizing Your Social Sciences Research Paper: The Research Problem/Question.

http://libguides.usc.edu/writingguide/introduction/resea
rchproblem

Wiki, H. (2014), How to Write a Critical Analysis,
        http://www.wikihow.com/Writing-a-Critical-Analysis

CHAPTER THIRTEEN

HOW TO DO YOUR BIBLIOGRAPHIC CITATIONS AND REFERENCING

13.1 Introduction

This chapter introduces us to yet another area where a majority of students do have difficulties in their academic writings - bibliographic citations and referencing. The chapter will teach us among other things: what is a bibliography, what is a citation and referencing in scholarly papers. It will also highlight the major bibliographic citations and reference formats with their examples.

13.2 What Is Bibliography

By bibliography, we mean a comprehensive list of all the sources you have used or cited in your scholarly or academic writings; whether a research work, term paper, seminar paper, journal article, websites or book. Conventionally, a bibliography includes: the author(s)' name(s), the year of publication, the title of the work cited or used, the name and location of the publisher, the volume, page chapter or number, as the case may be. A bibliography should include all the sources consulted whether they are directly cited or not.

13.3 What Is Bibliographic Citation

A bibliographic citation is a very short acknowledgment or identifier to a book, article, web page, or any other published material(s) used in your work. Citations usually carry the author(s') surname(s) and year of publication, or surnames with numbers or reference numbers only for footnotes and endnotes, depending on the style adopted. According to University of Pittsburgh (2017), a citation is a way of giving credit to individuals for their creative and intellectual works that you utilized to support your research. It can also be used to locate particular sources and combat plagiarism. Typically, a citation can include the author's name, date, the location of the publishing company, journal title, or DOI (Digital Object Identifier).

There are different citation styles peculiar to different academic writings, like a scientific citation, legal citation, prior art, the arts, and the humanities. Depending on the method approved by your university, in-text citations may take different forms which include:

Footnotes: These appear at the bottom of the page of your text, peculiar to legal citations.

Endnotes: These appear at the end of the written text of your work, peculiar to legal citations.

Bracketed References: These appear inside the body text. When it is coming at the end of a sentence or write-up, both the author(s) surnames and year of publication should be inside a bracket, like (Odigbo, 2014; or Eze & Odigbo, 2016). But when it is coming at the beginning or middle of a sentence, the author(s) surnames should be outside the bracket, followed by the year of publication in parenthesis, like Odigbo (2014) or Eze & Odigbo (2016). It is peculiar to the arts, management, humanities and social sciences.

Students are, however, advised to adopt a uniform pattern of citation style through the entire length and breadth of their term papers, seminar papers, essays, projects, thesis or dissertations. This is universally and conventionally acceptable as a mark for good scholarly or academic writings.

13.4 What Is Bibliographic Referencing

A bibliographic referencing is a full acknowledgment or identifier to a book, article, web page, or any other published material(s) used in your work. It usually carries the author(s') surname(s), followed by the full names or initials, then the year of publication, the title of the work cited or used, the name and location of the publisher, the volume, page chapter or number. An end-of-page referencing is a list of all the work, authors or materials cited in a particular page, like in a footnote. An end-of-chapter referencing is a list of all the work, authors or materials cited in a particular chapter of a text. While, an end-of-work referencing is a list of all the work, authors or materials cited in the entire work, from chapter one to the last chapter. However, where there is chapter by chapter referencing, end-of-work referencing is called a bibliography, which is a pool or an aggregation of all the chapters' references.

Students must make sure that all the citations in the body text of their work are fully referenced at the end. Many students fall foul of this and are usually embarrassed over this, during their projects, thesis, dissertation or other academic materials' defenses.

13.5 Importance of Bibliographic Citations and Referencing

Bibliographic citations and referencing have the following benefits to an author or authors of any academic material:

It is a mark of your intellectual honesty and integrity.

It shields you from being accused of plagiarism.

It boosts the scholarly or academic quality ratings of your work.

It shows you have read widely and have sufficient knowledge of your subject matter or topic.

It helps the reader of your work in searching for more information on any area of the subject matter.

It is a fundamental requirement for any academic text and often affects your score or grading.

It shows to a large extent that your work is free from certain ethical breaches.

13.6 Bibliographic Citations and Referencing Styles

A citation style is any format that shows the types and degree of information to be contained in a citation and the full referencing, including how they will be structured, ordered, punctuated and formatted. There are many citations and referencing styles, and different universities adopt one or two of these, depending on the area of studies' peculiarities. The popular citation and referencing styles include:

The American Psychological Association (APA),

Harvard Style,

Oxford Style,

Modern Language Association (MLA) style,

Chicago/Turabian style,

American Medical Association (AMA) style,
Chicago citation style,
Etc.

We will now try to present two of the styles commonly used by the majority of universities across the globe, the Harvard and APA styles. However, students are advised to stick to any method approved by their university, because none of the forms is superior or more important than the other. It is a matter of style.

13.6.1 The Harvard Style of Referencing

Citethisforme (2017), gave a compendium of guides to Harvard referencing with little amendments from us as follows:

Harvard In-Text Citations: The in-text citations could be done in four different ways as follows:
For public relations programme to be effective, it must be adequately monitored (Okigbo, 1993:112) – This one contains the author's surname, year of publication and page number.

For public relations programme to be effective, it must be adequately monitored (Okigbo, 1993) – This one contains the author's surname and year of publication only. Hence, the page number where the statement appeared must be identified in the full referencing.

Okigbo (1993), advises that for public relations programme to be effective, it must be adequately monitored.
It has been advised by Okigbo (1993), that for public relations programme to be effective, it must be adequately monitored.

Harvard Reference Lists: This is located at the end of the work and displays full citations for sources used in the assignment. Here is an example of a complete referencing for the citations above, which an article in a book, commonly called "a book chapter," done in a Harvard Reference style:

Okigbo, Charles (1993), "Public Relations Research and Evaluation," In Public Relations for Local Govt. in Nigeria, E.O. Salu (ed.), Lagos: Talkback Publishers, p112.

That is to say; the Harvard Reference List must contain information in the following order:

Name of the author(s)

Year published

Title

City published

Publisher

Pages used

Harvard Reference List citations follow this format:

Last name, First name or initial. (Year published). Title. City: Publisher, Page(s).

Citations are listed in alphabetical order by the author's last name. If there are multiple sources by the same author, then citations are listed in order by the date of publication.

Harvard Reference List Citations for Books by One Author: The structure for a Harvard Reference List citation for books with one author from Citethisforme (2017), includes the following:

Last name, First name or initial. (Year published). Title. Edition. (Only add the publication if it is not the first edition) The city published: Publisher, Page(s).

If the edition isn't listed, it is safe to assume that it is the first edition, and does not need to be included in the citation.

Example: One author and first edition:

Patterson, J. (2005). Maximum Ride. New York: Little, Brown.

Example: One author AND NOT the first edition

Dahl, R. (2004). Charlie and the chocolate factory. 6th ed. New York: Knopf.

Harvard Reference List Citations for Books with Two or More Authors

When creating a citation that has more than one author, place the names in the order in which they appear on the source. Use the word "and" to separate the names.

Last name, First name or initial and Last name, First initial. (Year published). Title. City: Publisher, Page(s).

Example:

Desikan, S. and Ramesh, G. (2006). Software testing. Bangalore, India: Dorling Kindersley, p.156.

Vermaat, M., Sebok, S., Freund, S., Campbell, J. and Frydenberg, M. (2014). Discovering Computers. Boston: Cengage Learning, pp.446-448.

Daniels, K., Patterson, G., and Dunston, Y. (2014). The ultimate student teaching guide. 2nd ed. Los Angeles: SAGE Publications, pp.145-151.

Note: When citing a book, only include the edition if it is NOT the first edition!

Harvard Reference List Citations for Chapters in Edited Books: When citing a chapter in an edited book, use the following format:

Last name, First name or initial. (Year published). Chapter title. In: First initial. Last name, ed., Book Title, 1st ed.* City: Publisher, Page(s).
Bressler, L. (2010). My Girl, Kylie. In: L. Matheson, ed., The Dogs That We Love, 1st ed. Boston: Jacobson Ltd., pp. 78-92.
Note: When citing a chapter in an edited book, the edition is displayed, even when it is the first edition.

Harvard Reference List Citations for Multiple Works By The Same Author: When there are multiple works by the same author, place the citations in order by year. When sources are published in the same year, put them in alphabetical order by the title. Example:
Odigbo, B. (2008). Public Relations Management. Enugu: John Jacobs Publishers.
Odigbo, B. (2012). Advertising Management. Lagos: Eagles Publishers.
Odigbo, B. (2013). Business Communications. Lagos: Eagles Publishers.

Harvard Reference List Citations for Print Journal Articles: The standard structure of a print journal citation in Harvard style includes the following components:
Last name, First name or initial. (Year published). Article title. Journal, Volume (Issue), Page(s). Examples:
Odigbo, Ben E., Samaila, Mande & Okonkwo, Raphael V. (2017), Assessment of public relations strategies employed by major international oil companies for crisis management in Nigeria. Developing Country Studies, Vol.7, No.7, p.1-11.
Odigbo, Ben; Samaila, Mande & Effiong, Etim Okon (2017), Assessment of Marketing Communications for the Prevention

and Control of Malaria in Nigeria. Journal of Biology, Agriculture and Healthcare Vol. 7, No. 14, p.14-21.

Odigbo, Ben; Ugwu-Ogbu, Silk & Odigbo, Rose Adannia (2014), The Correlation between Social Violence and the Comments of Nigerian Politicians during Electioneering Campaigns: A Political Marketing Study. Journal of Law, Policy, and Globalization, Vol.26, p.1-12.

Harvard Reference List Citations for Journal Articles Found on a Database or a Website.

When citing journal articles found on a database or through a website, including all of the components found in a citation of a print journal, but also include the medium ([online]), the website URL, and the date that the article was accessed. The standard structure of an online journal citation in Harvard style includes the following components:

Last name, First name or initial. (Year published). Article Title. Journal, [online] Volume(Issue), pages. Available at: URL [Accessed Day Mo. Year].

Example:

Kasomo, Daniel (2012), Factors Affecting Women Participation in Electoral Politics in Africa. International Journal of Psychology and Behavioral Sciences, [online] Volume 2(3), p.57-63. Available at: DOI: 10.5923/j.ijpbs.20120203.01. [Accessed 12th May 2017].

Harvard Reference List Citations for Print Newspaper

Articles: When citing a newspaper, use the following structure:

Last name, First name or initial. (Year published). Article title. Paper, Date published, Page(s).

Example:

Fawehinmi, Gani (2008), The Nigeria Electoral Reform, Real of Deceit. Vanguard Newspaper, Thursday, August 5, p.4.

Harvard Reference List Citations for Newspaper Articles Found on a Database or a Website: To cite a newspaper found either on a database or a website, use the following structure:
Last name, First name or initial. (Year published). Article title. Newspaper, [online] pages. Available at: URL [Accessed Day Mo. Year].
Example:
Oshiomhole, Adams   (2008). Support Yar'Adua's bid to stop electoral fraud, Oshiomhole tells Nigerians. TheNation [online] p.12,   Available   at: http://www.thenationonlineng.net/archive2/tblnews_Detail.ph p?id=73024, [Accessed 22 Jan. 2013].

Harvard Reference List Citations for Print Magazines: When citing magazines, use the following structure:
Last name, First name or initial. (Year published). Article title. Magazine, (Volume), Page(s).

Example:
Davidson, J. (2008). Speak her language. Men's Health, (23), pp.104-106.

Harvard Reference List Citations for Websites: When citing a website, use the following structure:
Last name, first name or initial (Year published). Page title. [online] Website name. Available at: URL [Accessed Day Mo. Year].

When no author is listed, use the following structure:
Website name, (Year published). Page title. [online] Available at URL [Accessed Day Mo. Year].

Example:
Messer, L. (2015). 'Fancy Nancy' Optioned by Disney Junior. [online] ABC News. Available at: http://abcnews.go.com/Entertainment/fancy-nancy-optioned-disney-junior-2017/story?id=29942496#.VRWbWJwmbs0.twitter [Accessed 31 Mar. 2015].
Mms.com, (2015). M&M'S Official Website. [online] Available at: http://www.mms.com/ [Accessed 20 Apr. 2015].

Harvard Reference List Citations for eBooks and PDFs: When citing eBooks and PDFs, include the edition, even if it's the first edition, and follow it with the type of resource in brackets (either [ebook] or [pdf]). Include the URL at the end of the citation with the date it was accessed in brackets. Use the following structure:
   Last name, First name or initial. (Year published). Title. Edition. [format] City: Publisher, page(s). Available at: URL [Accessed Day Mo. Year].
   Example:
Zusack, M. (2015). The Book Thief. 1st ed. [ebook] New York: Knopf. Available at: http://ebooks.nypl.org/ [Accessed 20 Apr. 2015].
Robin, J. (2014). A handbook for professional learning: research, resources, and strategies for implementation. 1st ed. [pdf] New York: NYC Department of Education. Available at http://schools.nyc.gov/ [Accessed 14 Apr. 2015].

Harvard Reference List Citations for Archive Material: Archival materials are information sources used to provide evidence of past events. They are collected and stored by governments, organizations, institutions, libraries, repositories, or historical societies. The structure for archival materials includes:

Last name, First name or initial. (Year published). Title of the article. [format] Name of the university, library, organization, Collection name, code, or number. City.

Examples:

Pearson, J. (1962). Letter to James Martin. [letter] The Jackson Historical Society, Civil Rights Collection. Jackson.

Marshall, S. and Peete, L. (1882). Events Along the Canal. [program] Afton Library, Yardley History. Yardley.

Harvard Reference List Citations for Artwork: To cite artwork, use the following structure:

Last name, First name or initial. (Year created). Title. [Medium]. The city that the artwork is/was displayed in Gallery or Museum.

Example:

Gilbert, S. (1795-1796). George Washington. [Oil on canvas] New York: The Frick Collection.

Jensen, L., Walters, P. and Walsh, Q. (1994). Faces in the Night. [Paint Mural] Trenton: The Trenton Free Library.

Harvard Reference List Citations for Blogs: Blogs are regularly updated web pages that are run by an individual. When citing a blog post, use the following format:

Last name, First name or initial. (Year published). Post title. [Blog] Blog name. Available at: URL [Accessed Day Mo. Year].

Example:

Cohen, M. (2013). Re-election Is Likely for McConnell, but Not Guaranteed. [Blog] FiveThirtyEight. Available at: http://fivethirtyeight.blogs.nytimes.com/2013/07/01/re-election-is-likely-for-mcconnell-but-not-guaranteed/ [Accessed 4 Apr. 2015].

Harvard Reference List Citations for Radio or TV Broadcasts:
To cite a radio or tv broadcast, use the following structure:
Series title, (Year published). [Type of Programme] Channel number: Broadcaster.
Examples:
Modern Family, (2010). [TV programme] 6: Abc.
The Preston and Steve Morning Show (2012). [Radio Programme] 93.3: WMMR.
Harvard Reference List Citations for Conference Proceedings:
These are papers presented or used at a conference. Use the following structure to cite a conference proceeding:
If published online:
Last name, First name or initial. (Conference Year). Title of Paper or Proceedings. In: Name or Title of Conference. [online] City: Publisher of the Proceedings, pages. Available at: URL [Accessed Day Mo. Year].
If not published online:
Last name, First name or initial. (Conference Year). Title of Paper or Proceedings. In: Name or Title of Conference. City: Publisher of the Proceedings, pages.
Examples:
Fox, R. (2014). Technological Advances in Banking. In: American Finance Association Northeast Regional Conference. Hartford: AFA, p. 24.

Harvard Reference List Citations for Court Cases: To cite a court case, use the following format:
Case name [Year published]Report abbreviation Volume number (Name or abbreviation of court); First page of the court case.

Example:
Young v. United Parcel Service, Inc. [2015]12-1226 (Supreme Court of the United States); 1.

Harvard Reference List Citations for Dictionary Entry: When citing a dictionary entry in print, use the following structure:
Last name, First name or initial. (Year published). Entry title. In: Dictionary Title, Edition. City: Publisher, page.
When citing a dictionary entry found online, use the following structure:

Last name, First name or initial. (Year published). Entry title. In: Dictionary Title, Edition. City: Publisher, page. Available at: URL [Accessed Day Mo. Year].

**If no author/editor/or contributor is given, omit it from the citation.

**If the publishing year is unavailable, use the abbreviation n.d., which stands for no date

Examples:

Sporadic (1993). In: Webster Dictionary, 8th ed. New York: Webstin LLC, page 223.

Reference. (n.d.) In: Merriam-Webster [online] Springfield: Merriam-Webster, Inc. Available at: http://www.merriam-webster.com/dictionary/reference [Accessed 12 Dec. 2014].

Harvard Reference List Citations for Dissertations: Use the following structure to create a citation for a dissertation:

Last name, First name or initial. (Year published). Dissertation title. Academic Level of the Author. Name of University, College, or Institution.

Example:
Shaver, W. (2013). Effects of Remediation on High-Stakes Standardized Testing. Ph.D. Yeshiva University.

Harvard Reference List Citations for DVD, Video, and Film:
When citing a DVD, Video, or Film, use the following format:

Film title. (Year published). [Format] Place of origin: Filmmaker.

**The place of origin refers to the place where the DVD, film, or video was made. E.g.: Hollywood

**The filmmaker can be the director, studio, or main producer.

Example:

Girls Want To Have Fun. (1985). [film] Chicago: Alan Metter.

Harvard Reference List Citations for Emails: For Email citations, use the following format:

Sender's Last name, First name or initial. (Year published). Subject Line of Email. [email].

Example:

Niles, A. (2013). Update on my health. [email].

Harvard Reference List Citations for Print Encyclopedia Articles: Use this format to cite an encyclopedia:

Last name, First name or initial. (Year published). Article title. In: Encyclopedia title, Edition. The city published: Publisher, page(s).

Example:

Harding, E. (2010). Anteaters. In: The International Encyclopedia of Animals, 3rd ed. New York: Reference World, p. 39.

Harvard Reference List Citations for Government Publications: Government publications consist of documents that are issued by local, state, or federal governments, offices, or subdivisions. Use the following format to cite the government publications:

Government Agency OR Last name, First name or Initial., (Year published). Title of Document or Article. The city published: Publisher, Page(s).

Examples:

Pennsylvania Department of Transportation, (2012). Bicycle PA Routes. Harrisburg: PENNDOT, p.1.

Harvard Reference List Citations for Interviews: When citing an interview, use the following format:

Last name of Interviewer, First name or the initial and Last name of Interviewee, First name or initial. (Year of Interview). Title or Description of Interview.

Example:

Booker, C. and Lopez, J. (2014). Getting to know J. Lo.

Harvard Reference List Citations for Music or Recordings: To cite a music piece or recording, use the following format:

Performer or Writer's Last name, First name or initial. (Year published). Recording title. [Medium] City published: Music Label.

When citing a music piece or recording found online, use the following structure:

Performer or Writer's Last name, First name or initial. (Year published). Recording title. [Online] City published: Music Label. Available at: URL [Accessed Day Mo. Year].

Examples:

Jackson, M. (1982). Thriller. [CD] West Hollywood: Epic.

Kaskade, (2015). Never Sleep Alone. [Online] Burbank: Warner Bros/Arcade. Available at: https://soundcloud.com/kaskade/kaskade-never-sleep-alone [Accessed 7 Apr. 2015].

Harvard Reference List Citations for Online Images or Videos:
To cite an image or video found electronically, use the following structure:

Last name, First name or initial. OR Corporate Author. (Year published). Title/description. [format] Available at URL [Accessed Day Mo. Year].

Examples:

Williams, A. (2013). DJ Gear. [image] Available at: https://flic.kr/p/fbPZyV [Accessed 8 Apr. 2015].

7UP (2015). 7UP Team Up Tiesto. [video]. Available at: https://youtu.be/TMZqgEgy_Xg [Accessed 8 Apr. 2015].

Harvard Reference List Citations for Patents: When citing patents, use the following structure:

Last name, First name or initial. OR Corporate Author (Year published). Title or Description of Patent. Patent number.

**It should be noted that even if the information is found online, no online information needs to be included.

Example:

Masuyama, T., Suzuki, M. and Fujimoto, H. (1993). Structure for securing batteries used in an electric vehicle. 5,392,873.

Harvard Reference List Citations for Podcasts: When citing a podcast, use the following format:

Last name, First name or initial. OR Corporate Author (Year published) Episode title. [podcast]. Podcast title. Available at: URL [Accessed Day Mo. Year].

Example:

Provenzano, N. (2012). #NerdyCast Episode 5. [podcast]. #NerdyCast. Available at: https://itunes.apple.com/us/podcast/nerdycast/id514797904?mt=2 [Accessed 14 Dec. 2014].

Harvard Reference List Citations for Presentations and Lectures: To cite a presentation or lecture, use the following structure:

Last name, First initial. (Year) Presentation Title.

Example:

Valenza, J. (2014). Librarians and Social Capital.

Harvard Reference List Citations for Press Releases: When citing a press release in print, use the following format:

Corporate Author, (Year published). Title.

If found online, use the following format:

Corporate Author, (Year published). Title. [online] Available at URL [Accessed Day Mo. Year].

Examples:

Imagine Easy Solutions, (2015). Research Ready Jr. Now Available For Elementary Age Students.

EBSCO, (2014). EBSCO adds EasyBib Citation Integration. [online] Available at: http://campustechnology.com [Accessed 11 Jan. 2015].

Harvard Reference List Citations for Religious Texts: To cite any religious text, such as the Bible, Torah, Quran, use the following format:

Title (Year published). The city published: Publisher, pages used.

Example:

New American Standard Bible, (1998). Anaheim: Foundation Publications, Inc, pp.332-340.

Harvard Reference List Citations for Reports: When citing a report, use the following format:

Last name, First name or Initial. OR Corporate Author (Year published). Title. [online] City published: Publisher, Pages used. Available at: URL [Accessed Day Mo. Year].

Example:

Certify, (2015). First Quarter, 2015 Business Expense Trends. [online] Portland: Certify, p.2. Available at: http://www.certify.com/CertifySpendSmartReport.aspx [Accessed 8 Apr. 2015].

Harvard Reference List Citations for Software: When citing software, use the following format:

Title or Name of Software. (Year Published). Place or city where the software was written: Company or publisher.

Example:

Espanol. (2010). Arlington: Rosetta Stone.

Harvard In-Text Citations for Four or More Authors: Only use the first listed author's name in the in-text citation, followed by "et al." and the publishing year.

Example:
It can be said that "knowledge of the stages of growth and development helps predict the patient's response to the present illness or the threat of future illness" (Potter et al., 2013).

Example:
Potter et al. (2013) go on to explain that "among the most Catholic Filipinos, parents keep the newborn inside the home until after the baptism to ensure the baby's health and protection."

Harvard In-Text Citations for Corporate Authors: Use the name of the organization in place of the author.

Example:
"Dr. Scharschmidt completed her residency in 2012, joined the Leaders Society in 2013, and became a new volunteer this year to encourage other young dermatologists in her area to join her in leadership giving" (Dermatology Foundation, 2014).
If the name of the organization is used in the text, place only the year in parentheses.

Example:
The Dermatology Foundation (2013) stated in their report that "industry also played an important role in the success of the

highly rated annual DF Clinical Symposia—Advances in Dermatology."

Harvard In-Text Citations for No Author: When an author's name cannot be found, place the title of the text in the parentheses, followed by the publishing year.

Example:
Lisa wasn't scared. She was only shocked and caught off guard to notice her father in such a peculiar place (Lost Spaces, 2014).

13.7 APA Style of Referencing
The Western Sydney University (2017), outlined some general rules governing the APA referencing style as follows:
Whenever you present a statement of evidence such as a quote, or when you use someone else's ideas, opinions or theories in your own words (paraphrasing), you must acknowledge your sources.

All sources appearing in the APA reference list must be ordered alphabetically by surname. The same thing goes for the bibliography if there is one.
Italics is the preferred format for titles of books, journals, and videos. Article and chapter titles are not italicised or put in quotation marks. Volume numbers are italicised, but issue numbers are not.

The reference list should be double-spaced (no line spaces between references) with hanging indents used for the second and subsequent lines of each entry. A hanging indent is where the left line starts at the left margin and subsequent lines are indented (approx. 1.3 cm or five spaces). You can use your word processor to format the double-spacing and hanging indents automatically.

APA does not require you to provide the page number unless you use a direct quote, however, if you paraphrase or summarize a specific paragraph or section you should consider including the page number.
When there are no page numbers, but the sources contain headings or numbered paragraphs, use a section name or paragraph number, e.g., Jones (2008, Introduction section) or Roberts (2008, para. 5). If the paragraphs are not numbered, cite the heading and the number of the item following the entry, e.g., Anderson (2005, Discussion section, para. 2).

For Capitalization in APA style, the following general rules apply: Book titles and Articles - capitalize the first letter of the first word of the title and the first letter of the first word after a colon. (e.g., Ageing and aged care in Australia and Brave new brain: Conquering mental illness in the era of the genome).

When referencing electronic resources, it is necessary to provide details about the location of the item. The 6th edition of the Publication Manual advises that wherever possible, the DOI (digital object identifier) should be provided in the reference. Electronic sources should be referenced in the same format as that for a "fixed-media source," such as a book, with the DOI included at the end. If a DOI is available, no further publication or location elements are required. If no DOI is available, provide the direct URL if the item is freely accessible or the home page URL if access is restricted.

You must acknowledge both the first and the secondary source when citing an original work from a secondary source. In these instances, you may want to quote or paraphrase a source (A) that is referred to within another source (B). You should not cite source A as though you read the original work. You must mention source A through the secondary source (B) which you read, as follows: Jones (as cited in Smith, 2009) agreed that the experiment failed to confirm this hypothesis. Or, the experiment failed to confirm this hypothesis (Jones, as cited in Smith, 2009).

Citing from an official APA website, Citethisforme (2017), gave a run-down of APA 6th edition referencing guides as follows:

In-text Citation with APA

The APA style calls for three kinds of information to be included in in-text citations. The author's last name and the work's date of publication must always appear, and these items must match exactly the corresponding entry in the references list. The third kind of information, the page number, appears only in a citation to a direct quotation.

Direct quote from the text:

"The potentially contradictory nature of Moscow's priorities surfaced first in its policies towards East Germany and Yugoslavia," (Crockatt, 1995, p. 1).

Other examples of the APA referencing style from Citethisforme (2017), could be seen in table 13.1 below:

Table 13.1: APA Referencing Styles

Material Type	Reference List/Bibliography
A book in print	Baxter, C. (1997). *Race equality in health care and education.* Philadelphia: Ballière Tindall.
A book chapter, print version	Haybron, D. M. (2008). Philosophy and the science of subjective well-being. In M. Eid & R. J. Larsen (Eds.), *The science of subjective well-being* (pp. 17-43). New York, NY: Guilford Press.
An eBook	Millbower, L. (2003). *Show biz training: Fun and effective business training techniques from the worlds of stage, screen, and song.* Retrieved from http://www.amacombooks.org/
An article in a print journal	Alibali, M. W. (1999). How children change their minds: Strategy change can be gradual or abrupt. *Developmental Psychology, 35,* 127-145.
An article in a journal without DOI	Carter, S., & Dunbar-Odom, D. (2009). The converging literacies center: An integrated model for writing programs. *Kairos: A Journal of Rhetoric, Technology, and Pedagogy, 14*(1), 38-48. Retrieved from http://kairos.technorhetoric.net/
An article in a journal with DOI	Gaudio, J. L., & Snowdon, C. T. (2008). Spatial cues more salient than color cues in cotton-top tamarins (saguinus oedipus) reversal learning. *Journal of Comparative Psychology, 122,* 441-444. doi: 10.1037/0735-7036.122.4.441
Websites - professional or personal sites	*The World Famous Hot Dog Site.* (1999, July 7). Retrieved January 5, 2008, from http://www.xroads.com/~tcs/hotdog/hotdog.html
Websites - online government publications	U.S. Department of Justice. (2006, September 10). Trends in violent victimization by age, 1973-2005. Retrieved from http://www.ojp.usdoj.gov/bjs/glance/vage.htm
Emails (cited in-text only)	According to preservationist J. Mohlhenrich (personal communication, January 5, 2008).
Mailing Lists (listserv)	Stein, C.(2006, January 5). Chessie rescue - Annapolis, MD [Message posted to Chessie-L electronic mailing list]. Retrieved from http://chessie-l-

	owner@lists.best.com
Radio and TV episodes - from library databases	DeFord, F. (Writer). (2007, August 8). Beyond Vick: Animal cruelty for sport [Television series episode]. In NPR (Producer), *Morning Edition.* Retrieved from Academic OneFile database.
Radio and TV episodes - from website	Sepic, M. (Writer). (2008). Federal prosecutors eye MySpace bullying case [Television series episode]. In NPR (Producer), *All Things Considered.* Retrieved from http://www.npr.org/templates/story/
Film Clips from website	Kaufman, J.C. (Producer), Lacy, L. (Director), & Hawkey, P. (Writer). (1979). *Mean Joe Greene* [video file]. Retrieved from http://memory.loc.gov/mbrs/ccmp/meanjoe_01g.ram
Film	Greene, C. (Producer), del Toro, G.(Director). (2015). *Crimson peak* [Motion picture]. United States: Legendary Pictures.
Photograph (from book, magazine or webpage)	Close, C. (2002). *Ronald.* [photograph]. Museum of Modern Art, New York, NY. Retrieved from http://www.moma.org/collection/object.php?object_id=108890
Artwork - from library database	Clark, L. (c.a. 1960's). *Man with Baby.* [photograph]. George Eastman House, Rochester, NY. Retrieved from ARTstor
Artwork - from website	Close, C. (2002). *Ronald.* [photograph]. Museum of Modern Art, New York. Retrieved from http://www.moma.org/collection/browse_results.php?object_id=108890

Exercises

1. Explain what you understand by bibliography, bibliographic citations and referencing.

2. With examples, explain the meaning of DOI (Digital Object Identifier), footnotes, endnotes and bracketed references.

3. List and explain the importance of bibliographic citations and referencing in research or any academic text.

4. Research and give three examples each of the following bibliographic citations and referencing styles:
    i.   The American Psychological Association (APA),
    ii. Harvard Style,
    iii. Oxford Style,
    iv. Modern Language Association (MLA) style,
    v.   Chicago/Turabian style,
    vi. American Medical Association (AMA) style, and
    vii. Chicago citation style.

References

America Psychology Association (2009), DOI and URL Flow Chart. Fhttp://lgimages.s3.amazonaws.com/data/imagemanager/18189/apa_doi_flowchart.jpg

Citethisforme (2017), Ultimate guide to Harvard referencing. http://www.citethisforme.com/harvard-referencing

University of Pittsburgh (2017), Citation Styles: APA, MLA, Chicago, Turabian, IEEE. URL: https://pitt.libguides.com/citationhelp

University of Pittsburgh (2017), Citation Styles: APA, MLA, Chicago, Turabian, IEEE: APA 6th Edition. http://pitt.libguides.com/c.php?g=12108&p=64730

Western Sydney University (2017), American Psychological Association (APA) Referencing Style Guide. Sydney: Western Sydney University Library, p.2-4.

CHAPTER FOURTEEN

TEST MARKETING

14.1 Introduction

This chapter introduces us to test marketing, the uses of test marketing, the place of test marketing and why organizations are interested in test-marketing, including why you as a student should bother yourself about test marketing. This is done through a clear explanation of the meaning of test marketing, the need for test marketing, the advantages and disadvantages of test marketing, tips for operating a successful test marketing, types of test marketing strategies, the problems and pitfalls in test marketing and how to avoid the pitfalls in test marketing.

14.2 What is Test Marketing

Test marketing, in the field of business and marketing, is the use of a geographic region or demographic group to gauge the viability or otherwise of a product or service in that selected market, prior to a full-scale launch in the mass market. In experimental research, test marketing is an exercise conducted in a selected geographic area comprising of target consumers and real-life buying situations, to ascertain the consumers' reaction to a new product, product price, quality, taste, promotion, distribution and many more. It is a tool used by companies to provide insight into the probable market success or failure of a new product or effectiveness of a marketing campaign (Study.com, 2017). Businessjargons (2016), defines test marketing as an experiment conducted before the commercialization (launch) of a new product to find out the facts about the product such as: Is the product the right one? Is the product reasonably priced? Etc. On the basis of such findings, the firm may either accept or drop the product idea.

It is also a tool used by the commercial organizations to check the viability of their new product(s) or a marketing campaign before it is being launched in the market on a large scale. It is generally carried out to ascertain the probable market success concerning new product's performance, its level of acceptance and the suitability of each of the marketing-mix elements. In the non-commercial marketing fields, especially in social marketing campaigns, test marketing is used to determine the level of target publics' perceptions and acceptability of a new policy, programme, project, idea, etc. So, not only commercial organizations engage in test-marketing, a government can use it to gauge the public acceptability of a new policy, programme or project. The United Nations or any of its agencies can use it to test peoples' feelings about a new programme. The World Bank can use it to test the acceptability or viability of a new farming incentive to farmers in a geographic region.

14.3 The Need for Test Marketing

The need for test marketing accrues from the fact that it is not right to make marketing decisions based on mere instincts, feelings, hunches or guesswork. It is not also good to make marketing decisions based on what worked in the past. We are in a dynamic world, and people and things are changing fast, especially in the contemporary technological age. Customers' variables are changing quickly, competitors are constantly evolving their strategies while new competitors are emerging every day. In fact, the whole marketing demographic, sociographic, economic, political, international and ecosystem dynamics are changing by the day. Hence, the need for test marketing to still stay afloat and competitively viable.

Keep on test marketing, and don't assume that just because you tested it last year and it worked, it will continue to work well this year or next year. Even when you think you have found the right combinations, still keep testing. Although it may not be evident at the moment, every crucial aspect of your marketing plan is changing slowly. Your customers are changing; your staff is evolving, and your competition is adjusting. The things that worked quite well 6–12 months ago may be losing their effectiveness. Don't assume you have it all figured out, test (CBSnews, 2007; Gorchels, 2005, Harvard Business Revie, 1975).

14.4 Advantages of Test Marketing

Test Marketing has numerous benefits or importance, which include the following:

- Risk Minimization: It reduces the risk of a full-scale launch since significant costs will be saved in a test marketing if the product fails, unlike if it were in a mass-marketing campaign.

- It offers companies the leeway to test the marketing-mix elements before a full product launch.
- It can be used by an organization to test multiple marketing scenarios and select the most promising for expansion (Entrepreneur, 2017).
- It is one of the ways to determine the revenue potentials of a new or improved product before its full launch.
- It is a way of involving customers in a new product's development process, which could make them feel more regarded and develop attachment and brand loyalty to the product and by extension to your organization, later.
- Information gathered during test-marketing helps an organization in modifying and developing the right product(s) for consumers.
- Test marketing arms an organization with knowledge of consumers' attributes for informed marketing decision-making.
- Test marketing helps organizations to ensure that their product(s), services and marketing strategies are sound.
- Test marketing helps organizations to ascertain the effectiveness of their promotional strategies, marketing strategies, distribution channels and other issues. They can use their test marketing results to identify weak points in those areas and refine them.

14.5 Disadvantages of Test Marketing

In spite of the numerous advantages of test-marketing, there are still some disadvantages which include the following:

Some people or organizations nurse the fears that their competitors might be learning about the product(s) they are test-marketing, and come up with a counter-product before the full launch. But, we wish to state, categorically, that the benefits from a successful test-marketing out-weighs this factor.

There is the notion that test markets do not usually serve a true representative of the full mass market. Hence, the results could lead to inappropriate generalization and decisions.

Test marketing, sometimes, leads to delays in full product launch to the mass markets, consequently, bring about a loss of revenue opportunities in the mass markets.

Test marketing is sometimes costly and time-consuming to administer.

14.6 Tips for Operating a Successful Test Marketing

+Our 10-points steps for operating a successful test-marketing exercise are as follows:

Produce a reliable new product or modify or improve an existing one.

Decide on the type of test-marketing style to adopt and the time-frame.

Set out your test-marketing goals, objectives, and targets, which will serve as a benchmark for evaluation at the end of the exercise.

Design the test marketing plan to be used.

Select an area in line with your organizational goals, objectives, and targets.

Ensure that the selected test market area, is indeed representative of the full market, in demographic, sociographic, economic, political, ecological and other characteristics.

Accommodate a variety of advertising media that reflects what you plan to use nationally in the press, radio, television, and online.

Train your sales force and acquaint your channel distribution members on your plan. Try to carry them along.

Implement your test-marketing project in line with the set time-frame.

Conduct evaluative research to determine the extent you attained your set test-marketing goals and objectives, the areas you got it right, the areas you got it wrong, and how to do it better the next time.

14.7 Types of Test Marketing

There are several forms of test marketing styles to be adopted by organizations. They are as follows:

14.7.1 Using a Small Group of Customers Who Provide Direct Product Feedback

Some organizations may prefer to use a small group of customers to test-market a product, service, programme or project. This is called beta testing, which helps the organization in gathering valuable feedback, for future decision-making. The small group of customers which may include select final consumers, retailers, wholesalers, and distributors, test the product or service and provide feedback the organization will analyze and refine/fine tune their product or the marketing-mix strategies before the full product launch. Small and medium-scale enterprises may adopt this type of test-marketing plan.

14.7.2 Conducting A Regional Product Launch

For more prominent organizations with the necessary financial muscles, Conducting A Regional Product Launch could suffice. This is most likely to capture a representative sample characteristic of variables in the national or mass market, rather than the small group option. However, for multinational organizations with global marketing reach, it is advisable for them to conduct this regional product launch in select nations, that could harbor the characteristics of their global market.

14.7.3 Online Test Marketing

According to the Harvard Business Review (1975), testing products on the Internet offers the advantage of speed and allows you to evaluate a broader geographic region with minimal expense. Other benefits include:

You can carry out your test anywhere throughout the world.

You can test a full product range without physical limits.

You can easily customize displays, pricing, and products for different customer groups.

You can obtain a high volume of information in a short period.

14.7.4 Using A Targeted Direct Marketing Program

Some organizations prefer to use direct marketing in their test-marketing programmes to divulge only minimal information to their competitors. Through this test-marketing option, the competitors will be less able to measure your organization's market size and scope. However, this style may be limited in scope. Meanwhile …says that one of its advantages is that it is easy to evaluate the effectiveness of a direct marketing campaign. The most effective will be the one that has the highest response levels.

14.8 How to Avoid/Overcome the Problems and Pitfalls of Test Marketing

Various measures that could be adopted to checkmate the pitfalls accruable from test-marketing include the following:

Be mindful of the significant investment your organization is spending in the exercise, and bring it all amount of seriousness and carefulness into it.

Be sure you use the result of your test-marketing to make refinements to your product, services, marketing strategy or marketing-mix elements.

Choose a test area that serves a truly representative sample of the mass market or total market in your full product launch.

Be sure to make effective and optimal use of the media to disseminate information about your product or service to the target consumers and channel members.

Never neglect to evaluate your test-marketing programme, to track factors critical to the success or failure of the exercise.

Exercises

1. Define test marketing? What is the implications to businesses and marketing.
2. Carefully illustrate how test-marketing can be employed by government and non-governmental organizations.
3. Outline and explain the merits and demerits of test marketing to an organization of your choice.
4. List and explain the basic steps for operating a successful test-marketing exercise.
5. Outline and explain at least four types of test marketing styles that can be employed by an organization.
6. List and explain various measures that could be adopted to checkmate the pitfalls in test-marketing.

References

Businessdictionary (2017), What is test marketing? Definition and meaning. http://www.businessdictionary.com/definition/test-marketing.html

Businessjargons (2016), What is Market Test? Definition and meaning. https://businessjargons.com/market-test.html

CBSnews (2007), Conducting effective test markets. https://www.cbsnews.com/news/conducting-effective-test-marketing/

Entrepreneur (2017), Market Testing. https://www.entrepreneur.com/encyclopedia/market-testing

Gorchels, Linda (2005), The Product Manager's Handbook. 3rd ed. Chicago: McGraw Hill.

Harvard Business Review (1975), When, Where, and How to Test Market. https://hbr.org/1975/05/when-where-and-how-to-test-market

Study.com (2017), What Is Test Marketing? - Definition, Types & Examples. https://study.com/academy/lesson/what-is-test-marketing-definition-types-examples.ht

CHAPTER FIFTEEN

RESEARCH: DEVELOPING COUNTRIES' PROBLEMS AND CHALLENGES

15.1 Introduction

Research in developing countries is fraught with many problems, challenges and in some cases dangers. This chapter tries to highlight some of those problems, so that students or organizations wishing to go into research in Africa, Asia, Latin America or middle East will be abreast of such environmental pitfalls and arm themselves adequately towards mitigating them. We will also give you tips for successfully avoiding or handling the problems, where necessary.

15.2 Highlight of Some of the Developing Countries' Research Problems

Even though the problems differ from one country to another or from one continent to another, in general terms, the developing countries' research problems and challenges include the following:

- Local populace research phobia and suspicions.
- Lack of cooperation from government officials.
- Dearth of data.
- Unreliability of data from government agencies.
- Traditional taboos.
- Religious taboos.
- Gender discrimination.
- Difficulty in securing official approvals.
- Students' research phobia.
- Lack of funds.
- Lack of interest in research by policymakers.
- Poor research culture.
- Poor research writing skills.
- Lack of motivation by peers, and,
- Heavy workload.
- Poor facilities.
- Epileptic power supplies.
- Poor data analysis knowledge and skills.

Some brief explanations of the points above can be given as follows:

15.2.1 Local Populace Research Phobia and Suspicions

In some African and other developing countries, the local natives view researchers with great suspicion, as people who have come to spy on them or sap from them information for government that would be used to impose taxes on the people. In other cases, they see researchers as strangers who have come to desecrate their environment and expose them to ominous dangers. Reports have been heard of researchers who were either lynched or driven away by such local natives as could be seen in figure 15.1.

Fig. 15.1: Example of local populace research phobia and suspicions: A male and female researcher suspected to be spies, tied to a tree, and local natives carrying stones and clubs to deal with them. Both of you should confess your real mission to this community.

Tips for Successfully Avoiding or Handling this Problem

The researcher(s) should seek out and reach out to enlightened opinion leaders from the area, and brief them on their mission, the purpose and benefits of the research to the people and society. This may include the traditional rulers, the religious leaders, the teachers, government representatives, university students, town union leaders and other reliable prominent men and women from the area. Try to convince them and solicit their cooperation and support, so that they will assist you in convincing the less enlightened local natives. Once this is achieved, you will enjoy the love, cooperation and traditional hospitality of the natives.

15.2.2 Lack of Cooperation from Government Officials

Often times, due to high rate of corruption in official quarters in developing countries, government workers especially the top managers view researchers as people who have come to expose them. Hence, they do everything within their powers to frustrate innocent researchers who are on genuine missions. They also punish severely any of their subordinates who vouch such information to a researcher without authorization, which rarely comes. This author had such an ugly experience when I was doing my doctoral studies and the topic was on social marketing and public relations for enhanced immunization campaigns in Nigeria. Notwithstanding the fact that the study was being conducted at a time when the country was experiencing a globally recognized challenges in its immunization records, I went to a popular health center and administered questionnaire to twelve nurses, who gladly collected the copies from me and promised to fill same.

However, before I could reach the gate of the compound I heard the footsteps of someone hotly pursuing me from the back. "Sir, they said you should come back," he gasped. I followed him humbly and when I got back to the office, the twelve nurses handed back the questionnaire copies to me. "Our Matron said if you want us to fill the questionnaire, you should go and get a written permission from the Commissioner for Health," they told me. Well, I knew that was a mission impossible. So, I devised a strategy and served my 520 questionnaire copies on public health personnel through the assistant of a friendly nurse, who told them it was her own.

Tips for Successfully Avoiding or Handling this Problem

Write to the government officials in charge, explaining the reasons for the study and assuring them the study is not meant for any untoward motive, and will not in no way harm their interest. This may also involve some leg walks for a face-to-face meeting and convincing of the official(s). It is not really an easy task, but you will win if you persevere.

15.2.3 Dearth of Data

While data can be easily sourced and procured on any subject matter in developed countries (see figures 15.2a – 15.2e), in the developing countries, it is usually an uphill task for researchers sourcing reliable secondary data for their studies. In Africa and other developing countries, the culture of acquiring and banking data is still a far cry from governments and governmental agencies. This paucity of data is a major challenge to researchers in those countries. Where such data exist at all, getting them is a story for another day.

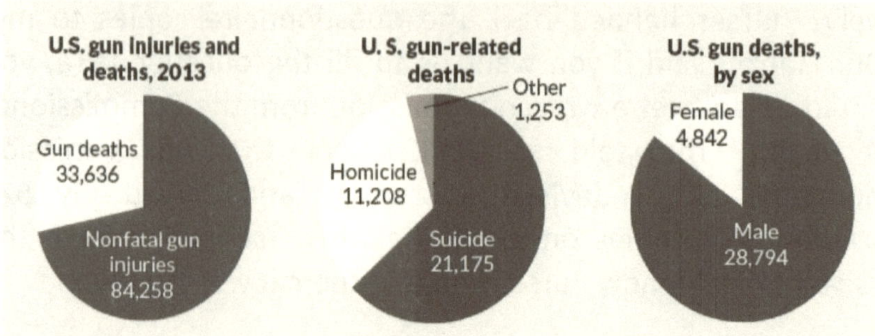

Fig. 15.2a: Gun-related injuries and deaths in US, 2013. Example of data can be easily sourced and procured on any subject matter in developed countries. Source: CDC (USA).

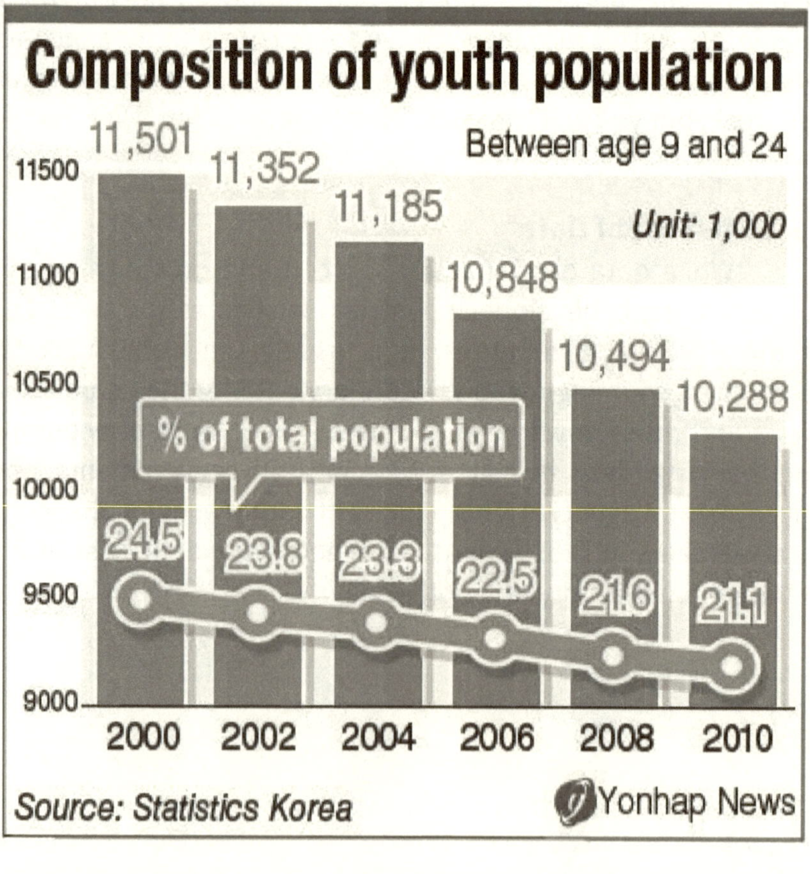

Fig. 15.2b: Youth population data in Korea. Example of data can be easily sourced and procured on any subject matter in developed countries.

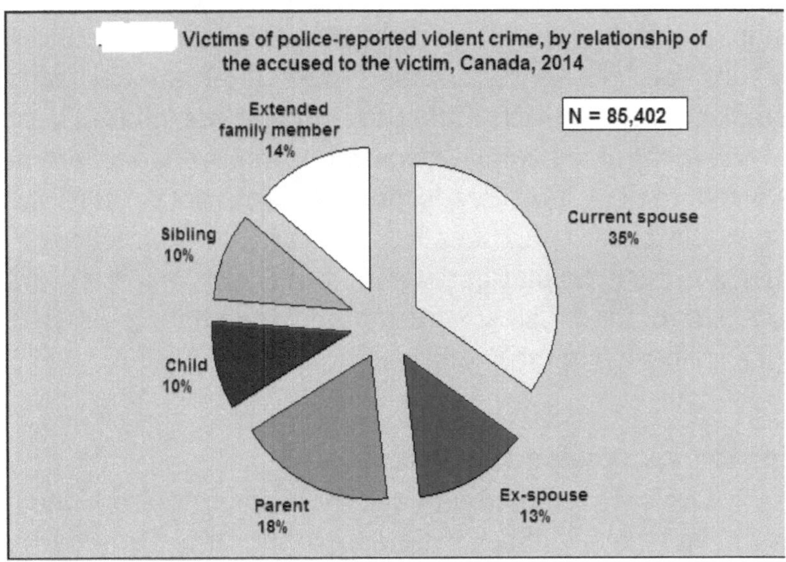

Fig. 15.2c: Rent statistics in Scotland. Data can be easily sourced and procured on any subject matter in developed countries.

Fig. 15.2d: Crime-related statistics in Canada. Example of data can be easily sourced and procured on any subject matter in developed countries.

Tips for Addressing this Problem

You may have to rely more on primary data generated by yourself or under your control. However, if the study is such that secondary data is quite inevitable, then work hard at getting the ones available, through the assistance of some top government officials or civil servants. Giving a few monetary inducements in some poor developing countries could also open the shut doors for you.

15.2.4 Unreliability of Data from Government Agencies

In Africa and other developing countries, official data are often doctored for political, economic or social gains. For instance, politicians inflate census figures in their areas in order to gain more political positions and economic shares. That is why most census figures are often a subject for disputes and controversies in many developing countries. Health statistics are manipulated by government agencies in order to increase amount of grants receivable from international funding organizations. Contracts and budget figures are inflated in order to receive far above actual costs, while import figures are over-invoiced to line individual's pockets. The police will always underestimate the number of casualties in social violence or any crisis; and even the number of people in detention. This problem plays out in almost all spheres of life where data is needed for research in developing countries.

Tips for Addressing this Problem

Don't rely on the secondary data given to you alone; you may have to really check it up and confirm the authenticity or reliability before using it. You could also do a confirmatory adhoc primary study to confirm the secondary data. However, you may also have to look towards international organizations with reliable and up to date data like The United Nation's Agencies, the World Bank, the United States' of America agencies like the Centre for Disease Control (CDC), and other developed countries where research data are hold sacrosanct. Some of them also commission and bank data in vital areas of the developing countries' affairs, as shown in figure 15.5.

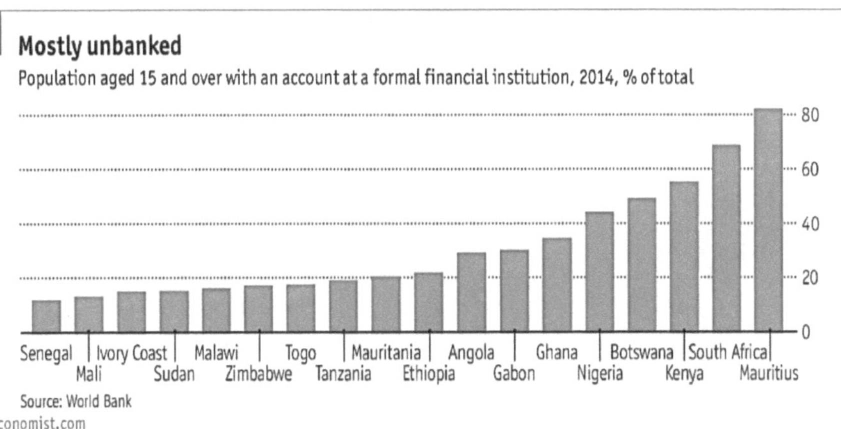

Fig. 15.5: You may rely more on data from credible international organizations like the World Bank.

15.2.5 Traditional Taboos

In some African and Asian communities, you have sacred places and sacred days. The people will not take it kindly with a researcher that desecrates their sacred places or sacred days. It may also be viewed a serious taboo to trespass some places of worship by orthodox or traditional religionists. For the traditional religionists, it may need the intervention of their gods or goddesses through the chief priest to pronounce the judgement on the erring researcher, with the consequent penalties, as depicted in figure 15.6.

Fig. 15.6: Example of traditional taboos: A white lady with hands tied. 'You walked through our sacred grove on a forbidden day, and thus desecrated the land. You will bring two white cocks, two pigeons and two turtles to appease the gods.'

Tips for Avoiding or Handling this Problem

Ask before you enter any community. Get as much information as possible about the people, their culture, traditions and norms. Find out if there are no-go-areas in the community, and if possible, look for tour guides or research assistants from amongst the people. It may also be advisable to pay a courtesy visit to one or two village-heads, traditional rulers, religious leader or opinion leader in the community and intimate him/her about your mission, then, listen for advice and their blessings.

15.2.6 Religious Taboos

Religious beliefs, dogmas and practices are some of the problems and challenges of conducting research in Africa and other developing countries. For instance, in countries where Hinduism hold sway, the use of cow as experimental animal is prohibited, while in some other climes the use of other animals like royal python, green snake, pig, rabbit, guinea fowl and many more may be forbidden on religious or traditional grounds. Female researchers are also advised not to wear revealing clothes, shorts or trousers going about the Streets during a survey in Muslim-dominated societies.

Fig. 15.7: Example of religious taboos: In some parts of India and few other countries, cows are religiously sacred and the use of a cow as experimental specimen is highly prohibited.

Tips for Avoiding or Handling this Problem

Every researcher going into a foreign land or a new environment must first of all study the religious sensibilities of the people and try to accommodate such in your research planning, decisions and actions. Respect the peoples' holy days and holy places. Don't wear dresses that may be considered religiously offensive by the people. Make sure that your questionnaire does not contain words that offend their religious inclinations. Finally, don't make comments or exhibit manners that may be religiously frowned at by the people.

15.2.7   Gender Discrimination
Culturally, in some developing countries women are to be seen and not heard, their place belongs to the kitchen. In some other places women may be secluded in sacred confines like the purdah or fattening rooms, on religious or traditional grounds. A researcher entering such confined places to interview or administer questionnaire on the inmates, without express permission from the right authorities, may be asking for real trouble.

Fig. 15.8: Example of gender discrimination: Lady, don't be sad, women are forbidden to trespass this environment, be it for interview, questionnaire administration or whatever.

Tips for Avoiding or Handling this Problem
Make sure that permissions are duly secured from the right quarters before entering such places. Male researchers are advised to avoid such places to save their heads. The use of female researchers in such places will be more advisable. Make

yourself conversant with the religious cum cultural gender-based beliefs and practices of the people and try to respect them. You can use credible female research assistants from the area or go with one if you must be there.

15.2.8 Difficulty in Securing Official Approvals

Certain research requires official approvals before a researcher could enter an office or an environment to interview workers or administer questionnaire on them. Other studies might call for approvals to use some official facilities like corporate libraries, organizational data banks, organizational records like sales statistics, staff records and many more. In some developing countries, it is easier for the camel to pass through the needle's eye than for researchers to get such approvals.

Tips for Avoiding or Handling this Problem

Persistency and perseverance is the key to success here. Keep knocking and knocking until the door of approval opens to you. Convince the top officials that the study will in no way hurt their corporate interest. Try to seek out someone that could help you talk to the relevant managers and secure the authorization. Do not breach their corporate rules and security. It is painful to a researcher to hear afterwards that a worker is sacked, queried or suspended because of attending to him/her. So, save yourself from such burden of conscience by doing the right thing at the right time.

15.2.9 Research Phobia and Lack of Interest in Research by Policymakers

In some developing countries, the fear of research by public officers is the rule rather than the exception. In countries where this plays out, government officials see research as a sheer waste of resources, hence, corporate planning, decisions and action are not based on research. Students from such countries also dread research as a difficult and abstract task. Hence, securing the peoples' cooperation as research assistants may be an uphill task, except when you're ready to part with some money.

Tips for Avoiding or Handling this Problem

Try to harp on the benefits of the research to the people. Show them the results of research-based decisions and actions from the developed countries of the world. However, in doing so, avoid unnecessary arguments and conflict of interests. Be patient with them, it is a developmental problem.

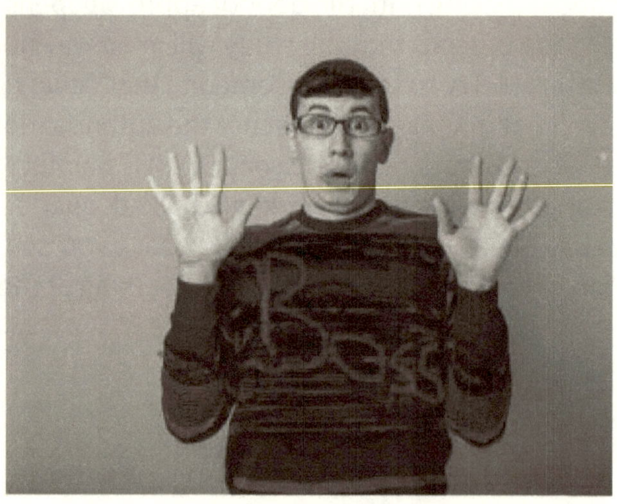

Fig. 15.10: Research phobia and lack of interest in research by policymakers: Aaarh, research? Count me out!

15.2.10 Lack of Funds

The paucity of funds is a major problem confronting genuine researchers in developing countries of the world. Either due to poverty or lack of interest in research, most developing countries do not give grants to students be it undergraduate or graduate. Such grants only come from the developed countries, international organizations and foundations. However, majority of the researchers in developing countries are not aware of the grant sources and when they do, lack the proposal-writing skills.

Tips for Addressing this Problem

The United Nations should make an Act mandating all member nations to devote a certain percentage of their annual budgets to research. Research grants should also be given to postgraduate students, especially those pursuing their doctoral studies. Research proposal writing skills should also be organized periodically for researchers and students in developing countries.

15.2.11 Poor Research Culture and Lack of Motivation

The research culture is yet to catch up in many developing countries. This very problem affects all spheres of life of the people: government, commerce, education, health, economy and many more. It is a problem that brings with it lack of motivation and encouragement to foreign researchers coming from other backgrounds, as it inhibits the chances of securing the peoples' goodwill, cooperation, research assistants and receiving any kind of motivation from them.

Tips for Addressing this Problem

Engage university students from the area or community as your research assistants. Ask them to go in advance, inform and sensitize their people about your coming. You can also use them as your research tour guides, so that they will show you forbidden places and places to trespass. You can also ask them to teach you a few of their native greetings. African natives are very happy and highly amused when you greet them in their local languages, no matter how poorly delivered. Another way to blow their minds is for a foreigner to dress in the local native's traditional costumes. These ways, you open the doors to their hearts and earn their maximum cooperation.

African natives clapping for two foreign researchers dressed in Africa traditional wears. A sure way to win their cooperation and support

Fig. 15.11: How to win their cooperation: A white lady and white man researchers dressed in African costume, and the natives cheering them up.

15.2.12   Poor Research Writing Skills

Notwithstanding the fact that research is a basic requirement for obtaining any higher academic qualification, majority of students in developing countries fear it and display poor research-writing skills. Hence, supervising research work in many developing countries could, sometimes, translate to an inevitable nightmare.

Tips for Addressing this Problem

Continued training and re-training of students in research skills is the answer. Try to allay their fears that research is not as difficult as some believe, but just like any other course of study. Also, let them know that it is a matter of practice-makes-perfect, just like any other endeavor in life.

15.2.13   Poor Facilities

The poor facility problem is another big headache for researchers in developing countries. For instance, if you must reach the rural dwellers where over 70 percent of the populace reside, you will be confronted with the problem of bad roads, lack of power supply, lack of hotels or poor hotel accommodations, poor transportation facilities and many more. Library resources may also be hard to come by, where they exist, many are poorly equipped while others are furnished with obsolete books. Again, Internet services are often either poor, very slow or unreliable in many developing countries.

Tips for Addressing this Problem

If it is possible and convenient for you, provide yourself with the facilities you need, like computers, laptops, internet-connection items, and others. If your study is in the rural areas, locate a city nearby and book for a good hotel there. Power supply and transportation may also be better in the cities, and so do Internet facilities. However, if the city is very far away or it's inevitable that you must stay and interact with the natives to conduct your study effectively, then make use of what you see and try to make yourself as comfortable as possible by mingling with the natives, eating their food and sharing with them.

15.2.14   Epileptic Power Supplies

Electricity power supply is very erratic and quite unreliable in many developing countries. Hence, many resort to their personal alternative power supplies like the use of standby generating-sets, with its attendant air and noise pollution. This problem often hampers researchers' work in the field and also during data analysis.

Tips for Addressing this Problem

If it is possible and convenient for you, provide yourself with a standby generating-set. You can also search for and book into a hotel that guarantees steady power supply.

15.2.15   Poor Data Analysis Facilities

Data analysis resources and facilities, especially computer-aided data analysis tools, may also be hard to come by in some developing countries. This problem, however, differs from one country to another.

Tips for Addressing this Problem

Be mindful of this problem and arm yourself with the requisite data analysis materials, facilities and computer-aided data analysis tools you may use in your research.

Other authors like Ajinomoh (2017), outlines some problems and challenges confronting researchers in   Africa some of which buttressed the points we aforementioned in this text here to include:

i. Laziness on the part of the researchers.
Scarcity of research facilities.
Illiteracy.
Security.
Inadequate statistics.
Political instability.
Inadequate research funds.
Scanty information base.
Secrecy.
Dominance of small scale organizations.
Lack of Coordination.

i. **Laziness on the Part of Researchers:** Most of the researchers in Africa and some other developing countries are very lazy. They often refuse to go through the rigor of a research process, rather, they go out looking for 'cheap' ways of solving their research problems or questions. The consequences of this is that whatever conclusion drawn by such dubious research cannot be reliable or valid.

ii. Scarcity of Research Facilities: A researcher must have access to research facilities such as research centers, laboratories, and libraries for his research to be meaningful. Dearth of research centers and laboratories in Africa and other developing countries make the work of researchers difficult and, on many occasions, inconclusive. Again, most of the libraries in these countries are poorly equipped because of lack of funds.

iii. Illiteracy: Due to the high illiteracy rates in Africa and other developing countries, many cannot appreciate the value of research undertakings. Hence, the lethargy to cooperate with researchers by supplying relevant information to them, and the inability to complete research questionnaires or grant interviews.

iv. Security: The problem of insecurity arising from conflicts in many parts of Africa and other developing countries frustrates the researcher in his effort to generate meaningful data.

v. Inadequate Statistics: The problem of shortage or lack of relevant secondary data limits the degree of some researchers' effectiveness and by extension their research findings in Africa and other developing countries.

vi. Political Instability: Many developing countries are saddled with a near-perennial problem of political instability, which sometimes inhibits research in those countries. This is because research takes time and can only be done in a safe and conducive environment.

vii. Inadequate Research Funds: Conducting a purposeful research requires a good chunk of money for many things including: printing and distributing of questionnaire, obtaining all necessary equipment, travelling here and there, and many more. When the needed fund is not available, it discourages research of all forms.

viii. **Scanty Information Base**: The scanty research information data base in many developing countries narrows down the quantity and quality of literature available to a researcher. That is to say, not as much research findings have been accumulated in many developing countries from where a researcher can draw from.

ix. **Secrecy**: The task of data collection is not always easy in many developing countries. For example, even in government ministries, information that otherwise would be for public consumption is considered 'secret'. The officials are often reluctant to cooperate in rendering some vital information to researchers. Sometimes, they are biased with sentiments or ego, feeling it will promote the status of their offices, organizations and/or themselves.

x. Dominance of Small Scale Organizations

Directors and managers of many private sector organizations in developing countries do not sufficiently understand nor appreciate the values of research in industries and business, so, cannot budget for, nor fund research studies.

xi. Lack of Coordination: In many developing countries, there is usually no clear coordinating body for research, hence, the dissemination and utilization of research results is poor. In practice, many of the research reports remain on the shelves unused and only gather dust. Research in these countries is neither used for the setting of national priorities, national planning, plan implementations, monitoring or evaluation (Ajinomoh, 2017).

Meanwhile, Chukwu, Ebue, Obikeguna, Arionu, Agbawodikeizu & Agwu (2016), add that cultural and ethical issues affect the conduct of research in many developing countries negatively. With regards to ethics, the absence of a veritable yardstick in curbing and penalizing plagiarism issues in some developing countries impedes on the performance of social researchers. More so, the traditional culture in some developing countries like ethnic biases, religious biases and political prejudices result in conflict of values that influence the perceptions and apathy to research and researchers, especially from other ethnic or religious backgrounds. Again, the problem of superstitious belief makes it difficult for the people to imbibe the scientific concept of causality which teaches that effects could be traced to certain causes that must be scientifically investigated for truth to be discovered, and which predicates problem solving and development on the continuum. This impedes on the efficacy of the scientific community in the social sciences in the developing countries.

For this reason, most nations in Africa fall short of comprehensiveness and thus usually have issues with accuracy of data, which in turn tell negatively on the research and consequently, interventions. More so, the kind of politics practiced in most African nations abhor truth telling and to such end, also affect the quality of social research, especially when information is sought after from politicians or civil servants (Chukwu, Ebue, Obikeguna, Arionu, Agbawodikeizu & Agwu, 2016).

Mutula (2009), also adds that there are several challenges

facing researchers in a digital environment, especially within the context of the developing world (in this instance, in Africa). Mutula et al. (2006), in an empirical study of e-learning at the University of Botswana, identified the following problems:

Shortage of computers.

Lack of clarity of online content.

Poor Internet connectivity.

Difficulty in finding information on the Internet.

Students' inability to cope with research workload.

Poor formats of presenting online contents.

The lack of appeal of online contents.

Exercises

1. Outline and explain at least ten problems or challenges of conducting research in developing countries.
2. List and explain ten antidotes to the research problems or challenges mentioned in question one above.
3. If you're conducting research in Africa, explain how you would effectively handle local populace research phobia and traditional taboos.
4. Mention some of the research-based religious taboos in India and how to contain them wisely.
5. It is reported that secrecy and lack of cooperation is the norm amongst government officials in developing countries. Explain how to address this problem and secure the needed data or information from them.
6. If you're a female going for research in Africa or other developing countries, explain some of the hazards and how you would avoid them.

References

Ajinomoh, Merciful (2017), Problems facing research in Nigeria. http://infotechcommunication.blogspot.com/2015/11/problems-facing-research-in-nigeria_21.html

Chukwu, Ngozi; Ebue Malachy; Obikeguna Christy; Arionu Ngozi; Agbawodikeizu Patricia;
Agwu Prince (2016), *Problems of Social Research in Nigeria.* Research on Humanities and Social Sciences Vol.6, No.12, 2016, p58-65. Available from: https://www.researchgate.net/publication/305683573_Problems_of_Social_Research_in_Nigeria.

Mutula, Stephen (2009), Challenges of doing research in sub-Saharan African universities: digital scholarship opportunities. Journal of Humanities and Social Sciences, Vol 1 No 1, p1-7.

CHAPTER SIXTEEN

ACHIEVING A GOOD OPENER

16.1 Introduction

Many students score low grades in their articles, seminar papers, projects, thesis or dissertations due to poor kick-off of the reports. This is because the opener, starting-point or kick-off of the work tells a lot about you and the work. It gives the reader the over-all first impression of the entire work. The first kick-off is your background of the study and the Abstract. Hence, this chapter is devoted to our understanding and mastery of how to write successful background of the study and Abstract.

What Is A Background of the Study?

A background of the study for a thesis or article is a brief overview, mirror or picture of the issues, challenges or problems (in applied research) that occasioned a study. It should be supported with verifiable data or reports from relevant authorities or experts in the very subject matter. It must paint a convincing picture or rendition of how the claimed issue or problem has been playing out in history or perspectives.

16.2 Why Study Background of the Study

➤ It is the first door-opener in your research.

➢ It gives the first impression about you and your work.
➢ First impression matters most (First cut is the deepest-effect).
➢ It makes the reader either favourably or negatively disposed to the entire work.
➢ It sets the mood for the grade to be awarded the work.

What A Background of the Study Is Not
➢ Definition of key terms in the topic.
➢ A Generalist Highlight of the importance or benefits.
➢ Another Literature Review.
➢ Essay-like or newspaper report format.

What A True Background of the Study Must Be and Observe:
✓ Topical, interesting, captivating, striking and be able to hold the reader spell-bound.
✓ Give proof of any claim.
✓ Citations must meet three standards (Authority-based, Source Credibility, Believability).
✓ A compelling justification for the study.
✓ Convince the reader on why resources (time, money, human efforts, etc) should be invested in a study.
✓ Must be free from channel noise:
  - wrong ideas,
  - wrong definitions,
  - grammatical errors,
  - punctuation errors,
  - editing errors,
  - proof-reading errors and many more. Be conscious and mindful of your audience (academia).

- ✓ Must be able to educate the reader, including the supervisor on the issue concerned.
- ✓ All citations must be fully referenced afterwards.
- ✓ Finally, it should end with a thesis statement that summarizes the key point, claim or basis of the study.

Types of Background of Study

There are four major types of background of study – historical, analytical, perspectival, and expository.

i.   Historical Background of the Study

The historical background of the study tries to give a historical account or rendition of the issues that prompted a study, in order to convince the audience that the research is really worth it. For instance, a doctoral seminar paper by Basil (2017), which followed the historical approach went as follows:

ii.   Analytical Background of the Study

An analytical background of the study tries to break down the issue or motivating problem for the study into its component parts, evaluates the issue or idea, and presents this breakdown and evaluation to the audience. It follows the approach of a critical analysis, because in it, a researcher critiques what other researchers or reports hold or say on an issue, and tries to locate a gap or missing element, which his/her own study is trying to fill.

iii.   Perspectival Background of the Study

This entails the presentation of your background of the study, not really in a historical fashion, but perspective by perspective. It paints a picture to the reader(s) of different perspectives of how the issue or problem that motivated the study has been playing out, and its negative effects, hence, the justification for the study.

iv. An Expository Background of the Study

In this type of background of the study, the author tries to marshal many points and defend them intelligently as the justification for the study. He/she lays emphasis in the explanation of the issues or motivating problems pointed out, for the audience to see and convinced that the study is worth the time, effort and resources to be invested in it.

Practical Examples of the Four Types of Background of Study

i. **Historical Background:** A good example here is a Ph.D seminar paper presented at the Department of Marketing, University of Calabar on the topic: "Effect of unethical marketing practices by independent petroleum marketers and kerosene explosions in Nigeria" by Dr Basil, Glory:

> "Over the years, there have been perennial incidence of kerosene explosions with fingers pointing at unethical marketing practices of independent marketers as the root cause. Records show that the first major kerosene explosion in Nigeria occurred in March 1984 in Lagos. There have been several other kerosene explosions in Nigeria since then particularly in the oil petroleum producing areas of the South-South zone of Nigeria. For instance, a major kerosene explosion disaster occurred in oil-producing area of Ondo State, Nigeria in

October 2001. One hundred and twenty-five burn patients were treated at the Lagos State University Teaching Hospital from that incidence, as reported by the News Agency of Nigeria (NAN, 2012).

In 2003, another fuel explosion occurred in Delta State, Nigeria, where 10 persons died and 30 others were seriously injured. The explosions occurred in their homes from adulterated kerosene, the local press reported. Several homes in Warri and Effurun in the oil-producing state were affected by the explosions, which occurred as the victims tried to light their cooking stoves or lanterns, which had been filled with the adulterated kerosene. Among the victims were a nursing mother and her eight-week-old baby, both of whom were badly burnt after the family's cooking stove exploded, notes the Department of Petroleum Resources (DPR, 2015).

In 2007, following the reduction of the pump price of petrol to N65, while the street price of kerosene dangled between N140 to N150, many unscrupulous marketers started mixing kerosene with petrol, leading to kerosene explosion in many parts of the country, as witnessed in PortHarcourt, Potiskum, Lagos, Lokoja, Delta, Kano, Abuja and Abia State respectively. In the process many Nigerians met their untimely deaths, while hundreds sustained indelible injuries, reports the Petroleum Products Pricing Regulatory Agency (PPPRA, 2007).

In 2009, six members of a family in Kano State were hospitalized at the Murtala Mohammed Specialist Hospital over explosion from adulterated kerosene. One of them died immediately after admission (Ogun, 2010). Then, in 2011 kerosene explosions occurred almost at the same time in Rivers and Edo states of the South-South zone of Nigeria. The explosions killed many and either incapacitated or disfigured other permanently (NAN, 2011).

Again in 2012, Badejo (2012), reports that kerosene explosions occurred in both Delta and Edo States between February 1 and March 14, which claimed the lives of eleven persons, while several people were hospitalised for serious degrees of burns. Nine of the victims later died at the University of Benin Teaching Hospital (UBTH). Two others died in other hospitals. The explosions were said to have occurred in boundary villages between Edo and Delta while others happened in Warri and Irrua. Some of the victims said the explosion occurred when they attempted to pour kerosene into their lanterns (Badejo, 2012).

Recently, in August 2015, nine children were rushed to Warri Central Hospital following severe burns they got in the explosions caused by suspected adulterated kerosene in Warri South and Udu local government areas of Delta State. The victims were said to have suffered between 50 to 90 degrees of burns. The incidents occurred on August 15 and 16 when the children attempted to fuel lit lanterns, while others said the explosions occurred while they were pouring kerosene into a lantern (NAN, 2011).

There have been controversies over the sources of the adulterations. Blames were traded between the Nigerian National Petroleum Corporation, NNPC, Petroleum Products Marketing Company (PPMC) and the independent marketers with each body passing the bulk. Recently, the President of the National Union of Petroleum and Gas Workers (NUPENG) confirmed that some major dealers mix kerosene with other products in various proportions to obtain higher monetary value and to make abnormal profits (Udeme, 2011). In their own investigations, the Petroleum and Natural Gas Senior Staff Association of Nigeria (PENGASSAN) reported that, some marketers adulterated products in their tank farms (Ogun, 2010). Kerosene was also adulterated through deliberate addition of water to increase its volume (NAN, 2011).

All these motivated this study for a critical appraisal of the correlation between unethical marketing practices by independent petroleum marketers in Nigeria, and the rates of kerosene explosions in the country (Basil, 2017).

i.   **An Example of Expository Background:** This type of research report lays emphasis in the explanation of the issue or motivating problem for the study to the audience. See an example below from a Ph.D seminar paper presented at the Department of Marketing, University of Calabar on the topic: "A critical analysis of corporate social responsibility (CSR) tax practices of tourism organizations towards the development of Cross River State, Nigeria" (Ekom, 2017):

The tax payment corporate citizenship CSR practices of tourism/hospitality organisations in Cross River State do not contribute significantly to the economic development of the State and its people. This is quite disheartening, considering the fact that tourism/hospitality is a leading business sector in the State. This fact is attested to an economic and financial expert from the State, Mr. Fidelis Ugbo, immediate past Secretary to the Cross-River State Government (SSG) and retired Director of the Central Bank of Nigeria, who is now the Secretary of the National Planning Commission (NPC), and also Secretary of the National Economic Council (NEC).   Ugbo (2013) attributed this problem to some internal structural problems which he said distorted emphasis on internally generated revenue in the State. There are a lot of players in the informal sector, especially in tourism and hospitality in the State, and they generate a lot of revenue and pay little or no tax (Ugbo, 2013).

Another financial expert and immediate past Accountant General of the State, Dr Peter Oti, buttressed the same point by stating that the internal revenue portfolio in Cross River State is still poor and the sooner the state starts paying more attention to this, the better for the economic development of the people, because there will be enough for governmental socio-economic development (Oti, 2015). The two experts lamented that the internally generated revenue contributions to the per capita income of the people of Cross River State is still poor in comparative terms with other States, which shows that IGR from this sector including tourism/hospitality organisations in Cross River State have not contributed significantly to the economic development of the State and its people, as can be seen in figures 1 and 2 below:

S/N	STATE	2012 IGR (N)	Population	IGR/Capita (N)
1	LAGOS	219,202,426,843.89	20,200,000.00	10,851.61
2	RIVERS	66,275,698,676.01	6,100,000.00	3,280.98
3	DELTA	45,566,897,481.00	4,800,000.00	2,255.79
4	EDO	18,880,055,380.83	3,800,000.00	934.66
5	OYO	14,598,808,723.10	6,500,000.00	722.71
6	EBONYI	14,033,391,157.02	2,600,000.00	694.72
7	AKWA IBOM	13,516,810,150.00	4,600,000.00	669.15
8	CROSS RIVER	12,734,560,333.00	3,400,000.00	630.42
9	OGUN	12,438,765,025.22	4,400,000.00	615.78
10	ENUGU	12,209,587,683.00	3,800,000.00	604.44

Fig. 16.1: Ten States' IGR/Per capita in Nigeria, 2012. Source: Ugbo, Fidelis (2013), How States Can Boost IGR Without Multiple Taxation. http://www.theguardianmobile.com/readNewsItem1.php?nid=19021

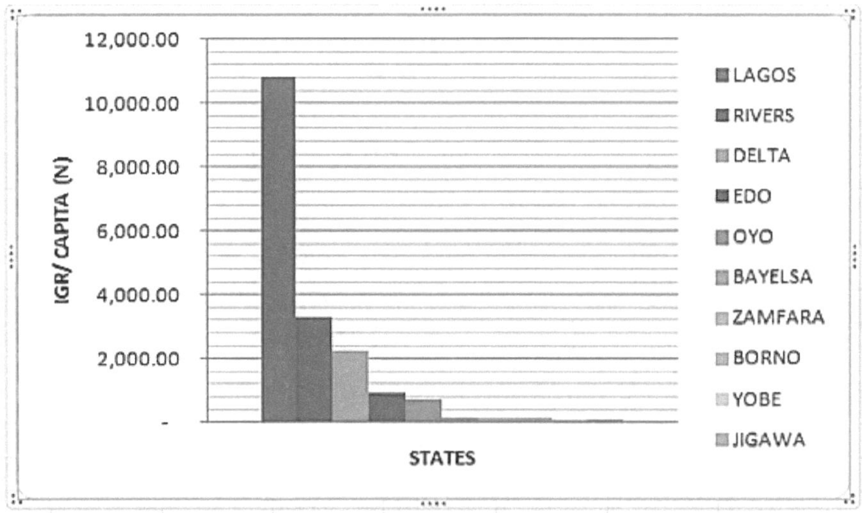

Fig. 16.2: States' with best IGR/Per capita in Nigeria, 2013. Source: Ugbo, Fidelis (2013), How States Can Boost IGR Without Multiple Taxation. http://www.theguardianmobile.com/readNewsItem1.php?nid=19021

iii. Example of Perspectival Background: Remember we said this type of background report presents in perspectives how the issue or problem that motivated the study has been playing out. The perspectives could be a state by state account, social class by social class, gender by gender, age group by age group, and many more. See an example from a Ph.D thesis titled: "Social marketing public relations (SMPR) and enhanced immunisation campaigns' success against childhood killer diseases in Nigeria," (Odigbo, 2014).

Global reports have it that Nigeria has one of the worst immunization records in the world leading to a high rate of infant and maternal mortality. That the country's national coverages in full immunization is less than 13%, one of the lowest rates in the world, even lower than many countries in conflict, such as Democratic Republic of Congo, DRC. For instance, a study by the National Population Commission tagged the National Demographic Health Survey (NDHS, 2003), reveals that some states in Northern Nigeria even have coverage rates below 1%, and the average for the whole North West zone is just 4%. These coverage figures are much worse than in the neighbouring countries of Benin, Niger, Chad and Cameroon, reports the Global Alliance for Vaccines Initiative (GAVI, 2003) and one of the worst in the world (UNICEF, 2013). Among the 22.6 million children who did not receive three DTP doses (DTP3) during the first year of life, 16.3 million (72%) lived in 10 countries, among which 12.4 million (55%) lived in three countries: 30% in India (72% DTP3 coverage), 17% in Nigeria (41% DTP3 coverage), and 7% in Indonesia (64% DTP3 coverage). Figures 3 and 4 below give pictorial views of this position:

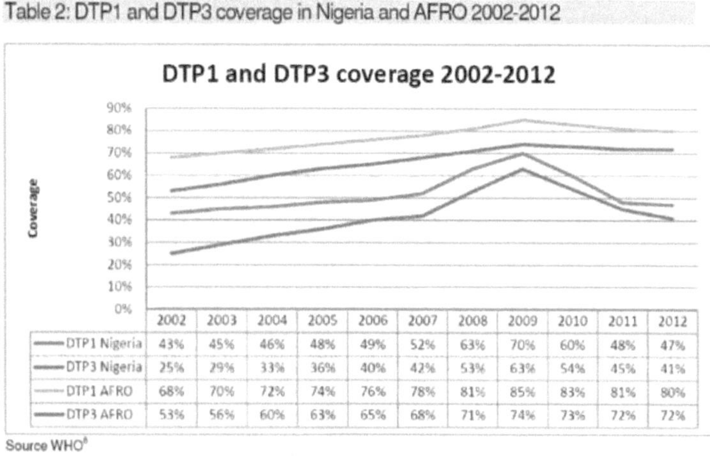

Table 2: DTP1 and DTP3 coverage in Nigeria and AFRO 2002-2012

	2002	2003	2004	2005	2006	2007	2008	2009	2010	2011	2012
DTP1 Nigeria	43%	45%	46%	48%	49%	52%	63%	70%	60%	48%	47%
DTP3 Nigeria	25%	29%	33%	36%	40%	42%	53%	63%	54%	45%	41%
DTP1 AFRO	68%	70%	72%	74%	76%	78%	81%	85%	83%	81%	80%
DTP3 AFRO	53%	56%	60%	63%	65%	68%	71%	74%	73%	72%	72%

Source WHO[8]

Fig. 16.3: Nigeria and Afro coverage rates 2002-2010. Source: WHO (2010), Compiled from data published at
http://apps.who.int/immunization_monitoring/globalsummary/ estimates?c=NGA.

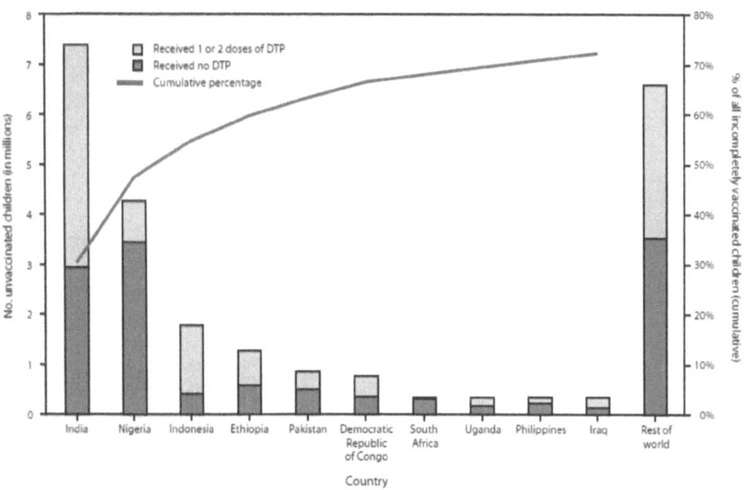

Figure 16.4: Estimated number of children who had not received 3 doses of diphtheria-tetanus-pertussis vaccine (DTP) during the first year of life among 10 countries with the largest number of children incompletely vaccinated

with DTP, by country, and cumulative percentage of all incompletely vaccinated children — worldwide, 2012. Source: US Center for Disease Control (CDC.gov, 2013).

The United States Agency for International Development (USAID, 2003) reports that in Nigeria, one child in five dies before its fifth birthday. This represented about 872,000 childhood deaths in 2002. Vaccine preventable diseases (VPDs) account for about 22% of deaths. Therefore, over 200,000 children a year are dying needlessly of VPDs. The result is even worse in the Northern part of Nigeria due to unfounded fears and dangerous rumours.

Transaid (2007: 1) also captured this sad situation thus: "immunisation rates in Northern Nigeria are some of the lowest in the world. According to the 2003 National Immunization Schedule the percentage of fully immunized infants on the States to be targeted was less than 1% in Jigawa, 1.5% in Yobe, 1.6% in Zamfara and 8.3% in Katsina. As a result, thousands of children are dying as victims of vaccine preventable diseases.

Furthermore, the Global Alliance for Vaccine Initiatives (GAVI, 2003), observed that in Nigeria there is excessively high rates of vaccine wastage. For instance, the relatively expensive Yellow Fever and Hepatitis B vaccines account for half of Nigeria's vaccine expenditure, but evidence from several northern states shows that 80% of Hepatitis B vaccine is wasted or unused. This is a vaccine that is in short supply globally, and these wasted vaccines could have been put to good use in other countries, (GAVI, 2003) regretted.

The World Health Organization ((WHO, 2005) report that international comparative data show Nigeria's immunization coverage rates are among the worst in the world.   That in Nigeria, vaccine-preventable diseases (VPDs) currently account for about 22% of deaths for children aged under five. In 2002 deaths in Nigerian children aged 0-5 years are estimated to have been 872,000; therefore, in that year estimates that close to 200,000 Nigerian children died from VPDs.

Again, UNICEF (2005), noted that close to 200,000 Nigerian children died from VPDs in 2005. Out of this, 17,000 Nigerian infants are estimated to have died due to neonatal tetanus. Deaths from measles have been estimated at 96,000 that year. The North is prone to epidemics of cerebrospinal meningitis. 75,000 cases of CSM were treated and 8,440 people died. None of these figures consider potential adverse health consequences, e.g. blindness resulting from measles. An effective immunization service would have averted this crisis.

NIGERIA's INFANT MORTALITY RATES, 2004 - 2010

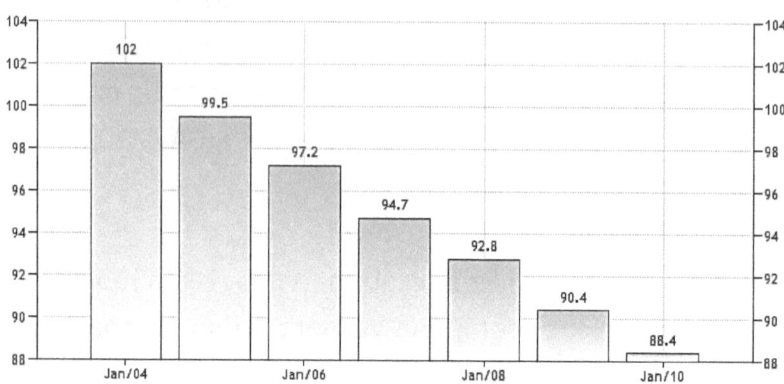

Fig. 16.5: NIGERIA'S INFANT MORTALITY RATES, 2004–2010, Source: WORLD BANK INDICATORS (2011).
http://data.worldbank.org/indicator/SP.DYN.IMRT.IN.

Infant mortality rate (deaths/1,000 live births) in Nigeria, 2000 – 2012

Country	2000	2001	2002	2003	2004	2005	2006	2007	2008	2009	2010	2011	2012
Nigeria	74.18	73.34	72.49	71.35	70.49	98.8	97.14	95.52	95.74	94.35	92.99	91.54	74.36

Fig. 16.6: Nigeria's INFANT Mortality RATES, 2000 – 2012. Source: CIA World Factbook (2013), Infant mortality rate, http://www.cia.gov/library/publications/the-world-factbook/nigeria.

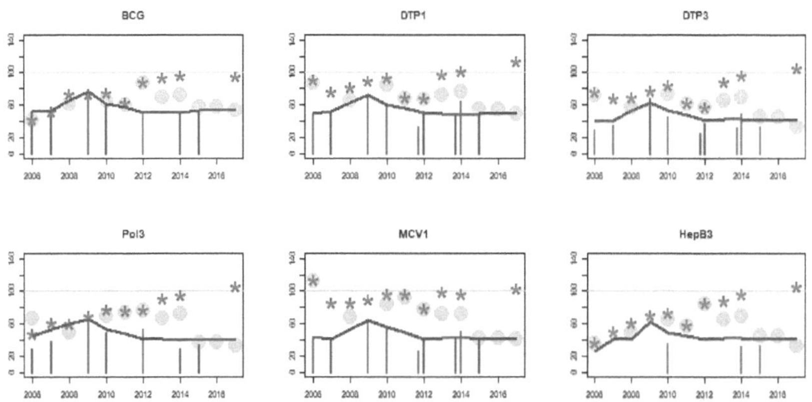

Fig. 16.7: Nigeria: WHO and UNICEF estimates of immunization coverage: 2013.Source: WHO and UNICEF data as of 30 June 2013.
http://www.who.int/immunization/monitoring_surveillance/data/nga.pdf

According to UNICEF (2013), every single day, Nigeria loses about 2,300 under-five year olds and 145 women of childbearing age. This makes the country the second largest contributor to the under–five and maternal mortality rate in the world. Underneath the statistics lies the pain of human tragedy, for thousands of families who have lost their children. Even more devastating is the knowledge that, according to recent research, essential interventions reaching women and babies on time would have averted most of these deaths.

iv. **Analytical Background:** This type of research report breaks down the issue or motivating problem for the study into its component parts, evaluates the issue or idea, and presents this breakdown and evaluation to the audience. For example, breaking the discussion into the key variables of the study.

v. An Argumentative Background: This type of research report tries to provide convincing evidence or justifications for the subject matter or topic. The target of an argumentative research report is to convince the audience that the thesis or claims of the study are true based on the convincing evidence provided.

Statement of the Problem

While the background of the study highlights the issues that informed a study, the statement of the problem is emphatic in explaining the problems that justifies the study. It tries to convince the reader that there is really a problem and that the consequences of the problem on the study population is worthy of the proposed research. According to the University of Southern California (2016), a research problem is a definite or clear expression [statement] about an area of concern, a condition to be improved upon, a difficulty to be eliminated, or a troubling question that exists in scholarly literature, in theory, or within existing practice that points to a need for meaningful understanding and deliberate investigation. It does not state how to do the problem, but gives:

A brief overview of the issues or problems existing in the concerned area selected for the research.

- ➢ The issue(s) prevalent in the area which drives the researcher to take interest in the study.
- ➢ To convince the reader further on the topic being studied and the parameters of what is to be investigated.
- ➢ Clarity and precision [a well-written statement does not make sweeping generalizations and irresponsible

pronouncements; it also does include unspecific determinates like "very" or "giant"],

➢ Demonstrate a researchable topic or issue [i.e., feasibility of conducting the study is based upon access to information that can be effectively acquired, gathered, interpreted, synthesized, and understood],

➢ Identification of what would be studied, while avoiding the use of value-laden words and terms,

➢ Identification of an overarching question or small set of questions accompanied by key factors or variables,

➢ Identification of key concepts and terms,

➢ Articulation of the study's boundaries or parameters or limitations,

➢ Some generalizability in regards to applicability and bringing results into general use,

➢ Conveyance of the study's importance, benefits, and justification [i.e., regardless of the type of research, it is important to demonstrate that the research is not trivial],

➢ Does not have unnecessary jargon or overly complex sentence constructions; and,

➢ Conveyance of more than the mere gathering of descriptive data providing only a snapshot of the issue or phenomenon under investigation.

For more details on statement of the problem, see chapter seven of this book.

Objectives of the Study

A good objective of the study should observe the following guidelines:

    i. Commence with a statement of the broad or general objective first, before the specific objectives.

    ii. Contain the dependent and independent variables.

    iii. Match or link each numbered specific objective to its corresponding number of the research question and hypothesis.

That is:

Objective 1 ➡ Research Question 1 ➡ Hypothesis 1.

Objective 2 ➡ Research Question 2 ➡ Hypothesis 2.

Objective 3 ➡ Research Question 3 ➡ Hypothesis 3.

The scope of the Study

Every good scope of the study must embody three technical items:

    i.   The subject scope: That is a tight summary of the subject matter of the study or the topic.

    ii.   The geographic scope: That is, the geographic area(s) to be covered in the study population.

    iii.   The sampling scope: That is, the select groups or class of people to be sampled amongst the study population.

Abstract

Whether for an article or thesis, a good Abstract must contain six basic technical items:

    i. A short statement of what the study/paper is all about.

ii. A short statement of the issues or problems that
     motivated it.
iii. A summary of the objectives.
iv. A summary of the research methodology.
v.   A summary of the results, and
vi. A summary of the recommendations.

References

Basil, Glory (2017), "Effect of unethical marketing practices by
     independent petroleum marketers and kerosene
     explosions in Nigeria" a Ph.D seminar paper presented at
     the Department of Marketing, University of Calabar,
     Nigeria.

Ekom, Francis Adibo (2017), "A critical analysis of corporate
     social responsibility (CSR) tax practices of tourism
     organizations towards the development of Cross River
     State, Nigeria," a Ph.D seminar paper presented at the
     Department of Marketing, University of Calabar, Nigeria.

Odigbo, B. E. (2014), "Social marketing public relations (SMPR)
     and enhanced immunisation campaigns' success against
     childhood killer diseases in Nigeria," a Ph.D seminar
     paper presented at the Department of Marketing,
     University of Nigeria.

University of Southern Carlifornia (2016), Organizing Your Social
     Sciences Research Paper: The Research
     Problem/Question.
     http://libguides.usc.edu/writingguide/introduction/resea
     rchproblem

APPENDIX

RESEARCH STATISTICAL TABLES

Table 1: Chi-square Distribution Table

df	$\chi^2_{.995}$	$\chi^2_{.990}$	$\chi^2_{.975}$	$\chi^2_{.950}$	$\chi^2_{.900}$	$\chi^2_{.100}$	$\chi^2_{.050}$	$\chi^2_{.025}$	$\chi^2_{.010}$	$\chi^2_{.005}$
1	0.000	0.000	0.001	0.004	0.016	2.706	3.841	5.024	6.635	7.879
2	0.010	0.020	0.051	0.103	0.211	4.605	5.991	7.378	9.210	10.597
3	0.072	0.115	0.216	0.352	0.584	6.251	7.815	9.348	11.345	12.838
4	0.207	0.297	0.484	0.711	1.064	7.779	9.488	11.143	13.277	14.860
5	0.412	0.554	0.831	1.145	1.610	9.236	11.070	12.833	15.086	16.750
6	0.676	0.872	1.237	1.635	2.204	10.645	12.592	14.449	16.812	18.548
7	0.989	1.239	1.690	2.167	2.833	12.017	14.067	16.013	18.475	20.278
8	1.344	1.646	2.180	2.733	3.490	13.362	15.507	17.535	20.090	21.955
9	1.735	2.088	2.700	3.325	4.168	14.684	16.919	19.023	21.666	23.589
10	2.156	2.558	3.247	3.940	4.865	15.987	18.307	20.483	23.209	25.188
11	2.603	3.053	3.816	4.575	5.578	17.275	19.675	21.920	24.725	26.757
12	3.074	3.571	4.404	5.226	6.304	18.549	21.026	23.337	26.217	28.300
13	3.565	4.107	5.009	5.892	7.042	19.812	22.362	24.736	27.688	29.819
14	4.075	4.660	5.629	6.571	7.790	21.064	23.685	26.119	29.141	31.319
15	4.601	5.229	6.262	7.261	8.547	22.307	24.996	27.488	30.578	32.801
16	5.142	5.812	6.908	7.962	9.312	23.542	26.296	28.845	32.000	34.267
17	5.697	6.408	7.564	8.672	10.085	24.769	27.587	30.191	33.409	35.718
18	6.265	7.015	8.231	9.390	10.865	25.989	28.869	31.526	34.805	37.156
19	6.844	7.633	8.907	10.117	11.651	27.204	30.144	32.852	36.191	38.582
20	7.434	8.260	9.591	10.851	12.443	28.412	31.410	34.170	37.566	39.997
21	8.034	8.897	10.283	11.591	13.240	29.615	32.671	35.479	38.932	41.401
22	8.643	9.542	10.982	12.338	14.041	30.813	33.924	36.781	40.289	42.796
23	9.260	10.196	11.689	13.091	14.848	32.007	35.172	38.076	41.638	44.181
24	9.886	10.856	12.401	13.848	15.659	33.196	36.415	39.364	42.980	45.559
25	10.520	11.524	13.120	14.611	16.473	34.382	37.652	40.646	44.314	46.928
26	11.160	12.198	13.844	15.379	17.292	35.563	38.885	41.923	45.642	48.290
27	11.808	12.879	14.573	16.151	18.114	36.741	40.113	43.195	46.963	49.645
28	12.461	13.565	15.308	16.928	18.939	37.916	41.337	44.461	48.278	50.993
29	13.121	14.256	16.047	17.708	19.768	39.087	42.557	45.722	49.588	52.336
30	13.787	14.953	16.791	18.493	20.599	40.256	43.773	46.979	50.892	53.672
40	20.707	22.164	24.433	26.509	29.051	51.805	55.758	59.342	63.691	66.766
50	27.991	29.707	32.357	34.764	37.689	63.167	67.505	71.420	76.154	79.490
60	35.534	37.485	40.482	43.188	46.459	74.397	79.082	83.298	88.379	91.952
70	43.275	45.442	48.758	51.739	55.329	85.527	90.531	95.023	100.425	104.215
80	51.172	53.540	57.153	60.391	64.278	96.578	101.879	106.629	112.329	116.321
90	59.196	61.754	65.647	69.126	73.291	107.565	113.145	118.136	124.116	128.299
100	67.328	70.065	74.222	77.929	82.358	118.498	124.342	129.561	135.807	140.169

Table 2: Z-Normal Distribution Table
Standard Normal Probabilities

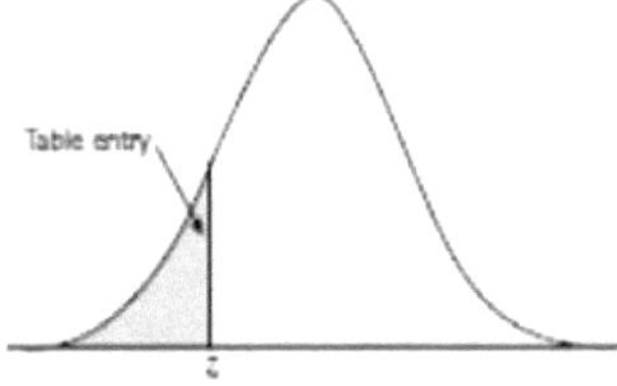

Table entry for z is the area under the standard normal curve to the left of z.

z	.00	.01	.02	.03	.04	.05	.06	.07	.08	.09
−3.4	.0003	.0003	.0003	.0003	.0003	.0003	.0003	.0003	.0003	.0002
−3.3	.0005	.0005	.0005	.0004	.0004	.0004	.0004	.0004	.0004	.0003
−3.2	.0007	.0007	.0006	.0006	.0006	.0006	.0006	.0005	.0005	.0005
−3.1	.0010	.0009	.0009	.0009	.0008	.0008	.0008	.0008	.0007	.0007
−3.0	.0013	.0013	.0013	.0012	.0012	.0011	.0011	.0011	.0010	.0010
−2.9	.0019	.0018	.0018	.0017	.0016	.0016	.0015	.0015	.0014	.0014
−2.8	.0026	.0025	.0024	.0023	.0023	.0022	.0021	.0021	.0020	.0019
−2.7	.0035	.0034	.0033	.0032	.0031	.0030	.0029	.0028	.0027	.0026
−2.6	.0047	.0045	.0044	.0043	.0041	.0040	.0039	.0038	.0037	.0036
−2.5	.0062	.0060	.0059	.0057	.0055	.0054	.0052	.0051	.0049	.0048
−2.4	.0082	.0080	.0078	.0075	.0073	.0071	.0069	.0068	.0066	.0064
−2.3	.0107	.0104	.0102	.0099	.0096	.0094	.0091	.0089	.0087	.0084
−2.2	.0139	.0136	.0132	.0129	.0125	.0122	.0119	.0116	.0113	.0110
−2.1	.0179	.0174	.0170	.0166	.0162	.0158	.0154	.0150	.0146	.0143
−2.0	.0228	.0222	.0217	.0212	.0207	.0202	.0197	.0192	.0188	.0183
−1.9	.0287	.0281	.0274	.0268	.0262	.0256	.0250	.0244	.0239	.0233
−1.8	.0359	.0351	.0344	.0336	.0329	.0322	.0314	.0307	.0301	.0294
−1.7	.0446	.0436	.0427	.0418	.0409	.0401	.0392	.0384	.0375	.0367
−1.6	.0548	.0537	.0526	.0516	.0505	.0495	.0485	.0475	.0465	.0455
−1.5	.0668	.0655	.0643	.0630	.0618	.0606	.0594	.0582	.0571	.0559
−1.4	.0808	.0793	.0778	.0764	.0749	.0735	.0721	.0708	.0694	.0681
−1.3	.0968	.0951	.0934	.0918	.0901	.0885	.0869	.0853	.0838	.0823
−1.2	.1151	.1131	.1112	.1093	.1075	.1056	.1038	.1020	.1003	.0985
−1.1	.1357	.1335	.1314	.1292	.1271	.1251	.1230	.1210	.1190	.1170
−1.0	.1587	.1562	.1539	.1515	.1492	.1469	.1446	.1423	.1401	.1379
−0.9	.1841	.1814	.1788	.1762	.1736	.1711	.1685	.1660	.1635	.1611
−0.8	.2119	.2090	.2061	.2033	.2005	.1977	.1949	.1922	.1894	.1867
−0.7	.2420	.2389	.2358	.2327	.2296	.2266	.2236	.2206	.2177	.2148
−0.6	.2743	.2709	.2676	.2643	.2611	.2578	.2546	.2514	.2483	.2451
−0.5	.3085	.3050	.3015	.2981	.2946	.2912	.2877	.2843	.2810	.2776
−0.4	.3446	.3409	.3372	.3336	.3300	.3264	.3228	.3192	.3156	.3121
−0.3	.3821	.3783	.3745	.3707	.3669	.3632	.3594	.3557	.3520	.3483
−0.2	.4207	.4168	.4129	.4090	.4052	.4013	.3974	.3936	.3897	.3859
−0.1	.4602	.4562	.4522	.4483	.4443	.4404	.4364	.4325	.4286	.4247
−0.0	.5000	.4960	.4920	.4880	.4840	.4801	.4761	.4721	.4681	.4641

Table 3: Z-Normal Distribution Table

Standard Normal Probabilities

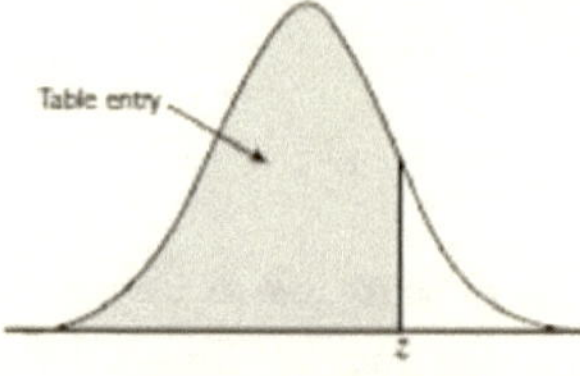

z	.00	.01	.02	.03	.04	.05	.06	.07	.08	.09
0.0	.5000	.5040	.5080	.5120	.5160	.5199	.5239	.5279	.5319	.5359
0.1	.5398	.5438	.5478	.5517	.5557	.5596	.5636	.5675	.5714	.5753
0.2	.5793	.5832	.5871	.5910	.5948	.5987	.6026	.6064	.6103	.6141
0.3	.6179	.6217	.6255	.6293	.6331	.6368	.6406	.6443	.6480	.6517
0.4	.6554	.6591	.6628	.6664	.6700	.6736	.6772	.6808	.6844	.6879
0.5	.6915	.6950	.6985	.7019	.7054	.7088	.7123	.7157	.7190	.7224
0.6	.7257	.7291	.7324	.7357	.7389	.7422	.7454	.7486	.7517	.7549
0.7	.7580	.7611	.7642	.7673	.7704	.7734	.7764	.7794	.7823	.7852
0.8	.7881	.7910	.7939	.7967	.7995	.8023	.8051	.8078	.8106	.8133
0.9	.8159	.8186	.8212	.8238	.8264	.8289	.8315	.8340	.8365	.8389
1.0	.8413	.8438	.8461	.8485	.8508	.8531	.8554	.8577	.8599	.8621
1.1	.8643	.8665	.8686	.8708	.8729	.8749	.8770	.8790	.8810	.8830
1.2	.8849	.8869	.8888	.8907	.8925	.8944	.8962	.8980	.8997	.9015
1.3	.9032	.9049	.9066	.9082	.9099	.9115	.9131	.9147	.9162	.9177
1.4	.9192	.9207	.9222	.9236	.9251	.9265	.9279	.9292	.9306	.9319
1.5	.9332	.9345	.9357	.9370	.9382	.9394	.9406	.9418	.9429	.9441
1.6	.9452	.9463	.9474	.9484	.9495	.9505	.9515	.9525	.9535	.9545
1.7	.9554	.9564	.9573	.9582	.9591	.9599	.9608	.9616	.9625	.9633
1.8	.9641	.9649	.9656	.9664	.9671	.9678	.9686	.9693	.9699	.9706
1.9	.9713	.9719	.9726	.9732	.9738	.9744	.9750	.9756	.9761	.9767
2.0	.9772	.9778	.9783	.9788	.9793	.9798	.9803	.9808	.9812	.9817
2.1	.9821	.9826	.9830	.9834	.9838	.9842	.9846	.9850	.9854	.9857
2.2	.9861	.9864	.9868	.9871	.9875	.9878	.9881	.9884	.9887	.9890
2.3	.9893	.9896	.9898	.9901	.9904	.9906	.9909	.9911	.9913	.9916
2.4	.9918	.9920	.9922	.9925	.9927	.9929	.9931	.9932	.9934	.9936
2.5	.9938	.9940	.9941	.9943	.9945	.9946	.9948	.9949	.9951	.9952
2.6	.9953	.9955	.9956	.9957	.9959	.9960	.9961	.9962	.9963	.9964
2.7	.9965	.9966	.9967	.9968	.9969	.9970	.9971	.9972	.9973	.9974
2.8	.9974	.9975	.9976	.9977	.9977	.9978	.9979	.9979	.9980	.9981
2.9	.9981	.9982	.9982	.9983	.9984	.9984	.9985	.9985	.9986	.9986
3.0	.9987	.9987	.9987	.9988	.9988	.9989	.9989	.9989	.9990	.9990
3.1	.9990	.9991	.9991	.9991	.9992	.9992	.9992	.9992	.9993	.9993
3.2	.9993	.9993	.9994	.9994	.9994	.9994	.9994	.9995	.9995	.9995
3.3	.9995	.9995	.9995	.9996	.9996	.9996	.9996	.9996	.9996	.9997
3.4	.9997	.9997	.9997	.9997	.9997	.9997	.9997	.9997	.9997	.9998

Table 4: Z-test Distribution Table

z	0.00	0.01	0.02	0.03	0.04	0.05	0.06	0.07	0.08	0.09
0.0	0.5000	0.5040	0.5080	0.5120	0.5160	0.5199	0.5239	0.5279	0.5319	0.5359
0.1	0.5398	0.5438	0.5478	0.5517	0.5557	0.5596	0.5636	0.5675	0.5714	0.5753
0.2	0.5793	0.5832	0.5871	0.5910	0.5948	0.5987	0.6026	0.6064	0.6103	0.6141
0.3	0.6179	0.6217	0.6255	0.6293	0.6331	0.6368	0.6406	0.6443	0.6480	0.6517
0.4	0.6554	0.6591	0.6628	0.6664	0.6700	0.6736	0.6772	0.6808	0.6844	0.6879
0.5	0.6915	0.6950	0.6985	0.7019	0.7054	0.7088	0.7123	0.7157	0.7190	0.7224
0.6	0.7257	0.7291	0.7324	0.7357	0.7389	0.7422	0.7454	0.7486	0.7517	0.7549
0.7	0.7580	0.7611	0.7642	0.7673	0.7704	0.7734	0.7764	0.7794	0.7823	0.7852
0.8	0.7881	0.7910	0.7939	0.7967	0.7995	0.8023	0.8051	0.8078	0.8106	0.8133
0.9	0.8159	0.8186	0.8212	0.8238	0.8264	0.8289	0.8315	0.8340	0.8365	0.8389
1.0	0.8413	0.8438	0.8461	0.8485	0.8508	0.8531	0.8554	0.8577	0.8599	0.8621
1.1	0.8643	0.8665	0.8686	0.8708	0.8729	0.8749	0.8770	0.8790	0.8810	0.8830
1.2	0.8849	0.8869	0.8888	0.8907	0.8925	0.8944	0.8962	0.8980	0.8997	0.9015
1.3	0.9032	0.9049	0.9066	0.9082	0.9099	0.9115	0.9131	0.9147	0.9162	0.9177
1.4	0.9192	0.9207	0.9222	0.9236	0.9251	0.9265	0.9279	0.9292	0.9306	0.9319
1.5	0.9332	0.9345	0.9357	0.9370	0.9382	0.9394	0.9406	0.9418	0.9429	0.9441
1.6	0.9452	0.9463	0.9474	0.9484	0.9495	0.9505	0.9515	0.9525	0.9535	0.9545
1.7	0.9554	0.9564	0.9573	0.9582	0.9591	0.9599	0.9608	0.9616	0.9625	0.9633
1.8	0.9641	0.9649	0.9656	0.9664	0.9671	0.9678	0.9686	0.9693	0.9699	0.9706
1.9	0.9713	0.9719	0.9726	0.9732	0.9738	0.9744	0.9750	0.9756	0.9761	0.9767
2.0	0.9772	0.9778	0.9783	0.9788	0.9793	0.9798	0.9803	0.9808	0.9812	0.9817
2.1	0.9821	0.9826	0.9830	0.9834	0.9838	0.9842	0.9846	0.9850	0.9854	0.9857
2.2	0.9861	0.9864	0.9868	0.9871	0.9875	0.9878	0.9881	0.9884	0.9887	0.9890
2.3	0.9893	0.9896	0.9898	0.9901	0.9904	0.9906	0.9909	0.9911	0.9913	0.9916
2.4	0.9918	0.9920	0.9922	0.9925	0.9927	0.9929	0.9931	0.9932	0.9934	0.9936
2.5	0.9938	0.9940	0.9941	0.9943	0.9945	0.9946	0.9948	0.9949	0.9951	0.9952
2.6	0.9953	0.9955	0.9956	0.9957	0.9959	0.9960	0.9961	0.9962	0.9963	0.9964
2.7	0.9965	0.9966	0.9967	0.9968	0.9969	0.9970	0.9971	0.9972	0.9973	0.9974
2.8	0.9974	0.9975	0.9976	0.9977	0.9977	0.9978	0.9979	0.9979	0.9980	0.9981
2.9	0.9981	0.9982	0.9982	0.9983	0.9984	0.9984	0.9985	0.9985	0.9986	0.9986
3.0	0.9987	0.9987	0.9987	0.9988	0.9988	0.9989	0.9989	0.9989	0.9990	0.9990
3.1	0.9990	0.9991	0.9991	0.9991	0.9992	0.9992	0.9992	0.9992	0.9993	0.9993
3.2	0.9993	0.9993	0.9994	0.9994	0.9994	0.9994	0.9994	0.9995	0.9995	0.9995
3.3	0.9995	0.9995	0.9995	0.9996	0.9996	0.9996	0.9996	0.9996	0.9996	0.9997
3.4	0.9997	0.9997	0.9997	0.9997	0.9997	0.9997	0.9997	0.9997	0.9997	0.9998
3.5	0.9998	0.9998	0.9998	0.9998	0.9998	0.9998	0.9998	0.9998	0.9998	0.9998
3.6	0.9998	0.9998	0.9999							

t Distribution: Critical Values of t

		Significance level					
Degrees of freedom	Two-tailed test: One-tailed test:	10% 5%	5% 2.5%	2% 1%	1% 0.5%	0.2% 0.1%	0.1% 0.05%
1		6.314	12.706	31.821	63.657	318.309	636.619
2		2.920	4.303	6.965	9.925	22.327	31.599
3		2.353	3.182	4.541	5.841	10.215	12.924
4		2.132	2.776	3.747	4.604	7.173	8.610
5		2.015	2.571	3.365	4.032	5.893	6.869
6		1.943	2.447	3.143	3.707	5.208	5.959
7		1.894	2.365	2.998	3.499	4.785	5.408
8		1.860	2.306	2.896	3.355	4.501	5.041
9		1.833	2.262	2.821	3.250	4.297	4.781
10		1.812	2.228	2.764	3.169	4.144	4.587
11		1.796	2.201	2.718	3.106	4.025	4.437
12		1.782	2.179	2.681	3.055	3.930	4.318
13		1.771	2.160	2.650	3.012	3.852	4.221
14		1.761	2.145	2.624	2.977	3.787	4.140
15		1.753	2.131	2.602	2.947	3.733	4.073
16		1.746	2.120	2.583	2.921	3.686	4.015
17		1.740	2.110	2.567	2.898	3.646	3.965
18		1.734	2.101	2.552	2.878	3.610	3.922
19		1.729	2.093	2.539	2.861	3.579	3.883
20		1.725	2.086	2.528	2.845	3.552	3.850
21		1.721	2.080	2.518	2.831	3.527	3.819
22		1.717	2.074	2.508	2.819	3.505	3.792
23		1.714	2.069	2.500	2.807	3.485	3.768
24		1.711	2.064	2.492	2.797	3.467	3.745
25		1.708	2.060	2.485	2.787	3.450	3.725
26		1.706	2.056	2.479	2.779	3.435	3.707
27		1.703	2.052	2.473	2.771	3.421	3.690
28		1.701	2.048	2.467	2.763	3.408	3.674
29		1.699	2.045	2.462	2.756	3.396	3.659
30		1.697	2.042	2.457	2.750	3.385	3.646
32		1.694	2.037	2.449	2.738	3.365	3.622
34		1.691	2.032	2.441	2.728	3.348	3.601
36		1.688	2.028	2.434	2.719	3.333	3.582
38		1.686	2.024	2.429	2.712	3.319	3.566
40		1.684	2.021	2.423	2.704	3.307	3.551
42		1.682	2.018	2.418	2.698	3.296	3.538
44		1.680	2.015	2.414	2.692	3.286	3.526
46		1.679	2.013	2.410	2.687	3.277	3.515
48		1.677	2.011	2.407	2.682	3.269	3.505
50		1.676	2.009	2.403	2.678	3.261	3.496
60		1.671	2.000	2.390	2.660	3.232	3.460
70		1.667	1.994	2.381	2.648	3.211	3.435
80		1.664	1.990	2.374	2.639	3.195	3.416
90		1.662	1.987	2.368	2.632	3.183	3.402
100		1.660	1.984	2.364	2.626	3.174	3.390
120		1.658	1.980	2.358	2.617	3.160	3.373
150		1.655	1.976	2.351	2.609	3.145	3.357
200		1.653	1.972	2.345	2.601	3.131	3.340
300		1.650	1.968	2.339	2.592	3.118	3.323
400		1.649	1.966	2.336	2.588	3.111	3.315
500		1.648	1.965	2.334	2.586	3.107	3.310
600		1.647	1.964	2.333	2.584	3.104	3.307
∞		1.645	1.960	2.326	2.576	3.090	3.291

Table 6: F-test Distribution Table

F Distribution: Critical Values of F (5% significance level)

ν_1 / ν_2	1	2	3	4	5	6	7	8	9	10	12	14	16	18	20
1	161.45	199.50	215.71	224.58	230.16	233.99	236.77	238.88	240.54	241.88	243.91	245.36	246.46	247.32	248.01
2	18.51	19.00	19.16	19.25	19.30	19.33	19.35	19.37	19.38	19.40	19.41	19.42	19.43	19.44	19.45
3	10.13	9.55	9.28	9.12	9.01	8.94	8.89	8.85	8.81	8.79	8.74	8.71	8.69	8.67	8.66
4	7.71	6.94	6.59	6.39	6.26	6.16	6.09	6.04	6.00	5.96	5.91	5.87	5.84	5.82	5.80
5	6.61	5.79	5.41	5.19	5.05	4.95	4.88	4.82	4.77	4.74	4.68	4.64	4.60	4.58	4.56
6	5.99	5.14	4.76	4.53	4.39	4.28	4.21	4.15	4.10	4.06	4.00	3.96	3.92	3.90	3.87
7	5.59	4.74	4.35	4.12	3.97	3.87	3.79	3.73	3.68	3.64	3.57	3.53	3.49	3.47	3.44
8	5.32	4.46	4.07	3.84	3.69	3.58	3.50	3.44	3.39	3.35	3.28	3.24	3.20	3.17	3.15
9	5.12	4.26	3.86	3.63	3.48	3.37	3.29	3.23	3.18	3.14	3.07	3.03	2.99	2.96	2.94
10	4.96	4.10	3.71	3.48	3.33	3.22	3.14	3.07	3.02	2.98	2.91	2.86	2.83	2.80	2.77
11	4.84	3.98	3.59	3.36	3.20	3.09	3.01	2.95	2.90	2.85	2.79	2.74	2.70	2.67	2.65
12	4.75	3.89	3.49	3.26	3.11	3.00	2.91	2.85	2.80	2.75	2.69	2.64	2.60	2.57	2.54
13	4.67	3.81	3.41	3.18	3.03	2.92	2.83	2.77	2.71	2.67	2.60	2.55	2.51	2.48	2.46
14	4.60	3.74	3.34	3.11	2.96	2.85	2.76	2.70	2.65	2.60	2.53	2.48	2.44	2.41	2.39
15	4.54	3.68	3.29	3.06	2.90	2.79	2.71	2.64	2.59	2.54	2.48	2.42	2.38	2.35	2.33
16	4.49	3.63	3.24	3.01	2.85	2.74	2.66	2.59	2.54	2.49	2.42	2.37	2.33	2.30	2.28
17	4.45	3.59	3.20	2.96	2.81	2.70	2.61	2.55	2.49	2.45	2.38	2.33	2.29	2.26	2.23
18	4.41	3.55	3.16	2.93	2.77	2.66	2.58	2.51	2.46	2.41	2.34	2.29	2.25	2.22	2.19
19	4.38	3.52	3.13	2.90	2.74	2.63	2.54	2.48	2.42	2.38	2.31	2.26	2.21	2.18	2.16
20	4.35	3.49	3.10	2.87	2.71	2.60	2.51	2.45	2.39	2.35	2.28	2.22	2.18	2.15	2.12
21	4.32	3.47	3.07	2.84	2.68	2.57	2.49	2.42	2.37	2.32	2.25	2.20	2.16	2.12	2.10
22	4.30	3.44	3.05	2.82	2.66	2.55	2.46	2.40	2.34	2.30	2.23	2.17	2.13	2.10	2.07
23	4.28	3.42	3.03	2.80	2.64	2.53	2.44	2.37	2.32	2.27	2.20	2.15	2.11	2.08	2.05
24	4.26	3.40	3.01	2.78	2.62	2.51	2.42	2.36	2.30	2.25	2.18	2.13	2.09	2.05	2.03
25	4.24	3.39	2.99	2.76	2.60	2.49	2.40	2.34	2.28	2.24	2.16	2.11	2.07	2.04	2.01
26	4.22	3.37	2.98	2.74	2.59	2.47	2.39	2.32	2.27	2.22	2.15	2.09	2.05	2.02	1.99
27	4.21	3.35	2.96	2.73	2.57	2.46	2.37	2.31	2.25	2.20	2.13	2.08	2.04	2.00	1.97
28	4.20	3.34	2.95	2.71	2.56	2.45	2.36	2.29	2.24	2.19	2.12	2.06	2.02	1.99	1.96
29	4.18	3.33	2.93	2.70	2.55	2.43	2.35	2.28	2.22	2.18	2.10	2.05	2.01	1.97	1.94
30	4.17	3.32	2.92	2.69	2.53	2.42	2.33	2.27	2.21	2.16	2.09	2.04	1.99	1.96	1.93
35	4.12	3.27	2.87	2.64	2.49	2.37	2.29	2.22	2.16	2.11	2.04	1.99	1.94	1.91	1.88
40	4.08	3.23	2.84	2.61	2.45	2.34	2.25	2.18	2.12	2.08	2.00	1.95	1.90	1.87	1.84
50	4.03	3.18	2.79	2.56	2.40	2.29	2.20	2.13	2.07	2.03	1.95	1.89	1.85	1.81	1.78
60	4.00	3.15	2.76	2.53	2.37	2.25	2.17	2.10	2.04	1.99	1.92	1.86	1.82	1.78	1.75
70	3.98	3.13	2.74	2.50	2.35	2.23	2.14	2.07	2.02	1.97	1.89	1.84	1.79	1.75	1.72
80	3.96	3.11	2.72	2.49	2.33	2.21	2.13	2.06	2.00	1.95	1.88	1.82	1.77	1.73	1.70
90	3.95	3.10	2.71	2.47	2.32	2.20	2.11	2.04	1.99	1.94	1.86	1.80	1.76	1.72	1.69
100	3.94	3.09	2.70	2.46	2.31	2.19	2.10	2.03	1.97	1.93	1.85	1.79	1.75	1.71	1.68
120	3.92	3.07	2.68	2.45	2.29	2.18	2.09	2.02	1.96	1.91	1.83	1.78	1.73	1.69	1.66
150	3.90	3.06	2.66	2.43	2.27	2.16	2.07	2.00	1.94	1.89	1.82	1.76	1.71	1.67	1.64
200	3.89	3.04	2.65	2.42	2.26	2.14	2.06	1.98	1.93	1.88	1.80	1.74	1.69	1.66	1.62
250	3.88	3.03	2.64	2.41	2.25	2.13	2.05	1.98	1.92	1.87	1.79	1.73	1.68	1.65	1.61
300	3.87	3.03	2.63	2.40	2.24	2.13	2.04	1.97	1.91	1.86	1.78	1.72	1.68	1.64	1.61
400	3.86	3.02	2.63	2.39	2.24	2.12	2.03	1.96	1.90	1.85	1.78	1.72	1.67	1.63	1.60
500	3.86	3.01	2.62	2.39	2.23	2.12	2.03	1.96	1.90	1.85	1.77	1.71	1.66	1.62	1.59
600	3.86	3.01	2.62	2.39	2.23	2.11	2.02	1.95	1.90	1.85	1.77	1.71	1.66	1.62	1.59
750	3.85	3.01	2.62	2.38	2.23	2.11	2.02	1.95	1.89	1.84	1.77	1.70	1.66	1.62	1.58
1000	3.85	3.00	2.61	2.38	2.22	2.11	2.02	1.95	1.89	1.84	1.76	1.70	1.65	1.61	1.58

Table 7: F-test Distribution Table

F Distribution: Critical Values of F (5% significance)

v_2 \ v_1	25	30	35	40	50	60	75	100	150	200
1	249.26	250.10	250.69	251.14	251.77	252.20	252.62	253.04	253.46	253.68
2	19.46	19.46	19.47	19.47	19.48	19.48	19.48	19.49	19.49	19.49
3	8.63	8.62	8.60	8.59	8.58	8.57	8.56	8.55	8.54	8.54
4	5.77	5.75	5.73	5.72	5.70	5.69	5.68	5.66	5.65	5.65
5	4.52	4.50	4.48	4.46	4.44	4.43	4.42	4.41	4.39	4.39
6	3.83	3.81	3.79	3.77	3.75	3.74	3.73	3.71	3.70	3.69
7	3.40	3.38	3.36	3.34	3.32	3.30	3.29	3.27	3.26	3.25
8	3.11	3.08	3.06	3.04	3.02	3.01	2.99	2.97	2.96	2.95
9	2.89	2.86	2.84	2.83	2.80	2.79	2.77	2.76	2.74	2.73
10	2.73	2.70	2.68	2.66	2.64	2.62	2.60	2.59	2.57	2.56
11	2.60	2.57	2.55	2.53	2.51	2.49	2.47	2.46	2.44	2.43
12	2.50	2.47	2.44	2.43	2.40	2.38	2.37	2.35	2.33	2.32
13	2.41	2.38	2.36	2.34	2.31	2.30	2.28	2.26	2.24	2.23
14	2.34	2.31	2.28	2.27	2.24	2.22	2.21	2.19	2.17	2.16
15	2.28	2.25	2.22	2.20	2.18	2.16	2.14	2.12	2.10	2.10
16	2.23	2.19	2.17	2.15	2.12	2.11	2.09	2.07	2.05	2.04
17	2.18	2.15	2.12	2.10	2.08	2.06	2.04	2.02	2.00	1.99
18	2.14	2.11	2.08	2.06	2.04	2.02	2.00	1.98	1.96	1.95
19	2.11	2.07	2.05	2.03	2.00	1.98	1.96	1.94	1.92	1.91
20	2.07	2.04	2.01	1.99	1.97	1.95	1.93	1.91	1.89	1.88
21	2.05	2.01	1.98	1.96	1.94	1.92	1.90	1.88	1.86	1.84
22	2.02	1.98	1.96	1.94	1.91	1.89	1.87	1.85	1.83	1.82
23	2.00	1.96	1.93	1.91	1.88	1.86	1.84	1.82	1.80	1.79
24	1.97	1.94	1.91	1.89	1.86	1.84	1.82	1.80	1.78	1.77
25	1.96	1.92	1.89	1.87	1.84	1.82	1.80	1.78	1.76	1.75
26	1.94	1.90	1.87	1.85	1.82	1.80	1.78	1.76	1.74	1.73
27	1.92	1.88	1.86	1.84	1.81	1.79	1.76	1.74	1.72	1.71
28	1.91	1.87	1.84	1.82	1.79	1.77	1.75	1.73	1.70	1.69
29	1.89	1.85	1.83	1.81	1.77	1.75	1.73	1.71	1.69	1.67
30	1.88	1.84	1.81	1.79	1.76	1.74	1.72	1.70	1.67	1.66
35	1.82	1.79	1.76	1.74	1.70	1.68	1.66	1.63	1.61	1.60
40	1.78	1.74	1.72	1.69	1.66	1.64	1.61	1.59	1.56	1.55
50	1.73	1.69	1.66	1.63	1.60	1.58	1.55	1.52	1.50	1.48
60	1.69	1.65	1.62	1.59	1.56	1.53	1.51	1.48	1.45	1.44
70	1.66	1.62	1.59	1.57	1.53	1.50	1.48	1.45	1.42	1.40
80	1.64	1.60	1.57	1.54	1.51	1.48	1.45	1.43	1.39	1.38
90	1.63	1.59	1.55	1.53	1.49	1.46	1.44	1.41	1.38	1.36
100	1.62	1.57	1.54	1.52	1.48	1.45	1.42	1.39	1.36	1.34
120	1.60	1.55	1.52	1.50	1.46	1.43	1.40	1.37	1.33	1.32
150	1.58	1.54	1.50	1.48	1.44	1.41	1.38	1.34	1.31	1.29
200	1.56	1.52	1.48	1.46	1.41	1.39	1.35	1.32	1.28	1.26
250	1.55	1.50	1.47	1.44	1.40	1.37	1.34	1.31	1.27	1.25
300	1.54	1.50	1.46	1.43	1.39	1.36	1.33	1.30	1.26	1.23
400	1.53	1.49	1.45	1.42	1.38	1.35	1.32	1.28	1.24	1.22
500	1.53	1.48	1.45	1.42	1.38	1.35	1.31	1.28	1.23	1.21
600	1.52	1.48	1.44	1.41	1.37	1.34	1.31	1.27	1.23	1.20
750	1.52	1.47	1.44	1.41	1.37	1.34	1.30	1.26	1.22	1.20
1000	1.52	1.47	1.43	1.41	1.36	1.33	1.30	1.26	1.22	1.19

Table 8: F-test Distribution Table

F Distribution: Critical Values of F (1% significance level)

ν_2 \ ν_1	1	2	3	4	5	6	7	8	9	10	12	14	16	18	20
1	4052.18	4999.50	5403.35	5624.58	5763.65	5858.99	5928.36	5981.07	6022.47	6055.85	6106.32	6142.67	6170.10	6191.53	6208.73
2	98.50	99.00	99.17	99.25	99.30	99.33	99.36	99.37	99.39	99.40	99.42	99.43	99.44	99.44	99.45
3	34.12	30.82	29.46	28.71	28.24	27.91	27.67	27.49	27.35	27.23	27.05	26.92	26.83	26.75	26.69
4	21.20	18.00	16.69	15.98	15.52	15.21	14.98	14.80	14.66	14.55	14.37	14.25	14.15	14.08	14.02
5	16.26	13.27	12.06	11.39	10.97	10.67	10.46	10.29	10.16	10.05	9.89	9.77	9.68	9.61	9.55
6	13.75	10.92	9.78	9.15	8.75	8.47	8.26	8.10	7.98	7.87	7.72	7.60	7.52	7.45	7.40
7	12.25	9.55	8.45	7.85	7.46	7.19	6.99	6.84	6.72	6.62	6.47	6.36	6.28	6.21	6.16
8	11.26	8.65	7.59	7.01	6.63	6.37	6.18	6.03	5.91	5.81	5.67	5.56	5.48	5.41	5.36
9	10.56	8.02	6.99	6.42	6.06	5.80	5.61	5.47	5.35	5.26	5.11	5.01	4.92	4.86	4.81
10	10.04	7.56	6.55	5.99	5.64	5.39	5.20	5.06	4.94	4.85	4.71	4.60	4.52	4.46	4.41
11	9.65	7.21	6.22	5.67	5.32	5.07	4.89	4.74	4.63	4.54	4.40	4.29	4.21	4.15	4.10
12	9.33	6.93	5.95	5.41	5.06	4.82	4.64	4.50	4.39	4.30	4.16	4.05	3.97	3.91	3.86
13	9.07	6.70	5.74	5.21	4.86	4.62	4.44	4.30	4.19	4.10	3.96	3.86	3.78	3.72	3.66
14	8.86	6.51	5.56	5.04	4.69	4.46	4.28	4.14	4.03	3.94	3.80	3.70	3.62	3.56	3.51
15	8.68	6.36	5.42	4.89	4.56	4.32	4.14	4.00	3.89	3.80	3.67	3.56	3.49	3.42	3.37
16	8.53	6.23	5.29	4.77	4.44	4.20	4.03	3.89	3.78	3.69	3.55	3.45	3.37	3.31	3.26
17	8.40	6.11	5.18	4.67	4.34	4.10	3.93	3.79	3.68	3.59	3.46	3.35	3.27	3.21	3.16
18	8.29	6.01	5.09	4.58	4.25	4.01	3.84	3.71	3.60	3.51	3.37	3.27	3.19	3.13	3.08
19	8.18	5.93	5.01	4.50	4.17	3.94	3.77	3.63	3.52	3.43	3.30	3.19	3.12	3.05	3.00
20	8.10	5.85	4.94	4.43	4.10	3.87	3.70	3.56	3.46	3.37	3.23	3.13	3.05	2.99	2.94
21	8.02	5.78	4.87	4.37	4.04	3.81	3.64	3.51	3.40	3.31	3.17	3.07	2.99	2.93	2.88
22	7.95	5.72	4.82	4.31	3.99	3.76	3.59	3.45	3.35	3.26	3.12	3.02	2.94	2.88	2.83
23	7.88	5.66	4.76	4.26	3.94	3.71	3.54	3.41	3.30	3.21	3.07	2.97	2.89	2.83	2.78
24	7.82	5.61	4.72	4.22	3.90	3.67	3.50	3.36	3.26	3.17	3.03	2.93	2.85	2.79	2.74
25	7.77	5.57	4.68	4.18	3.85	3.63	3.46	3.32	3.22	3.13	2.99	2.89	2.81	2.75	2.70
26	7.72	5.53	4.64	4.14	3.82	3.59	3.42	3.29	3.18	3.09	2.96	2.86	2.78	2.72	2.66
27	7.68	5.49	4.60	4.11	3.78	3.56	3.39	3.26	3.15	3.06	2.93	2.82	2.75	2.68	2.63
28	7.64	5.45	4.57	4.07	3.75	3.53	3.36	3.23	3.12	3.03	2.90	2.79	2.72	2.65	2.60
29	7.60	5.42	4.54	4.04	3.73	3.50	3.33	3.20	3.09	3.00	2.87	2.77	2.69	2.63	2.57
30	7.56	5.39	4.51	4.02	3.70	3.47	3.30	3.17	3.07	2.98	2.84	2.74	2.66	2.60	2.55
35	7.42	5.27	4.40	3.91	3.59	3.37	3.20	3.07	2.96	2.88	2.74	2.64	2.56	2.50	2.44
40	7.31	5.18	4.31	3.83	3.51	3.29	3.12	2.99	2.89	2.80	2.66	2.56	2.48	2.42	2.37
50	7.17	5.06	4.20	3.72	3.41	3.19	3.02	2.89	2.78	2.70	2.56	2.46	2.38	2.32	2.27
60	7.08	4.98	4.13	3.65	3.34	3.12	2.95	2.82	2.72	2.63	2.50	2.39	2.31	2.25	2.20
70	7.01	4.92	4.07	3.60	3.29	3.07	2.91	2.78	2.67	2.59	2.45	2.35	2.27	2.20	2.15
80	6.96	4.88	4.04	3.56	3.26	3.04	2.87	2.74	2.64	2.55	2.42	2.31	2.23	2.17	2.12
90	6.93	4.85	4.01	3.53	3.23	3.01	2.84	2.72	2.61	2.52	2.39	2.29	2.21	2.14	2.09
100	6.90	4.82	3.98	3.51	3.21	2.99	2.82	2.69	2.59	2.50	2.37	2.27	2.19	2.12	2.07
120	6.85	4.79	3.95	3.48	3.17	2.96	2.79	2.66	2.56	2.47	2.34	2.23	2.15	2.09	2.03
150	6.81	4.75	3.91	3.45	3.14	2.92	2.76	2.63	2.53	2.44	2.31	2.20	2.12	2.06	2.00
200	6.76	4.71	3.88	3.41	3.11	2.89	2.73	2.60	2.50	2.41	2.27	2.17	2.09	2.03	1.97
250	6.74	4.69	3.86	3.40	3.09	2.87	2.71	2.58	2.48	2.39	2.26	2.15	2.07	2.01	1.95
300	6.72	4.68	3.85	3.38	3.08	2.86	2.70	2.57	2.47	2.38	2.24	2.14	2.06	1.99	1.94
400	6.70	4.66	3.83	3.37	3.06	2.85	2.68	2.56	2.45	2.37	2.23	2.13	2.05	1.98	1.92
500	6.69	4.65	3.82	3.36	3.05	2.84	2.68	2.55	2.44	2.36	2.22	2.12	2.04	1.97	1.92
600	6.68	4.64	3.81	3.35	3.05	2.83	2.67	2.54	2.44	2.35	2.21	2.11	2.03	1.96	1.91
750	6.67	4.63	3.81	3.34	3.04	2.83	2.66	2.53	2.43	2.34	2.21	2.11	2.02	1.96	1.90
1000	6.66	4.63	3.80	3.34	3.04	2.82	2.66	2.53	2.43	2.34	2.20	2.10	2.02	1.95	1.90

Table 9: F-test Distribution Table

F Distribution: Critical Values of F (0.1% significance level)

ν_2 \ ν_1	1	2	3	4	5	6	7	8	9	10	12	14	16	18	20
1	4.05e05	5.00e05	5.40e05	5.62e05	5.76e05	5.86e05	5.93e05	5.98e05	6.02e05	6.06e05	6.11e05	6.14e05	6.17e05	6.19e05	6.21e05
2	998.50	999.00	999.17	999.25	999.30	999.33	999.36	999.37	999.39	999.40	999.42	999.43	999.44	999.44	999.45
3	167.03	148.50	141.11	137.10	134.58	132.85	131.58	130.62	129.86	129.25	128.32	127.64	127.14	126.74	126.42
4	74.14	61.25	56.18	53.44	51.71	50.53	49.66	49.00	48.47	48.05	47.41	46.95	46.60	46.32	46.10
5	47.18	37.12	33.20	31.09	29.75	28.83	28.16	27.65	27.24	26.92	26.42	26.06	25.78	25.57	25.39
6	35.51	27.00	23.70	21.92	20.80	20.03	19.46	19.03	18.69	18.41	17.99	17.68	17.45	17.27	17.12
7	29.25	21.69	18.77	17.20	16.21	15.52	15.02	14.63	14.33	14.08	13.71	13.43	13.23	13.06	12.93
8	25.41	18.49	15.83	14.39	13.48	12.86	12.40	12.05	11.77	11.54	11.19	10.94	10.75	10.60	10.48
9	22.86	16.39	13.90	12.56	11.71	11.13	10.70	10.37	10.11	9.89	9.57	9.33	9.15	9.01	8.90
10	21.04	14.91	12.55	11.28	10.48	9.93	9.52	9.20	8.96	8.75	8.45	8.22	8.05	7.91	7.80
11	19.69	13.81	11.56	10.35	9.58	9.05	8.66	8.35	8.12	7.92	7.63	7.41	7.24	7.11	7.01
12	18.64	12.97	10.80	9.63	8.89	8.38	8.00	7.71	7.48	7.29	7.00	6.79	6.63	6.51	6.40
13	17.82	12.31	10.21	9.07	8.35	7.86	7.49	7.21	6.98	6.80	6.52	6.31	6.16	6.03	5.93
14	17.14	11.78	9.73	8.62	7.92	7.44	7.08	6.80	6.58	6.40	6.13	5.93	5.78	5.66	5.56
15	16.59	11.34	9.34	8.25	7.57	7.09	6.74	6.47	6.26	6.08	5.81	5.62	5.46	5.35	5.25
16	16.12	10.97	9.01	7.94	7.27	6.80	6.46	6.19	5.98	5.81	5.55	5.35	5.20	5.09	4.99
17	15.72	10.66	8.73	7.68	7.02	6.56	6.22	5.96	5.75	5.58	5.32	5.13	4.99	4.87	4.78
18	15.38	10.39	8.49	7.46	6.81	6.35	6.02	5.76	5.56	5.39	5.13	4.94	4.80	4.68	4.59
19	15.08	10.16	8.28	7.27	6.62	6.18	5.85	5.59	5.39	5.22	4.97	4.78	4.64	4.52	4.43
20	14.82	9.95	8.10	7.10	6.46	6.02	5.69	5.44	5.24	5.08	4.82	4.64	4.49	4.38	4.29
21	14.59	9.77	7.94	6.95	6.32	5.88	5.56	5.31	5.11	4.95	4.70	4.51	4.37	4.26	4.17
22	14.38	9.61	7.80	6.81	6.19	5.76	5.44	5.19	4.99	4.83	4.58	4.40	4.26	4.15	4.06
23	14.20	9.47	7.67	6.70	6.08	5.65	5.33	5.09	4.89	4.73	4.48	4.30	4.16	4.05	3.96
24	14.03	9.34	7.55	6.59	5.98	5.55	5.23	4.99	4.80	4.64	4.39	4.21	4.07	3.96	3.87
25	13.88	9.22	7.45	6.49	5.89	5.46	5.15	4.91	4.71	4.56	4.31	4.13	3.99	3.88	3.79
26	13.74	9.12	7.36	6.41	5.80	5.38	5.07	4.83	4.64	4.48	4.24	4.06	3.92	3.81	3.72
27	13.61	9.02	7.27	6.33	5.73	5.31	5.00	4.76	4.57	4.41	4.17	3.99	3.86	3.75	3.66
28	13.50	8.93	7.19	6.25	5.66	5.24	4.93	4.69	4.50	4.35	4.11	3.93	3.80	3.69	3.60
29	13.39	8.85	7.12	6.19	5.59	5.18	4.87	4.64	4.45	4.29	4.05	3.88	3.74	3.63	3.54
30	13.29	8.77	7.05	6.12	5.53	5.12	4.82	4.58	4.39	4.24	4.00	3.82	3.69	3.58	3.49
35	12.90	8.47	6.79	5.88	5.30	4.89	4.59	4.36	4.18	4.03	3.79	3.62	3.48	3.38	3.29
40	12.61	8.25	6.59	5.70	5.13	4.73	4.44	4.21	4.02	3.87	3.64	3.47	3.34	3.23	3.14
50	12.22	7.96	6.34	5.46	4.90	4.51	4.22	4.00	3.82	3.67	3.44	3.27	3.14	3.04	2.95
60	11.97	7.77	6.17	5.31	4.76	4.37	4.09	3.86	3.69	3.54	3.32	3.15	3.02	2.91	2.83
70	11.80	7.64	6.06	5.20	4.66	4.28	3.99	3.77	3.60	3.45	3.23	3.06	2.93	2.83	2.74
80	11.67	7.54	5.97	5.12	4.58	4.20	3.92	3.70	3.53	3.39	3.16	3.00	2.87	2.76	2.68
90	11.57	7.47	5.91	5.06	4.53	4.15	3.87	3.65	3.48	3.34	3.11	2.95	2.82	2.71	2.63
100	11.50	7.41	5.86	5.02	4.48	4.11	3.83	3.61	3.44	3.30	3.07	2.91	2.78	2.68	2.59
120	11.38	7.32	5.78	4.95	4.42	4.04	3.77	3.55	3.38	3.24	3.02	2.85	2.72	2.62	2.53
150	11.27	7.24	5.71	4.88	4.35	3.98	3.71	3.49	3.32	3.18	2.96	2.80	2.67	2.56	2.48
200	11.15	7.15	5.63	4.81	4.29	3.92	3.65	3.43	3.26	3.12	2.90	2.74	2.61	2.51	2.42
250	11.09	7.10	5.59	4.77	4.25	3.88	3.61	3.40	3.23	3.09	2.87	2.71	2.58	2.48	2.39
300	11.04	7.07	5.56	4.75	4.22	3.86	3.59	3.38	3.21	3.07	2.85	2.69	2.56	2.46	2.37
400	10.99	7.03	5.53	4.71	4.19	3.83	3.56	3.35	3.18	3.04	2.82	2.66	2.53	2.43	2.34
500	10.96	7.00	5.51	4.69	4.18	3.81	3.54	3.33	3.16	3.02	2.81	2.64	2.52	2.41	2.33
600	10.94	6.99	5.49	4.68	4.16	3.80	3.53	3.32	3.15	3.01	2.80	2.63	2.51	2.40	2.32
750	10.91	6.97	5.48	4.67	4.15	3.79	3.52	3.31	3.14	3.00	2.78	2.62	2.49	2.39	2.31
1000	10.89	6.96	5.46	4.65	4.14	3.78	3.51	3.30	3.13	2.99	2.77	2.61	2.48	2.38	2.30

Table 10: Cumulative Poisson Probabilities

$$P(X \le x) = \sum_{t=0}^{x} \frac{e^{-\lambda}\lambda^t}{t!}$$

x	0.01	0.01	0.02	0.03	0.04	0.05	0.06	0.07	0.08	0.09
0	0.9950	0.9900	0.9802	0.9704	0.9608	0.9512	0.9418	0.9324	0.9231	0.9139
1	1.0000	1.0000	0.9998	0.9996	0.9992	0.9988	0.9983	0.9977	0.9970	0.9962
2	1.0000	1.0000	1.0000	1.0000	1.0000	1.0000	1.0000	0.9999	0.9999	0.9999
3	1.0000	1.0000	1.0000	1.0000	1.0000	1.0000	1.0000	1.0000	1.0000	1.0000

x	0.10	0.20	0.30	0.40	0.50	0.60	0.70	0.80	0.90	1.00
0	0.9048	0.8187	0.7408	0.6703	0.6065	0.5488	0.4966	0.4493	0.4066	0.3679
1	0.9953	0.9825	0.9631	0.9384	0.9098	0.8781	0.8442	0.8088	0.7725	0.7358
2	0.9998	0.9989	0.9964	0.9921	0.9856	0.9769	0.9659	0.9526	0.9371	0.9197
3	1.0000	0.9999	0.9997	0.9992	0.9982	0.9966	0.9942	0.9909	0.9865	0.9810
4	1.0000	1.0000	1.0000	0.9999	0.9998	0.9996	0.9992	0.9986	0.9977	0.9963
5	1.0000	1.0000	1.0000	1.0000	1.0000	1.0000	0.9999	0.9998	0.9997	0.9994
6	1.0000	1.0000	1.0000	1.0000	1.0000	1.0000	1.0000	1.0000	1.0000	0.9999
7	1.0000	1.0000	1.0000	1.0000	1.0000	1.0000	1.0000	1.0000	1.0000	1.0000

x	1.10	1.20	1.30	1.40	1.50	1.60	1.70	1.80	1.90	2.00
0	0.3329	0.3012	0.2725	0.2466	0.2231	0.2019	0.1827	0.1653	0.1496	0.1353
1	0.6990	0.6626	0.6268	0.5918	0.5578	0.5249	0.4932	0.4628	0.4337	0.4060
2	0.9004	0.8795	0.8571	0.8335	0.8088	0.7834	0.7572	0.7306	0.7037	0.6767
3	0.9743	0.9662	0.9569	0.9463	0.9344	0.9212	0.9068	0.8913	0.8747	0.8571
4	0.9946	0.9923	0.9893	0.9857	0.9814	0.9763	0.9704	0.9636	0.9559	0.9473
5	0.9990	0.9985	0.9978	0.9968	0.9955	0.9940	0.9920	0.9896	0.9868	0.9834
6	0.9999	0.9997	0.9996	0.9994	0.9991	0.9987	0.9981	0.9974	0.9966	0.9955
7	1.0000	1.0000	0.9999	0.9999	0.9998	0.9997	0.9996	0.9994	0.9992	0.9989
8	1.0000	1.0000	1.0000	1.0000	1.0000	1.0000	0.9999	0.9999	0.9998	0.9998
9	1.0000	1.0000	1.0000	1.0000	1.0000	1.0000	1.0000	1.0000	1.0000	1.0000

x	2.10	2.20	2.30	2.40	2.50	2.60	2.70	2.80	2.90	3.00
0	0.1225	0.1108	0.1003	0.0907	0.0821	0.0743	0.0672	0.0608	0.0550	0.0498
1	0.3796	0.3546	0.3309	0.3084	0.2873	0.2674	0.2487	0.2311	0.2146	0.1991
2	0.6496	0.6227	0.5960	0.5697	0.5438	0.5184	0.4936	0.4695	0.4460	0.4232
3	0.8386	0.8194	0.7993	0.7787	0.7576	0.7360	0.7141	0.6919	0.6696	0.6472
4	0.9379	0.9275	0.9162	0.9041	0.8912	0.8774	0.8629	0.8477	0.8318	0.8153
5	0.9796	0.9751	0.9700	0.9643	0.9580	0.9510	0.9433	0.9349	0.9258	0.9161
6	0.9941	0.9925	0.9906	0.9884	0.9858	0.9828	0.9794	0.9756	0.9713	0.9665
7	0.9985	0.9980	0.9974	0.9967	0.9958	0.9947	0.9934	0.9919	0.9901	0.9881
8	0.9997	0.9995	0.9994	0.9991	0.9989	0.9985	0.9981	0.9976	0.9969	0.9962
9	0.9999	0.9999	0.9999	0.9998	0.9997	0.9996	0.9995	0.9993	0.9991	0.9989

x										
10	1.0000	1.0000	1.0000	1.0000	0.9999	0.9999	0.9999	0.9998	0.9998	0.9997
11	1.0000	1.0000	1.0000	1.0000	1.0000	1.0000	1.0000	1.0000	0.9999	0.9999
12	1.0000	1.0000	1.0000	1.0000	1.0000	1.0000	1.0000	1.0000	1.0000	1.0000

λ

x	3.10	3.20	3.30	3.40	3.50	3.60	3.70	3.80	3.90	4.00
0	0.0450	0.0408	0.0369	0.0334	0.0302	0.0273	0.0247	0.0224	0.0202	0.0183
1	0.1847	0.1712	0.1586	0.1468	0.1359	0.1257	0.1162	0.1074	0.0992	0.0916
2	0.4012	0.3799	0.3594	0.3397	0.3208	0.3027	0.2854	0.2689	0.2531	0.2381
3	0.6248	0.6025	0.5803	0.5584	0.5366	0.5152	0.4942	0.4735	0.4532	0.4335
4	0.7982	0.7806	0.7626	0.7442	0.7254	0.7064	0.6872	0.6678	0.6484	0.6288
5	0.9057	0.8946	0.8829	0.8705	0.8576	0.8441	0.8301	0.8156	0.8006	0.7851
6	0.9612	0.9554	0.9490	0.9421	0.9347	0.9267	0.9182	0.9091	0.8995	0.8893
7	0.9858	0.9832	0.9802	0.9769	0.9733	0.9692	0.9648	0.9599	0.9546	0.9489
8	0.9953	0.9943	0.9931	0.9917	0.9901	0.9883	0.9863	0.9840	0.9815	0.9786
9	0.9986	0.9982	0.9978	0.9973	0.9967	0.9960	0.9952	0.9942	0.9931	0.9919
10	0.9996	0.9995	0.9994	0.9992	0.9990	0.9987	0.9984	0.9981	0.9977	0.9972
11	0.9999	0.9999	0.9998	0.9998	0.9997	0.9996	0.9995	0.9994	0.9993	0.9991
12	1.0000	1.0000	1.0000	0.9999	0.9999	0.9999	0.9999	0.9998	0.9998	0.9997
13	1.0000	1.0000	1.0000	1.0000	1.0000	1.0000	1.0000	1.0000	0.9999	0.9999
14	1.0000	1.0000	1.0000	1.0000	1.0000	1.0000	1.0000	1.0000	1.0000	1.0000

λ

x	4.10	4.20	4.30	4.40	4.50	4.60	4.70	4.80	4.90	5.00
0	0.0166	0.0150	0.0136	0.0123	0.0111	0.0101	0.0091	0.0082	0.0074	0.0067
1	0.0845	0.0780	0.0719	0.0663	0.0611	0.0563	0.0518	0.0477	0.0439	0.0404
2	0.2238	0.2102	0.1974	0.1851	0.1736	0.1626	0.1523	0.1425	0.1333	0.1247
3	0.4142	0.3954	0.3772	0.3594	0.3423	0.3257	0.3097	0.2942	0.2793	0.2650
4	0.6093	0.5898	0.5704	0.5512	0.5321	0.5132	0.4946	0.4763	0.4582	0.4405
5	0.7693	0.7531	0.7367	0.7199	0.7029	0.6858	0.6684	0.6510	0.6335	0.6160
6	0.8786	0.8675	0.8558	0.8436	0.8311	0.8180	0.8046	0.7908	0.7767	0.7622
7	0.9427	0.9361	0.9290	0.9214	0.9134	0.9049	0.8960	0.8867	0.8769	0.8666
8	0.9755	0.9721	0.9683	0.9642	0.9597	0.9549	0.9497	0.9442	0.9382	0.9319
9	0.9905	0.9889	0.9871	0.9851	0.9829	0.9805	0.9778	0.9749	0.9717	0.9682
10	0.9966	0.9959	0.9952	0.9943	0.9933	0.9922	0.9910	0.9896	0.9880	0.9863
11	0.9989	0.9986	0.9983	0.9980	0.9976	0.9971	0.9966	0.9960	0.9953	0.9945
12	0.9997	0.9996	0.9995	0.9993	0.9992	0.9990	0.9988	0.9986	0.9983	0.9980
13	0.9999	0.9999	0.9998	0.9998	0.9997	0.9997	0.9996	0.9995	0.9994	0.9993
14	1.0000	1.0000	1.0000	0.9999	0.9999	0.9999	0.9999	0.9999	0.9998	0.9998
15	1.0000	1.0000	1.0000	1.0000	1.0000	1.0000	1.0000	1.0000	0.9999	0.9999
16	1.0000	1.0000	1.0000	1.0000	1.0000	1.0000	1.0000	1.0000	1.0000	1.0000

λ

x	5.10	5.20	5.30	5.40	5.50	5.60	5.70	5.80	5.90	6.00
0	0.0061	0.0055	0.0050	0.0045	0.0041	0.0037	0.0033	0.0030	0.0027	0.0025
1	0.0372	0.0342	0.0314	0.0289	0.0266	0.0244	0.0224	0.0206	0.0189	0.0174
2	0.1165	0.1088	0.1016	0.0948	0.0884	0.0824	0.0768	0.0715	0.0666	0.0620
3	0.2513	0.2381	0.2254	0.2133	0.2017	0.1906	0.1800	0.1700	0.1604	0.1512
4	0.4231	0.4061	0.3895	0.3733	0.3575	0.3422	0.3272	0.3127	0.2987	0.2851
5	0.5984	0.5809	0.5635	0.5461	0.5289	0.5119	0.4950	0.4783	0.4619	0.4457

x										
6	0.7474	0.7324	0.7171	0.7017	0.6860	0.6703	0.6544	0.6384	0.6224	0.6063
7	0.8560	0.8449	0.8335	0.8217	0.8095	0.7970	0.7841	0.7710	0.7576	0.7440
8	0.9252	0.9181	0.9106	0.9027	0.8944	0.8857	0.8766	0.8672	0.8574	0.8472
9	0.9644	0.9603	0.9559	0.9512	0.9462	0.9409	0.9352	0.9292	0.9228	0.9161
10	0.9844	0.9823	0.9800	0.9775	0.9747	0.9718	0.9686	0.9651	0.9614	0.9574
11	0.9937	0.9927	0.9916	0.9904	0.9890	0.9875	0.9859	0.9841	0.9821	0.9799
12	0.9976	0.9972	0.9967	0.9962	0.9955	0.9949	0.9941	0.9932	0.9922	0.9912
13	0.9992	0.9990	0.9988	0.9986	0.9983	0.9980	0.9977	0.9973	0.9969	0.9964
14	0.9997	0.9997	0.9996	0.9995	0.9994	0.9993	0.9991	0.9990	0.9988	0.9986
15	0.9999	0.9999	0.9999	0.9998	0.9998	0.9998	0.9997	0.9996	0.9996	0.9995
16	1.0000	1.0000	1.0000	0.9999	0.9999	0.9999	0.9999	0.9999	0.9999	0.9998
17	1.0000	1.0000	1.0000	1.0000	1.0000	1.0000	1.0000	1.0000	1.0000	0.9999
18	1.0000	1.0000	1.0000	1.0000	1.0000	1.0000	1.0000	1.0000	1.0000	1.0000

$$\lambda$$

x	6.10	6.20	6.30	6.40	6.50	6.60	6.70	6.80	6.90	7.00
0	0.0022	0.0020	0.0018	0.0017	0.0015	0.0014	0.0012	0.0011	0.0010	0.0009
1	0.0159	0.0146	0.0134	0.0123	0.0113	0.0103	0.0095	0.0087	0.0080	0.0073
2	0.0577	0.0536	0.0498	0.0463	0.0430	0.0400	0.0371	0.0344	0.0320	0.0296
3	0.1425	0.1342	0.1264	0.1189	0.1118	0.1052	0.0988	0.0928	0.0871	0.0818
4	0.2719	0.2592	0.2469	0.2351	0.2237	0.2127	0.2022	0.1920	0.1823	0.1730
5	0.4298	0.4141	0.3988	0.3837	0.3690	0.3547	0.3406	0.3270	0.3137	0.3007
6	0.5902	0.5742	0.5582	0.5423	0.5265	0.5108	0.4953	0.4799	0.4647	0.4497
7	0.7301	0.7160	0.7017	0.6873	0.6728	0.6581	0.6433	0.6285	0.6136	0.5987
8	0.8367	0.8259	0.8148	0.8033	0.7916	0.7796	0.7673	0.7548	0.7420	0.7291
9	0.9090	0.9016	0.8939	0.8858	0.8774	0.8686	0.8596	0.8502	0.8405	0.8305
10	0.9531	0.9486	0.9437	0.9386	0.9332	0.9274	0.9214	0.9151	0.9084	0.9015
11	0.9776	0.9750	0.9723	0.9693	0.9661	0.9627	0.9591	0.9552	0.9510	0.9467
12	0.9900	0.9887	0.9873	0.9857	0.9840	0.9821	0.9801	0.9779	0.9755	0.9730
13	0.9958	0.9952	0.9945	0.9937	0.9929	0.9920	0.9909	0.9898	0.9885	0.9872
14	0.9984	0.9981	0.9978	0.9974	0.9970	0.9966	0.9961	0.9956	0.9950	0.9943
15	0.9994	0.9993	0.9992	0.9990	0.9988	0.9986	0.9984	0.9982	0.9979	0.9976
16	0.9998	0.9997	0.9997	0.9996	0.9996	0.9995	0.9994	0.9993	0.9992	0.9990
17	0.9999	0.9999	0.9999	0.9999	0.9998	0.9998	0.9998	0.9997	0.9997	0.9996
18	1.0000	1.0000	1.0000	1.0000	0.9999	0.9999	0.9999	0.9999	0.9999	0.9999
19	1.0000	1.0000	1.0000	1.0000	1.0000	1.0000	1.0000	1.0000	1.0000	1.0000
20	1.0000	1.0000	1.0000	1.0000	1.0000	1.0000	1.0000	1.0000	1.0000	1.0000

$$\lambda$$

x	7.10	7.20	7.30	7.40	7.50	7.60	7.70	7.80	7.90	8.00
0	0.0008	0.0007	0.0007	0.0006	0.0006	0.0005	0.0005	0.0004	0.0004	0.0003
1	0.0067	0.0061	0.0056	0.0051	0.0047	0.0043	0.0039	0.0036	0.0033	0.0030
2	0.0275	0.0255	0.0236	0.0219	0.0203	0.0188	0.0174	0.0161	0.0149	0.0138
3	0.0767	0.0719	0.0674	0.0632	0.0591	0.0554	0.0518	0.0485	0.0453	0.0424
4	0.1641	0.1555	0.1473	0.1395	0.1321	0.1249	0.1181	0.1117	0.1055	0.0996
5	0.2881	0.2759	0.2640	0.2526	0.2414	0.2307	0.2203	0.2103	0.2006	0.1912
6	0.4349	0.4204	0.4060	0.3920	0.3782	0.3646	0.3514	0.3384	0.3257	0.3134
7	0.5838	0.5689	0.5541	0.5393	0.5246	0.5100	0.4956	0.4812	0.4670	0.4530
8	0.7160	0.7027	0.6892	0.6757	0.6620	0.6482	0.6343	0.6204	0.6065	0.5925
9	0.8202	0.8096	0.7988	0.7877	0.7764	0.7649	0.7531	0.7411	0.7290	0.7166

x										
8	0.4426	0.4296	0.4168	0.4042	0.3918	0.3796	0.3676	0.3558	0.3442	0.3328
9	0.5742	0.5611	0.5479	0.5349	0.5218	0.5089	0.4960	0.4832	0.4705	0.4579
10	0.6941	0.6820	0.6699	0.6576	0.6453	0.6329	0.6205	0.6080	0.5955	0.5830
11	0.7932	0.7832	0.7730	0.7626	0.7520	0.7412	0.7303	0.7193	0.7081	0.6968
12	0.8684	0.8607	0.8529	0.8448	0.8364	0.8279	0.8191	0.8101	0.8009	0.7916
13	0.9210	0.9156	0.9100	0.9042	0.8981	0.8919	0.8853	0.8786	0.8716	0.8645
14	0.9552	0.9517	0.9480	0.9441	0.9400	0.9357	0.9312	0.9265	0.9216	0.9165
15	0.9760	0.9738	0.9715	0.9691	0.9665	0.9638	0.9609	0.9579	0.9546	0.9513
16	0.9878	0.9865	0.9852	0.9838	0.9823	0.9806	0.9789	0.9770	0.9751	0.9730
17	0.9941	0.9934	0.9927	0.9919	0.9911	0.9902	0.9892	0.9881	0.9870	0.9857
18	0.9973	0.9969	0.9966	0.9962	0.9957	0.9952	0.9947	0.9941	0.9935	0.9928
19	0.9988	0.9986	0.9985	0.9983	0.9980	0.9978	0.9975	0.9972	0.9969	0.9965
20	0.9995	0.9994	0.9993	0.9992	0.9991	0.9990	0.9989	0.9987	0.9986	0.9984
21	0.9998	0.9998	0.9997	0.9997	0.9996	0.9996	0.9995	0.9995	0.9994	0.9993
22	0.9999	0.9999	0.9999	0.9999	0.9999	0.9998	0.9998	0.9998	0.9997	0.9997
23	1.0000	1.0000	1.0000	1.0000	0.9999	0.9999	0.9999	0.9999	0.9999	0.9999
24	1.0000	1.0000	1.0000	1.0000	1.0000	1.0000	1.0000	1.0000	1.0000	1.0000

$$\lambda$$

x	11.00	12.00	13.00	14.00	15.00	16.00	17.00	18.00	19.00	20.00
0	0.0000	0.0000	0.0000	0.0000	0.0000	0.0000	0.0000	0.0000	0.0000	0.0000
1	0.0002	0.0001	0.0000	0.0000	0.0000	0.0000	0.0000	0.0000	0.0000	0.0000
2	0.0012	0.0005	0.0002	0.0001	0.0000	0.0000	0.0000	0.0000	0.0000	0.0000
3	0.0049	0.0023	0.0011	0.0005	0.0002	0.0001	0.0000	0.0000	0.0000	0.0000
4	0.0151	0.0076	0.0037	0.0018	0.0009	0.0004	0.0002	0.0001	0.0000	0.0000
5	0.0375	0.0203	0.0107	0.0055	0.0028	0.0014	0.0007	0.0003	0.0002	0.0001
6	0.0786	0.0458	0.0259	0.0142	0.0076	0.0040	0.0021	0.0010	0.0005	0.0003
7	0.1432	0.0895	0.0540	0.0316	0.0180	0.0100	0.0054	0.0029	0.0015	0.0008
8	0.2320	0.1550	0.0998	0.0621	0.0374	0.0220	0.0126	0.0071	0.0039	0.0021
9	0.3405	0.2424	0.1658	0.1094	0.0699	0.0433	0.0261	0.0154	0.0089	0.0050
10	0.4599	0.3472	0.2517	0.1757	0.1185	0.0774	0.0491	0.0304	0.0183	0.0108
11	0.5793	0.4616	0.3532	0.2600	0.1848	0.1270	0.0847	0.0549	0.0347	0.0214
12	0.6887	0.5760	0.4631	0.3585	0.2676	0.1931	0.1350	0.0917	0.0606	0.0390
13	0.7813	0.6815	0.5730	0.4644	0.3632	0.2745	0.2009	0.1426	0.0984	0.0661
14	0.8540	0.7720	0.6751	0.5704	0.4657	0.3675	0.2808	0.2081	0.1497	0.1049
15	0.9074	0.8444	0.7636	0.6694	0.5681	0.4667	0.3715	0.2867	0.2148	0.1565
16	0.9441	0.8987	0.8355	0.7559	0.6641	0.5660	0.4677	0.3751	0.2920	0.2211
17	0.9678	0.9370	0.8905	0.8272	0.7489	0.6593	0.5640	0.4686	0.3784	0.2970
18	0.9823	0.9626	0.9302	0.8826	0.8195	0.7423	0.6550	0.5622	0.4695	0.3814
19	0.9907	0.9787	0.9573	0.9235	0.8752	0.8122	0.7363	0.6509	0.5606	0.4703
20	0.9953	0.9884	0.9750	0.9521	0.9170	0.8682	0.8055	0.7307	0.6472	0.5591
21	0.9977	0.9939	0.9859	0.9712	0.9469	0.9108	0.8615	0.7991	0.7255	0.6437
22	0.9990	0.9970	0.9924	0.9833	0.9673	0.9418	0.9047	0.8551	0.7931	0.7206
23	0.9995	0.9985	0.9960	0.9907	0.9805	0.9633	0.9367	0.8989	0.8490	0.7875
24	0.9998	0.9993	0.9980	0.9950	0.9888	0.9777	0.9594	0.9317	0.8933	0.8432
25	0.9999	0.9997	0.9990	0.9974	0.9938	0.9869	0.9748	0.9554	0.9269	0.8878
26	1.0000	0.9999	0.9995	0.9987	0.9967	0.9925	0.9848	0.9718	0.9514	0.9221
27	1.0000	0.9999	0.9998	0.9994	0.9983	0.9959	0.9912	0.9827	0.9687	0.9475
28	1.0000	1.0000	0.9999	0.9997	0.9991	0.9978	0.9950	0.9897	0.9805	0.9657
29	1.0000	1.0000	1.0000	0.9999	0.9996	0.9989	0.9973	0.9941	0.9882	0.9782

30	1.0000	1.0000	1.0000	0.9999	0.9998	0.9994	0.9986	0.9967	0.9930	0.9865
31	1.0000	1.0000	1.0000	1.0000	0.9999	0.9997	0.9993	0.9982	0.9960	0.9919
32	1.0000	1.0000	1.0000	1.0000	1.0000	0.9999	0.9996	0.9990	0.9978	0.9953
33	1.0000	1.0000	1.0000	1.0000	1.0000	0.9999	0.9998	0.9995	0.9988	0.9973
34	1.0000	1.0000	1.0000	1.0000	1.0000	1.0000	0.9999	0.9998	0.9994	0.9985
35	1.0000	1.0000	1.0000	1.0000	1.0000	1.0000	1.0000	0.9999	0.9997	0.9992
36	1.0000	1.0000	1.0000	1.0000	1.0000	1.0000	1.0000	0.9999	0.9998	0.9996
37	1.0000	1.0000	1.0000	1.0000	1.0000	1.0000	1.0000	1.0000	0.9999	0.9998
38	1.0000	1.0000	1.0000	1.0000	1.0000	1.0000	1.0000	1.0000	1.0000	0.9999
39	1.0000	1.0000	1.0000	1.0000	1.0000	1.0000	1.0000	1.0000	1.0000	0.9999
40	1.0000	1.0000	1.0000	1.0000	1.0000	1.0000	1.0000	1.0000	1.0000	1.0000

References and Further Readings

Dougherty C. (2002), Introduction to Econometrics (second edition 2002), Oxford University Press, Oxford.

https://home.ubalt.edu/ntsbarsh/Business-stat/StatistialTables.pdf

http://health.uottawa.ca/biomech/courses/apa3381/Binomial%20table.pdf